THE LAW OF ABUNDANCE

S. D. Buffington

First Edition

The Law of Abundance
© 2008 S. D. Buffington

Cover design;   Randall Reiserer

Editor: Gina E. Morgan

Manufactured in the United States of America

ISBN: 978-0-9708926-0-7

QuinStar Publishing - Dallas, Texas

ACKNOWLEDGEMENTS

I wish to extend my deepest gratitude and appreciation to my family, friends and advisors for all the help, support and encouragement each has given so generously. In particular I want to acknowledge:

My husband, George, who has encouraged and supported me in every endeavor. His unconditional love and faith in me, even when I stumble and occasionally fall, have been a great source of strength over the years. Our deep philosophical discussions around the elements of this book have added insights and helped me expand concepts. His responsible approach and self-sufficiency that keeps me free to pursue grand goals, and his patience with my sometimes crazy schedule are priceless and much appreciated gifts.

My daughter and business partner, Gina, who has been a constant source of inspiration, my right arm and a frequent savior. She has been my champion as I tried new ventures and tackled mountains that sometimes seemed too steep to climb. Her tireless dedication and attention to detail has not just improved this book, it has saved me countless hours and increased the quality of just about every aspect of our business over the years. Her deep wisdom, eternal patience, and ability to get things done efficiently are awe inspiring.

My son, Randall, who provided excellent feedback from the perspective of a scientist. He challenged me to keep searching for deeper understanding of concepts that were new to me and provided many valuable insights. He also designed the Celtic Knot that graces the cover of this book and each chapter heading. The endless pattern represents the infinite nature of our abundant universe and the eternal motion of energy. Woven into the design are hearts and diamonds, which symbolize inner and outer abundance.

My Son, Ron, whose expertise lies in the world of electronics. He pored through the first draft of this book, providing great insight and clarity to a once unfamiliar subject; the laws of energy. His knowledge of electricity has been invaluable in helping me unravel complex concepts and convert technical jargon into layman's terms. He provided rough sketches for many of the illustrations in this book and made many down to earth explanations possible.

My son-in-law, Ron, who invested many hours cleaning up and refining the illustrations in this book and who provided some excellent analogies. He has been there through thick and thin, always willing to do whatever it takes to achieve the goal and realize the collective dream. His active support has been a blessing in so many ways.

My grandson, Bryan, who also invested many hours creating or improving the illustrations in this book and who is one of the finest examples of integrity I have ever seen in a young man. And to each of my other grandchildren. They have each been endless sources of joy and a constant reminder of how beautiful and capable the human spirit is when it is free to express authentically.

My extended family, all of whom have added much love and enjoyment to my life. Special thanks to my step-daughter, Sue Hough, who took time from a busy schedule to proof the final draft and provide valuable suggestions.

My friends and colleagues, Steve Wilson, who contributed many hours proofing and correcting the manuscript, Tim Cocklin, who designed the page layout, Brooke Snow, who prepared the book for printing, and Marc Schwartz and Jill Pickett, who provided excellent feedback on the original draft.

To all who have been there in ways both large and small, thank you. Without you this book could not have been written.

CONTENTS

PART 3 - APPLYING THE PRINCIPLES OF ABUNDANCE

PART 4 - EPILOGUE AND APPENDIXES

FOREWORD

The Law of Abundance

It's time to start living the life you've imagined
Henry James

If you don't already have an abundance of everything you desire in life; happiness, contentment, fulfilling relationships, financial health, physical fitness, personal success and deep satisfaction, it is certain that you are not in complete alignment with the Law of Abundance. And, once you are in alignment, it is just as certain that all of these things *will* be yours to whatever degree you choose.

This is a certainty because the same energy that directs the universe, and everything in it, every moment of every day; that precisely and predictably determines the form, nature, path and outcomes of all things, also precisely and predictably directs the life and outcomes of every person on this planet.

For millennia the few who have understood how to apply this energy correctly have used it to gain mastery over their own lives, amass great wealth and shape the world we live in. Yet, until now, no one has taken this magnificent power, which works so perfectly that all science, industry and technology have emerged from it, and presented it in a way that can be applied with the same precision to humanity.

Because the principles that govern energy have remained a mystery in *human* terms, very few have chanced upon the right formula. And, because those few who arrived did so by chance, explaining the formula completely enough to allow any and everyone who so chose to reproduce their successes has proven impossible. Nonetheless, the evidence those fortunate few presented has induced many, if not most of us, to keep trying.

Yet, without the whole formula our efforts have been mostly just experiments that sometimes work, but mostly fail. Still, the masses keep searching for answers and trying harder and harder to master life and realize their dreams. More often than not, though, what they end up with is not a realized dream, but feelings of greater discontent. People en masse report feeling more drained and more concerned about the future as they observe society stepping up the pace, yet falling father and farther behind. There is greater and greater dissatisfaction, and almost no one can say why or what to do to reverse this unwelcome trend.

There is a reason why life in the world we have created has grown less satisfying and more stressful as we try harder and harder to meet the demands of the day; why in spite of all our efforts, most of us have not produced the outcomes we have envisioned or the life we dream of. There is also an unfailing solution; a clear model that anyone can follow based in a law as completely predictable and dependable as the Law of Gravity. This book is about that law—the Law of Abundance.

The Law of Abundance is a science-based set of principles that work *all the time, every time, for anyone and everyone, bringing each of us absolutely predictable outcomes.* This book removes the mystery from the process of creating abundance in whatever way you define it and hands you an unfailing formula for mastering your life and outcomes.

The principles that underlie the Law of Abundance impact each of us on every level: personally, in families, in communities, nationally and globally. Just as energy works perfectly and predictably to power your home, it works perfectly and predictably to power your life, and does it in a completely non-discriminating way. Each of us always receives an abundance of whatever we consciously or unconsciously set into motion, whether good or bad. It behooves us then, to understand the principles that drive our outcomes and consciously choose our path.

If you believe that you have already tried everything, including every wealth or prosperity building technique on the planet, and have still not met with success, it may seem incomprehensible that abundance is not only available to everyone, but exists as an unfailing law. But the law does not dictate what we will have an abundance of. That is entirely dependent on how we use it. The fact is we all have an abundance of *something*. Those who are struggling are typically receiving an abundance of things they *do not want*, and the struggle is actually part of the problem.

Everything in the universe suggests that the natural flow of energy is toward positive abundance—that is, a sufficient and ever increasing supply of conditions that result in improved outcomes. The universe is expanding, for example, and life is evolving toward greater adaptability and fitness.

For humans, positive abundance expresses as satisfaction, contentment, joy, health, great relationships, prosperity and an abiding sense of well-being. That we all seek these things and try to avoid their opposite is evidence enough that positive abundance is our natural state of being. But to have the things we desire in abundance, we must understand the Law of Abundance as fully as we understand the Law of Gravity and adhere to its principles just as closely.

The reason the vast majority of people are struggling is because there has been no reliable means for clearly understanding how the law that guides every outcome works, so we have been inadvertently misapplying our energies and efforts. The Law of Abundance makes it clear that we either set things in motion toward an outcome—positive or negative—or we stall energy and stay stuck in one place. It also explains precisely how and why this is so. By knowing how and why we are getting every result, we can make purposeful adjustments that allow us to work in harmony with the law so we are moving consistently toward an abundance of the things we desire.

When we have learned in larger measure how to use this unfailing law to our advantage, there is no question that we can literally change the world. We can create the life we dream of, and not just for ourselves, but for our families, communities, nations and globally. And that is the goal of this book.

PART 1

The Basics of Abundance

*The eternal mystery of the world
is its comprehensibility.*

Albert Einstein

CHAPTER 1

Gathering the Pieces of the Puzzle

None of us can change our yesterdays,
but every one of us can change our tomorrows.
William Jefferson Clinton

Since recorded history, those who have tapped into the vast abundance of the universe have been trying to teach others how to do the same. Hundreds, perhaps thousands of pioneers have stepped forward to proclaim that the universe is abundant and that abundance is the natural condition. They have presented hundreds of methods and techniques for tapping into abundance, and on rare occasions, the entire equation has been presented, but without a clear explanation of why the formula worked or what to adjust when it failed to work, reproducing their results proved nearly impossible.

Too often, explanations place too much emphasis on one aspect of the law and too little on another. Sometimes the approach is too esoteric and shrouded in mystery and other times it is too methodical. The esoteric route tends to focus too heavily on the non-physical qualities of thoughts, feelings, and intent, where the methodical route tends to focus too heavily on the value of taking actions and directing events. Too great a focus in either direction can throw us off balance and cause us to miss essential information and important clues. And where essential information is missing, a predictable result is not possible.

WE CANNOT SOLVE A PROBLEM IF DATA IS MISSING

Just as we cannot solve a mathematical problem if essential variables are missing, neither can we achieve abundance with incomplete information. When we try, we keep getting inconsistencies that can neither be explained nor resolved and inconsistent results lead us to doubt the entire process. Once doubt creeps in, skepticism undermines any commitment we may have had. Without relatively consistent success or at least a clear awareness of why success did not occur, hope diminishes and confusion and skepticism grow.

IT'S OK TO BE SKEPTICAL

Skepticism is a valuable trait. It can prevent us from heading down paths that are dead ends or downright dangerous. It keeps us searching for the truth and questioning anything that fails to deliver consistent results. We look with skepticism on statements such as "Anything the mind can conceive and believe, it can achieve" or "Early to bed, early to rise makes a man healthy, wealthy and wise" or "Whenever you ask for something and fully believe you will receive it, the universe always grants your wish" because we know that we cannot apply such assertions to every possibility and get a consistent result.

We cannot, for example, conceive of being indestructible and then step in front of a fast moving bus without harm. We cannot simply go to bed early and get up at the crack of dawn and become healthier, wealthier or wiser. Neither can we conceive of or wish for an eternally young body, and never get a wrinkle. No matter how fervently we wish, hope, pray, positive think or believe we can, we cannot consistently get such outcomes. And where a rule does not apply across the board, it is human nature to discount the entire concept.

The fulfillment of such wishes would put us in violation of natural laws, which cannot be violated. Take wishing to be eternally young, for example; all complex organisms follow the path of birth, attrition, death, and renewal, as they must for energy to remain dynamic and for life to exist. It is through this process that potential energy becomes dynamic energy, and is freed to generate all that we know and are. Growing old is the process of attrition, an integral part of the life cycle, and the only way we can skip that step is to die young—not exactly a desirable alternative for most of us.

THERE IS NO MAGIC GENIE

We also know from personal observation or direct experience that we cannot ask for robust health or great wealth and then spend all of our spare time lounging around, eating junk food, and staring at a television set and hope to get fit or wealthy.

We cannot pray or positive think our way out of a rush-hour traffic jam. We cannot wish that an untended yard will just magically become green, lush, and well groomed and have that happen. We know that we can hope, wish, and pray from now until the end of time and no magical genie will ever show up to clean our house, groom our yard, hand us a fortune, make us fit, or keep us eternally young.

Yet many who aspire to teach success and abundance principles seem to be implying that such outcomes are possible. These people are almost never out to deceive anyone. In most cases, they have applied the formula they espouse to their own lives and have gotten the exact results they are promising you. Because the process worked for them, they truly believe that what they are presenting will work in the same way for others, provided they follow the same formula. And they are absolutely correct. It *will* work provided the *entire formula* is correctly applied. The problem is that the entire formula is often not consciously known and, unless it is, it can't even be presented fully much less correctly applied.

HOW DO YOU DO THAT?

A good example of being able to present only what is consciously known can be demonstrated using vehicle drivers. Some people are extremely good at driving and become rich and famous driving cars on racetracks such as Mario Andretti did, or by successfully pulling off daring stunts, like Evel Knievel. Others are extremely bad at it and are constantly wrecking vehicles and getting tickets for road violations. Most are just average drivers who lie somewhere between the two extremes. Yet, if you ask successful drivers, average drivers and bad drivers how to drive a vehicle, each will give you similar answers.

The professional drivers will certainly know more than the bad drivers and might give you some very good pointers, but they will not be able to tell you every single thing they do that makes them so much better at driving than most people. They can't tell you because they are not consciously aware of everything they do. The parts they are able to convey are often not all that different than what an average, but conscientious, driver might convey. To duplicate a top driver's success, however, you must know and be able to duplicate every significant thing they do. The same is true of creating abundance.

Over a twenty year period I interviewed successful people to discover what they do differently than those who are unsuccessful. No matter where they have been successful; losing weight and keeping it off, building really fit bodies, growing a business, amassing a fortune, creating successful relationships, being a superior salesperson, becoming a sports star, or any other great achievement, these people cannot usually convey *specifically* what it is they do differently. Like the exceptional driver, the information they provide isn't all that different from the information given by those who are working hard to succeed, but who keep falling short of their goals.

In spite of all the interviews and research, until I had the entire formula, I too was unable to see what was truly significant to success. Not only was I unable to determine exactly what others were doing, I couldn't even figure out what I was doing in the areas where I experienced success and not doing in areas where success was elusive. As a result, I—like everyone else who is missing essential information— was unable to purposefully correct my course and get better outcomes even though truly I wanted to and diligently tried.

NATURAL LAWS CANNOT BE VIOLATED

Let me try to put this problem into perspective. Imagine that there was a tribe of people who firmly believed that if they performed a particular ritual in just the right way, they could leap from a cliff and fly like a bird. They also believed they could not achieve greatness until they were able to fly like birds and were very driven to achieve greatness. So every day they would go through the ritual as it was currently understood and, to determine if they had the ritual just right, one member of the tribe would leap from a cliff. That member would fall to his death, but because the tribe didn't understand the Law of Gravity and didn't realize that natural laws can never be violated, the remaining tribe members would go back to camp and work on perfecting the ritual. The next day another member would jump with the same result. This adjusting and jumping process continued until every member of that tribe had jumped to his or her death.

This is a predictable outcome no matter how fervently the tribe believed they would eventually find the right formula and no matter how hard they tried. There is no way they could ever succeed because gravity is an inviolate law and its rules apply all the time and in every circumstance. Even though the members of the tribe were free to believe whatever they chose and to continue adjusting their approach to gravity in whatever way they chose, they were not able to change the rules of gravity.

The Law of Abundance is such a law and we, in trying to find the right formula, have been doing essentially the same thing as the mythical tribe. And, like the tribe, the vast majority of us have gotten results we did not want and did not intend. Because we have not understood the law, we have been trying to perfect the ritual for millennia. Different "tribe" leaders have offered different formulas, but the result has been essentially the same. We have failed to create abundance en masse though most of us long to do that and many of us have tried mightily to achieve that result.

THREE WAYS OF KNOWING

The information we have gathered to help us adjust the formula has mainly come from science, philosophy and religion, and each of these disciplines has contributed greatly to our understanding and well-being. Each has given us important parts of the equation, but like the proverbial blind men examining different parts of an elephant, each group has been examining the world, and us, from a different perspective, so we get conflicting information and can't say definitively who is right.

No single perspective has provided the entire picture and given us the means to affect our outcomes personally and globally in predictable and wholly beneficial ways, nor can it.

One of the many great benefits of the Law of Abundance is that it brings together each of the three ways of knowing—empirical evidence (science), reason (philosophy) and faith (religion)—so that a complete picture and a truly workable formula emerges.

It meets scientific ways of knowing in that the principles that drive abundance can be measured, quantified, and qualified. The results are completely predictable because the Law of Abundance follows precise rules from which it never varies.

It meets philosophical ways of knowing in that it encourages questioning, learning, and the pursuit of wisdom by intellectual means; it presents evidence that moral self-discipline is not just a nice philosophical idea, but a necessary part of an abundant life.

It meets religious ways of knowing in that it embraces the mysteries of life; it not only allows for faith, but shows precisely how, why and in what forms faith is necessary for sustaining abundance.

We need all three ways of knowing to have the entire picture. As many have discovered, we cannot take a few pieces of life's puzzle and apply them with the assumption that they make up the entire picture. Trying to do that is all too often a formula for failure. All we have to do to realize just how slim our odds of just happening upon the right formula are, is to look at the condition of the masses.

Nonetheless, one rule of the Law of Abundance is that nothing is ever lost, so whatever time, energy, and money we have invested, individually and collectively, seeking ways to live a happier, healthier, more abundant life have not been wasted. Everything we do in the search for fulfillment adds something useful, if only a new awareness.

There was a time when I would have argued this point because, after investing a whole lot of time and money on products and programs designed to improve my life, I was still experiencing very little success. Although much of the information I had gathered along the way made a lot of sense, it just wasn't working for me, and I couldn't for the life of me figure out why.

I studied everything I could get my hands on, from the most ancient wisdom right up to the latest scientific research. And, while my life was certainly better for it, it was not nearly what I hoped for and I had no idea why, until I finally had the entire formula and could see exactly what I had been doing wrong.

IN SEARCH OF ANSWERS

At one point, after years of searching, experimenting, and adjusting, I began to suspect that I just didn't have what it took to become successful in the grand ways I imagined. I feared that abundance just wasn't in the cards for me. I had become the quintessential skeptic, approaching every new theory with an odd combination of doubt that it would work and hope that it might. I suspect I would have eventually resigned myself to mediocrity except for the deep and passionate response I had to a quote I read back in 1976. The quote was by Henry David Thoreau, who wrote, *"The mass of men lead lives of quiet desperation."*

I knew that Thoreau's observation was all too true for me and for just about everyone else I knew or had ever known, and that was NOT alright with me. I knew that there *had* to be a reason for this sad reality and it had to be found. I believed that, if the cause could be found, so could the cure. I envisioned a world filled with happy, contented, joyous people, each living life so abundantly that the idea or thought of desperation never entered their minds. I wondered why, in a world filled with abundance, the majority of us were struggling on almost every level—financially, mentally, emotionally, physically, personally, spiritually and in relationships—and I needed to understand.

Unbeknownst to me at the time, that need—that longing to know—set into motion a series of events that would culminate in the writing of this book. The chronology of how this came about, for those who are interested, is presented at the back of the book. I put it there because this book is not about me. It's about a master law that works flawlessly all the time, every time, to bring us an abundance of whatever we are willing to allow, first collectively and then individually.

ASKING THE RIGHT QUESTIONS

The importance of the collective has been expressed since recorded history, but has been poorly understood. The ability to profit from the knowledge others have gained, to love and be loved, to amass wealth, or to have any other aspect of abundance is not possible outside of the collective. In fact, we cannot even have life outside of the collective. We will cover this subject in more detail later. It is presented here in brief because, without understanding that collective abundance *precedes* individual abundance, many questions will arise for which there will appear to be no answers. The answers always exist if we are asking the right questions and looking in the right places, but unless we begin from the right premise we can't even ask the right questions, much less answer them.

An often-posed hypothetical question might help to demonstrate this point. You've probably heard the question, "If a tree falls in the forest and there is no one there to hear it, does it still make a sound?" Stated in this form, this question can be debated forever. That's because, while the person who formulated this question undoubtedly had a clear idea as to exactly what he meant, the way the question is posed does not allow *us* to know. Did "no one" mean humans? Did it include animals, insects, and other hearing creatures? Did it factor for man-made recording devices? Since we don't know for sure, we have to assume, which is what makes the question as highly debatable as it is.

Suppose the question had been posed like this; "If a tree falls in the forest and there is *nothing* to receive the vibrations as sound, does the tree still make a sound?" We can see that the tree falling certainly provides the *potential* for sound to occur. The air is still displaced and still moves though space in waves that *could* result in sound, but with *nothing* to receive the air waves and translate them into sound, the potential would not be realized. That is unless, as some experiments suggest, plants have the capacity to "hear" sound.

Since plants have been shown to respond to music and being talked to, we would now have a whole new set of questions to ponder, but at least we would know where to look for the answers. In this case, we would have to define "sound" more clearly. Do plants only respond to vibrations; do mere vibrations count as sound? Is sound the translation of vibrations and, if so, what does the translation have to be to qualify as sound?

If sound reception is described as something that would evoke a response, then we could say that plants, and even glass, have the capacity to "hear," since both plants and glass respond to the vibrations produced by displaced air. When an explosion occurs nearby, glass shatters, for example.

The *Merriam-Webster Dictionary* defines sound as "*the sensation of hearing; also the mechanical energy transmitted by longitudinal pressure waves (sound waves).*" It describes "hearing" as "*the process, function, or power of perceiving sound; esp: the special sense by which noises and tones are received as stimuli.*" By these definitions, we could say that glass does not hear because it has no sense function to perceive the vibrations as sound. But, before we could answer the question about plants, we would have to determine whether they actually perceive the vibrations as sound. If they don't, then the answer to the "tree in the forest" question would have to be no, since there is nothing there (no humans, animals, insects or recording devices) to receive and translate it as sound. If studies conclusively proved that plants do perceive sound waves and receive them as stimuli, then the answer to the question would have to be yes.

Clearly, we still don't have a definitive answer to the question, but now we know where to look for it. We can now narrow our search to the tree itself and to the forest in which it resides. There is evidence that suggests that plants respond to sound, so the stimuli part may have been answered. If so, all we have to do now is determine whether plants have the capacity to perceive sound in the precise way the term perceive is intended. By clarifying each part of the equation, a precise answer is then possible.

SUBTLE BUT IMPORTANT DISTINCTIONS

Similarly, in our individual lives we can go in search of precise answers only when we understand exactly where to look and what we need to be focused upon. Yet, living abundantly has been presented much like the hypothetical question about the tree in the forest. Subtle, but important distinctions have been missing. And without those subtle distinctions, we cannot know where to look to find the right answer. We cannot know for certain whether the path we are on is taking us toward the right outcome or farther away. Everything is open to interpretation and, if we interpret wrong, we get the wrong outcome and don't know why.

When repeated efforts don't lead to intended outcomes and we can't determine why, we feel out of control and when we feel out of control, the result is often desperation.

Our birthright is abundance, however, not desperation. For those who are living desperate lives, I imagine this statement seems absurd and is very hard to buy. Statements such as this consistently lead to questions such as, "What about the people starving in Africa?" "What about people who have cancer through no fault of their own?" "What about tornadoes, hurricanes, floods and other disasters that destroy people's lives?" "What about innocent children who are suffering?"

These are legitimate questions, and we can see that they contain their own answers if we are paying attention to the subtleties that underlie such questions; subtleties that suggest why we are compelled to ask in the first place. We ask because, at some level, we realize that abundance must first occur collectively.

We cannot control nature, for example, but we can control how we respond to it and we respond better as a community. If we collectively put our minds to finding ways to live in this world safely and effectively rather than spending so much time trying to control and overpower one another, I have no doubt that we could find effective ways to live in harmony with one another and with nature, including finding ways to heal diseases and protect ourselves from most natural disasters.

The invention of the Doppler radar system is an example of human ingenuity that has given us a means of early warning to enable us to avoid many types of storms. And early warning for earthquakes, tsunamis and other ground-based disasters is not far from being perfected. There is very little we could not accomplish if we were all focused on enhancing one another's lives.

The creation of an ideal world is not as impossible as it sounds; it is unlikely on a broad scale perhaps, but surely not impossible. If we could all understand what leads to abundance and what prevents it, we could predict, with great accuracy, our own outcomes and those of every other person, group or nation.

We could know which actions and decisions would lead to greater abundance and which ones would prevent it. We could each know exactly why we are not getting the results we want, and could determine precisely how and where to make alterations to get the outcomes we are after. We could purposefully impact our future—both collectively and individually.

If everyone realized that *we can have sustained individual abundance only where collective abundance first exists*, perhaps we could let go of selfishness and greed and begin purposefully designing our lives to ensure abundance for everyone. In a world focused upon and experiencing abundance, fear would lose its grip and the whole world would be transformed.

The whole world may not be ready to make such a grand transformation, but perhaps you are. Everything suggested in the previous paragraph is possible—individually and collectively—through the proper application of Law of Abundance principles.

In this book, the means for properly applying the principles and achieving a life of abundance is yours.

Every great change begins somewhere. Let it begin with us.

> *Never doubt that a small group of thoughtful, committed people can change the world; indeed, it's the only thing that ever has.*
> Margaret Mead

CHAPTER 2

Abundance in a New Light

*The significant problems we face cannot be solved
by the same level of thinking that created them.*
Albert Einstein

The principles behind the Law of Abundance were identified, defined and proven scientifically valid many years ago. We just haven't realized how humans fit into that picture. So, although we have the science and benefit from it every single day, we haven't even come close to profiting from it as fully as we might. To fully profit, we must know how the principles that drive energy apply to us personally and to all humans and we must be able to see that the natural flow of energy in the human experience is toward positive abundance; that is, an ample supply of all the things that lead to satisfaction and happiness.

Whenever you flip on a light or start your car, you are using the principles that drive the Law of Abundance. This powerful, all encompassing force, which we call energy, produces every outcome and impacts each of us in far greater ways than most of us have ever imagined. It doesn't just power our sun and the many products we regularly enjoy; it powers, directs and defines our lives on every level and in every way. We direct energy to a far greater extent than most believe, and the way we manage it has a direct impact on our lives, from a personal level to a global one.

LIFE DOES NOT EXIST IN A VACUUM

The way we use energy always takes us closer to or farther away from the things we desire, directly impacts our outcomes, and precisely determines what we *regularly* experience. *Regularly* is the operative word here. For any of us to directly determine every single thing that occurred in our experience, life would have to exist in a vacuum where the intentions of others or other natural forces never impacted us in any way. No one lives in a vacuum. In fact, life cannot exist in a vacuum. Life is dynamic and, in a dynamic world, we can be doing exactly what we should be and still get hit with things that we did not intend and did not create.

While we may not attract or create all of the unwelcome events that occur in our lives, we do create what we *regularly* experience when we are in a position to choose our outcomes, which describes most adults in developed countries, as well as every government in the world. Our regular experiences are not happenstance. We directly impact them.

Those who misuse energy, whether purposely or inadvertently, create greater limitations and difficulties for themselves and for all who are directly subject to their decisions and actions. Those who use it wisely and purposefully to shape their own lives, will experience greater abundance for themselves and for all whom they directly impact. And, where greater abundance exists, we are far better equipped to handle the occasional difficulties that arise unexpectedly and unbidden.

The fact that energy naturally flows toward beneficial abundance does not mean that nothing bad will ever happen in our lives. Life is a symphony where many factors are constantly interacting with and impacting one another. Since the intentions of one can collide with the intentions of another, bad things really do happen to good people. But those who know how to use energy's natural flow and work with the Law of Abundance have a wealth of the things they desire, including the strength and ability to handle an occasional crisis. Those who ignore it or work against it have fewer resources.

KNOWLEDGE IS POWER

The reason the mass of humankind "lead lives of quiet desperation" is because the majority of us are unwittingly creating conditions that keep us stuck or that lead to an abundance of things *we do not want*. And, since we are all part of the whole, our individual actions impact the whole and we all feel the effect.

The patterns for getting a lot of things we *don't* want were set into motion many generations ago by our ancient ancestors out of ignorance and we, out of ignorance, have followed those patterns. The idea that we have to suffer to make gains is one of those misguided notions that has kept us stuck in limitation. But ignorance can exist only in the absence of sufficient information. Knowledge truly is power and, properly applied, it can literally transform the world.

HOW THE "IMPOSSIBLE" BECOMES POSSIBLE

The Law of Gravity existed long before Isaac Newton explained how it worked and, though people were using the law instinctively, no one was able to purposefully take advantage of the properties of gravity because they didn't know what they were. An understanding of the precision and predictability of the properties of gravity has made all kinds of things that once seemed impossible entirely possible. Through understanding how gravity works, we have accomplished some amazing feats, such as sending men to the moon and the Rover to explore Mars. Our early ancestors were unable to even *think* about such things.

Understanding the principles of the Law of Abundance can have a similar impact on your life. You will discover how things you once thought impossible are entirely possible. You will know exactly where you have been unwittingly using the law erroneously and you will know how to redirect your energies to get exactly the outcomes you want. Then you can set a purposeful course to arrive at exactly the place you intend just as effectively as scientists now use their understanding of gravity to put satellites into orbit and to send spacecraft to other planets in our solar system.

EVERYTHING IS ENERGY

If everything is energy, it stands to reason then that *everything*, including humans, must obey the laws that govern energy. But, just as a scientist must understand how to work with gravity to put a man on the moon, or an electrician must understand how to work with electricity to wire a house and make everything work properly, we must know how to work with energy, as it applies to the human condition, to determine and direct our outcomes.

Energy rightly used *always* results in abundance, but as anyone familiar with electricity can easily demonstrate, energy can be redirected, slowed, and even stopped.

We know and can apply the properties of electricity because it follows very precise and predictable rules. Electricity is harnessed energy and, as you will discover, the energy you and I harness in directing our lives is just as precise, just as predictable and just as powerful.

OUR ABUNDANT UNIVERSE

There is no question that we live in an abundant world or that we have an abundant universe. When we look at the world or at the universe, however, what many of us observe is that abundance appears to exist in pockets, rather than overall. The world-renowned scientist, Stephen Hawking, has observed this. Yet, his description of the universe as a whole certainly presents a picture of abundance as an overall occurrence. He describes our sun as "...just one of millions of stars in our own Milky Way galaxy. And our galaxy itself is just one of billions of galaxies, in a universe that is infinite and expanding."[1] If such abundance exists overall, imagine what is available in the pockets! Then realize that your home, Planet Earth, is the richest pocket in our known Universe.

The Universe is endless as far as any of us know. No matter which direction we look in, from infinitely small to infinitely large, what we see is abundance. It permeates all of nature and, if we observe the outcomes of people like Einstein, Edison, Newton, Gandhi, Mozart, Helen Keller, Marie Curie, Stephen Hawking, Bill Gates, Oprah Winfrey and hundreds of others who have accomplished something truly remarkable in their lifetimes, we can see it at work on a personal level too.

Everything necessary for an abundant life is available here on Earth. That we are not all receiving in abundance is a result of not applying the law properly, not a statement about abundance as a reality. Through proper application of the law, people have experienced great satisfaction, more-vibrant health, ample money, loving relationships, freedom, contentment, joy and anything else they desire. So too can you.

ABUNDANCE AND THE LAW OF ATTRACTION

The Law of Attraction as it is often presented suggests that we attract to ourselves energies or vibrations that match our thoughts and expectations. While that is essentially true, it is just one aspect of the abundance formula. Moreover, physicists argue with the assertion that we attract to ourselves *like* energies. That's because, energetically speaking, *opposites attract*. The positive energy of a magnetic pole, for example, is attracted to the negative pole. Like poles and like energy actually repel one another.

When we look at *how energy becomes matter*, however, which is how we manifest material wealth and physical abundance, we see that it is through the attraction of *complementary*, not identical and not opposing, energies.

DNA, the code that defines all of life, is a system of complementary pairings, for example. In DNA, identical nucleotides are never paired, but complementary ones always are, as you can see in Illustration 2.01.

DNA Strand Sequence

A	C	G	T	G	G	A	C
T	G	C	A	C	C	T	G

Illustration 2.01

This illustration represents only one small part of a DNA strand. There are actually many thousands of combinations, but no matter how many there are, the pairings never vary, which is why DNA can be decoded.

The thousands of combinations seen in DNA are derived from only four nucleotides. Adenine (A) and Guanine (G) are both nucleotides that belong to a group called Purines. Thymine (T) and Cytosine (C) belong to a group called Pyrimidines. Yet the two Purines and the two Pyrimidines never pair with one another. They pair with one of the nucleotides from the other set and always with the same one. Adenine (A) always pairs with Thymine (T) and Cytosine (C) always pairs with Guanine (G).

DNA "zips" together using hydrogen bonds that create an attraction between the A/T and C/G pairings in much the way water molecules are attracted to one another.

In water, the positive charge of the hydrogen molecules is attracted to the negative charge of the oxygen molecule.

Let's take a closer look at how attraction between opposites works by examining the structure of water (H^2O).

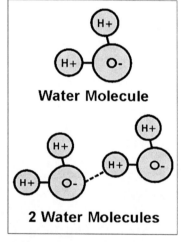

Water Molecule

2 Water Molecules

Illustration 2.02

As Illustration 2.02 shows, the positive charge of the two hydrogen atoms are attracted to the negative charge of the oxygen atom. The hydrogen atoms are not attracted to one another.

Multiple water molecules are joined together by an electrostatic attraction between the positive charge near the hydrogen atoms and the negative charge near the oxygen atoms. Here, as in all things, a plus/minus attraction is essential to the formation of matter.

OPPOSITES ATTRACT

This is an important aspect of the abundance formula, so let's take the same plus/minus principle that attracts atoms to one another and apply it to humans. Say for example, that a man is strongly attracted to a woman and wants to get to know her. They live in the same apartment complex, and every time he sees her, he goes out of his way to get her attention. He makes it clear that he is interested and does anything and everything he can to get in her good graces.

The man is the active (+) part of the equation. But he needs a receptive complement to complete the bond; so, unless the woman is receptive (-) to the actions and attentions of the man, everything he does is just wasted energy. If the woman is repelled by the man and his actions, not only is there no receptivity, the combination actually becomes repellent; so, not only is the man wasting his energy, if he continues to pursue her, there is likely to be trouble. This isn't a gender thing either. The same principle holds true for all relationships. If a woman is interested in a man, the man has to be receptive to her attentions and actions or no connection occurs there either.

For attraction to occur, both an active (+) and a receptive (-) charge must be present. It is this fact that the Law of Attraction, as it is usually presented, fails to make clear. The things we give our attention, focus, and faith to, are certainly factors that set energy into motion toward outcomes, both wanted and unwanted. But as you are about to discover, there is much more to it than that.

> *Somewhere something incredible*
> *is waiting to be known.*
>
> Dr. Carl Sagan

The Moment that any life,
however good, stifles you,
you can be sure it is not your real life

Arthur Christopher Benson

CHAPTER 3

The Four Energy Combinations

*The most beautiful thing we can experience is the mysterious.
It is the source of all true art and all science.*
Albert Einstein

There are only four possible energy combinations and only *one* of the four leads to an abundance of what we want. The other three lead to limitation in one way or another. One combination leads to negative outcomes, which can be described as *actively diminishing returns* or an abundance of things we *do not* want. The other two combinations keep us stuck, neither getting ahead nor falling into ruin.

As you examine each of the energy combinations, and how they apply to the principles that make up the Law of Abundance, you may find that there are areas that seem complex and perhaps a little confusing at first. You may also discover that some of what is presented seems *counter-intuitive*. It is precisely the seeming counter-intuitiveness of the law that has prevented its understanding and effective application. But, stick with it until you fully grasp the principles and you will have the key to creating a life filled with an abundance of the things you desire.

Thanks to the work of a long list of brilliant men (Benjamin Franklin, Nikola Tesla, Alessandro Volta, Thomas Edison, James Watt, and others), there exists today a clear understanding of electricity, which describes the primary conditions under which energy can be harnessed and directed in endlessly useful ways. We now know with certainty that energy, when harnessed, follows precise and predictable paths and, since humans harness energy, it must work exactly the same way for us. And, as you are about to discover, it does.

GETTING CLEAR ON POSITIVE (+) AND NEGATIVE (-) ENERGY

Physiologists and electricians use the term "positive "and "negative" when referring to properties of energy. These designations have absolutely nothing to do with positive or negative as those terms apply to how we use thoughts, feelings, actions, and intent. In energy, "positive" refers to the *active* aspect and "negative" refers to the *receptive* aspect. It is the active and receptive aspects of energy that I am referring to throughout this book when I use the symbols (+) and (-). When you see these symbols, it is essential that you recognize the distinctions between "positive" and "negative" as these terms apply to energy and as they apply to thoughts, feelings, actions, and intent. Understanding how active (+) and receptive (-) energies influence our outcomes, and how we influence them, is very important so let's examine these energies.

ENERGY OUT NEEDS A BOOST

In both electrical and in human terms, active (+) energy needs to be *induced* or boosted along. In humans, that inducement or boosting of energy feels like *effort*. If we are unwilling to put forth the effort to boost energy out from ourselves—that is, to make things happen—the energy our body generates goes nowhere. It gets stored as fat and, in time, useful energy begins to decline. When useful energy is sufficiently reduced, little to nothing good happens in our outer world.

RETURN ENERGY MUST FLOW FREELY

Receptive (-) energy flows freely and does not require a booster. In humans, the flow of receptive energy feels like *no effort* and *non-resistance*. Anything that sets up resistance will reduce the flow of *receptive* energy on its *return back to its source*. In the case of humans, we are the source.

You have probably noticed the resistance effect when you spend too much time working on something you don't enjoy or when you are in the presence of someone who irritates or frustrates you. Not only is there typically a feeling of resistance to such situations, when we must endure them for awhile, our energy levels drop.

THE FOUR ENERGY COMBINATIONS IN BRIEF

To understand how to correctly apply the active and receptive aspects of energy, you must understand the four possible energy combinations and how they impact your life and outcomes. Each path will be covered in greater detail later, but a brief explanation now will help provide clarity to the concepts that follow.

Humans harness and direct energy in much the same way as it is harnessed and directed for electricity. So the better you understand electricity, the better you will understand how to direct your own energies to get exactly the outcomes you desire.

In general, to harness energy and direct its flow there must be a complete circuit and it must have both an active (+) and a receptive (-) charge. A complete energy circuit has four elements:

(1) The source of the energy, such as a battery, a generator, or in human terms, a person.
(2) A path out from the generator, which for humans is *application*.
(3) A receiver, such as an appliance or a light bulb, or in human terms, a goal or purpose.
(4) A path back to the energy source, which for humans is *attitude*.

> As the terms are used in the descriptions of human energy paths, *application* refers to how we approach life (what we give or fail to give to life). *Attitude* refers to how we receive from life (what we are willing to accept).

Each of these four elements must be present for energy to flow.

THE LINE OUT

To get the desired results, the active and receptive charges must be properly directed so that energy flows where we want it to. For energy to flow in the proper direction, the *application* line must proceed *out* from the source of energy toward the receiver, but it only leaves the source when there is some catalyst to *boost it out*. As mentioned earlier, in humans, the catalyst is effort, which creates a positive or active (+) energy charge. Effort properly applied is responsible, disciplined, productive and courageous action.

When we apply *no effort*, no energy boost occurs. The no-effort path is that of being irresponsible, undisciplined, lazy or cowardly; in other words, taking the easiest route rather than the most productive one. The no-effort energy charge is "negative" or receptive (-). It is one of *allowing* things to happen rather than of acting purposefully.

THE LINE IN

For the energy, we send out to return to us, we must be *receptive* to its return. We must have little to no resistance on the return line and this is where positive thinking/feeling, faith and acceptance come in. This is also where many people get tripped up.

Why? Because energetically speaking, the *attitude* line must be passive or receptive (-) for energy to flow freely. Keep in mind that, in electricity, the receptive line is called "negative." That term can create confusion when applying it to the fact that positive thoughts, feelings, and expectations keep the "negative" line flowing freely. Until you reframe "negative" to *receptive*, this can be a real mind bender. Please do ponder this, but don't let it throw you. This will become clearer as each path is explained.

PATH 1 – THE PATH TO NEGATIVE ABUNDANCE
(A LOT OF WHAT WE DO NOT WANT)

The first combination we will explore is the *least desirable* one and the one you definitely want to avoid. This path has both an active (+) and receptive (-) charge so energy is flowing, but it is flowing *backwards—away from*, rather than toward, an abundance of good things. Just as powering an electric motor in reverse will result in the motor running backwards, so too does powering your life in reverse result in your moving *away from* the things you most desire.

Energy flows backwards on this path because the *application side* is *receptive* (-), which is being irresponsible, undisciplined, lazy, fearful and allowing life to just happen, and the *attitude* side is *active* (+). An active attitude is one of *resistance*, striving for or against an outcome, struggling, being non-accepting, disallowing, disbelieving, etc. Receptive application and active attitude result in a *reversal* (-/+) of energy flow, rather than the correct (+/-) flow, and a reversal of fortunes.

Since the application path is one of irresponsibility and lack of discipline, people on this path tend to avoid anything that feels like effort. Therefore, the effort necessary for building a good receiver (defining goals and laying out specific plans) has generally not been expended so goals are usually unclear and often altogether absent.

Where focus is clear, it is generally negative because those on this path don't expect good things in life, which is what makes the return line resistant and non-accepting (+). Add a negative focus to the backwards energy combination (-) and you have the formula for a lot of what *you do not want.* Illustration 3.01 shows what this path looks like.

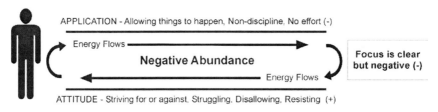

Illustration 3.01

> **In a Nut Shell:**
> When you (the generator) are undisciplined, act irresponsibly or allow things to just happen as they may (receptive application), when you struggle or strive for or against an outcome or are resistant, rigid or disallowing (active attitude), you have set up conditions for energy to flow backwards toward an abundance of the things you DO NOT want.

Negative focus does not necessarily mean that it is directed toward negative or harmful things. Negative can mean that there is excessive skepticism, fear, doubt or other negative emotions associated with the focus, which is more generally the case.

The people on this path are the ones that sit on the sofa eating junk food and watching television every night, feeling angry and frustrated because they are out of shape, don't enjoy their life and are envious of the TV characters that appear to have the healthy, wealthy, high-energy lifestyle the Couch Potato longs for. These are also the people who buy lots of self-help books, which they seldom finish reading and rarely heed, or health club memberships, which they rarely if ever use after the initial enthusiasm wears off.

Those on this path think that they are victims of everything from their genes to the neighbor next door. It isn't their fault that the New Years resolution they made to lose fifty pounds didn't pan out. It's their genes. They can't help it if the neighbor gets upset because their dog barks all night. The neighbor is too sensitive and the dog is uncontrollable. It isn't their fault that they are wasting their life away in a job they hate. It's the economy, the job market, and the breaks they never got in life.

THE FRUITLESS QUEST FOR INSTANT AND EFFORTLESS

This is the also group that makes the marketers of instant and effortless "cures" rich. They tend to fall prey to the gimmicks that promise quick and easy results. They are ever in search of that magic formula that will eliminate all of their problems with little to no effort on their part. But no such formula exists, or ever will exist. Until those in this group are ready to take responsibility for their own lives and outcomes, and quit blaming their problems on everyone and everything except themselves—until they can find something they can be passionate enough about to get off this very destructive path—they will continue to get more and more of the very things they want so badly to *avoid*.

Unfortunately, much of what is being perpetuated in the United

States today puts the majority of the population squarely on this path. Examples are everywhere. We are inundated with movies and television programs that promote irresponsible behaviors, which is "negative" application (-), and present violence as a typical solution to conflict. Violence always creates resistance, which leads to a non-accepting (+) attitude.

Politicians ignore the needs and even the will of the people and cater to those who finance their campaigns. This is not only irresponsible (-), but causes resistance in a large percentage of the population (+). Our political leaders turn a blind eye to problems that are inconvenient to deal with, such as illegal immigration, over-crowded prisons, a justice system that is badly broken, poor schools, the need for welfare reform and the imminent threat of global warming, and hope the problems will go away on their own. This is the epitome of irresponsible behavior (-) and it is a constant source of irritation for much of the population, which results in some level of resistance at a national level (+).

And the list goes on and on. You are probably aware of dozens of other examples. If you aren't, all you have to do is pick up a newspaper, turn on the evening news, or ponder the things that are passing for political correctness today, and ask yourself three questions:

1. Is this action or decision responsible, disciplined, courageous, and the right thing to do, not just in the moment, but for the long term good of the majority of citizens? (Active application)

   To answer this, you need to realize that for a decision or action to be responsible, according to the Law of Abundance, it must lead to responsible actions on the part of all it will affect. Enabling others toward dependency or dishonesty or greed is irresponsible and just as damaging as allowing special interest groups to get what they want at the expense of the majority of the population. Excusing undisciplined, irresponsible actions is never in anyone's best interest in the long term. Ultimately, it only serves to make everyone weaker and less capable.

2. Is this action or decision likely to be accepted by any reasonable, responsible citizen? In other words, is it so fair, just, and considerate of the majority that anyone without a personal agenda could clearly see its merits and accept the decision or action as one that serves the best interests of the majority, as opposed to just serving certain groups? (Receptive attitude)

3. Are there clear goals and a well thought out plan for ensuring that the proposed action results in a positive outcome?

THE STATE OF A NATION

We can learn a lot about the state of any nation and where it is headed by observing the path it is on. We can know the path it is on by observing what regularly occurs in that nation. But, be careful how you observe. If observation leads to feelings of anger, irritation, frustration or helplessness, it can actually be detrimental to you because such feelings create resistance, which will slow your own energies and outcomes and throw you onto the very path you would like to see others avoiding.

If you find yourself on the path of negative abundance, begin shifting your focus to the thoughts, feelings, and actions that will get you off of it. How to do that will be covered in detail in Chapter 19. In brief, the actions to focus upon are those that are responsible, disciplined, and courageous. The attitude is non-resistant; open, accepting, believing, and receptive to good outcomes. The outcomes you focus upon need to be very clear and positive as well.

As you observe the world around you, realize that you can positively impact it best when you are taking responsible, disciplined, courageous actions and when you are doing your part to heal yourself, your family, your workplace, your community, or whatever else you can directly impact. If enough of us are doing that, then our individual actions and attitudes can positively impact the whole world. No one person can change the world, of course, but we can each change some small part of it if we so choose.

PATH 2 – THE APPARENTLY POSITIVE PATH TO NOWHERE

The second energy combination is that of *active* (+) *application* (responsible, disciplined, courageous action) and *active* (+) *attitude* (striving for or against an outcome, worrying, struggling, fear, doubt, etc). Even when there is responsible action coupled with positive focus and intent, this combination does not produce the desired results because two active charges (+/+) do not allow energy to flow. It's the same effect as putting two new batteries into a perfectly good flashlight, but having one in backwards. Both batteries have plenty of potential energy, but it can't be released so the flashlight doesn't work.

If you are on this path, you may be sending out a lot of energy, but you have not provided an open channel for energy to return positive results to you. So like the flashlight, you have a lot of potential energy that is not getting to the intended source (your goal) and cannot return to you.

Those on this path are working very hard and diligently. They are being responsible and very disciplined, but are doing a lot of things they don't enjoy. Many on this path resist the idea that they can have what they want without working hard or struggling to get it. Typically, the idea of hard work, diligence, discipline and responsibility have been imposed on those in this group, either through early conditioning or as a result of current circumstances.

When the source is early conditioning, those in this group act responsibly because they believe they must "keep their nose to the grindstone" to have any worth or value. They don't enjoy all the hard work, but think it is what "decent" people are supposed to do. They typically impose these values on others as well and are frequently frustrated when others don't adhere to the same strict standards they hold themselves to.

There are many things that can put people on this path: the expectations of others, such as a critical parent, spouse or boss, or self-imposed expectations and beliefs.

When it is the expectations of others, people on this path tend to stay on it because they lack the courage to make better choices for themselves and/or lack the self-esteem to believe they deserve better. They either think that the needs and opinions of others are more valid and more important than their own or they are afraid that making and implementing better choices will create conflict.

Those who are stuck here because of self-imposed expectations are those who have bought into the idea that worth is measured by material wealth, shows of intelligence, or some other external marker. Their goals are driven by external ideals so, rather than being focused on finding their own personal and authentic source of happiness, they are working very hard to amass all the external trappings others have told them they should have.

Illustration 3.02 shows what this path looks like. In this case, the focus may be clear, but the fact that no energy is flowing back to the source keeps it from being realized.

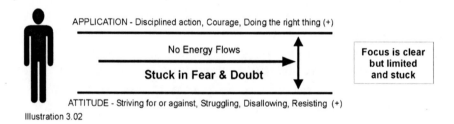

Illustration 3.02

> **In a Nut Shell:**
> When you (the generator) take responsible, disciplined, courageous action (active application) to achieve your goals and have a clear focus, but are also struggling, striving for or against an outcome, lack trust or confidence, or are resistant (active attitude), you have set up conditions where energy does not flow. Fear and doubt keep you stuck.

A STRUGGLE TO ESCAPE LIMITATIONS

Those in this group typically report that they are tired of getting nowhere in life and are diligently working to escape the limitations that they believe have prevented them from having the things they want. Perhaps, in addition to holding down a full time job, running a household and taking care of a family, they are also trying to do the work prescribed by the latest success expert. They are writing out affirmations and reciting them daily, setting goals and laying out plans, which they try to implement in those brief moments when they can catch a breather. They are working very hard to keep negative thoughts and feelings at bay. They are tired and overworked, and frequently frustrated, but are determined to do whatever it takes to get their life on track. In fact, "whatever it takes" is a frequent refrain.

The reason those in this group are stuck is because they are struggling to *get away from* limitations. They keep going through the motions that others have suggested, but are struggling with them. They struggle in the hope of getting to a place where they won't have to struggle anymore.

Though they practice positive thinking, in this instance it is an *application*, not an *attitude*. Their real attitude is one of worry, doubt, fear, and frustration. They are not really certain that the work they are doing will lead them to the outcomes they desire, but are willing to give it a shot anyway. Because they are frequently tired, negative events and petty frustrations regularly derail them. Underneath all the activity and the positive façade is frustration that things are not materializing as envisioned and fear that they never will.

FALTERING FAITH

For those on this path, the disciplined, responsible actions, positive thoughts, and/or courage to forge ahead create the correct application (+), yet this group lacks faith in the outcome. They continue to strive for abundance and struggle against limitation, which creates an active (+) attitude line and, in spite of all the diligence and hard work, two active energy lines (+/+) create a combination where NO energy is flowing so they are getting nowhere.

The lack of energy flow guarantees that events will *not* unfold as those on this path hope they will and, when they don't, faith diminishes even further and the striving and struggling to make things happen increases. If the resistance on the attitude line continues to *increase* and energy flow continues to *decrease*, eventually a complete shut down—or what we refer to as "burnout"—will occur.

THE REAL SECRET OF *"THE SECRET"*

It is the people in this group that report phenomenal results when they tap into a movement such as that which has been created by the video and book entitled, *The Secret* (Rhonda Byrne, Prime Time Productions, 2006). The reason they get the results is because they are encouraged to let go of the resistors and trust that they will receive the outcomes they desire. With encouragement and hope, a percentage of the people on this path will change their attitude from resistant to open and receptive and, of course, the moment they do that, energy begins to flow in the right direction because the active (resistant) attitude line is all that was preventing it from flowing in the first place.

The ones who don't get good results by following Law of Attraction advice such as that given in *The Secret,* are those who are either on the (+/+) path, and cannot let go of the resistors, or those on one of the receptive application paths—the negative abundance (-/+) path or the stuck in fear (-/-) path, which we will cover next. Those on either one of these paths fail to get good results because, for them, it's the *application* side of the equation that is not being properly applied. A better attitude won't correct that unless the attitude adjustment is great enough to result in the individual becoming consistently more responsible, self-disciplined and courageous, which is extremely rare.

PATH 3 – STUCK IN DELUSION
(THE "EASY" PATH TO NOWHERE)

The third possible energy combination is that of *receptive* (-) *application* combined with *receptive* (-) *attitude*. Receptivity on the application side is the path of least resistance. And remember, for energy to be sent out from its source (in this case a person) it must be *boosted*, which requires effort. Energy must have a catalyst to be set into motion and those who choose the effortless application route provide no catalyst.

This group does what is easiest in the moment. They are irresponsible, undisciplined, and often lazy. They avoid risk, stay in their comfort zone, and rarely do anything courageous. As with those on the negative abundance path, the application path of this group is one of irresponsibility and lack of discipline.

Goals are generally unclear too because of an unwillingness to expend the effort necessary for clarifying them. When combined with a receptive (-) attitude (trusting, believing, allowing things to happen as they may) the result is a double receptive (-/-) and NO energy flows. Illustration 3.03 shows what this path looks like. In this case, the focus is unclear due to lack of effort and the individual is stuck due to no energy flow.

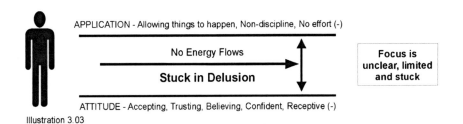

Illustration 3.03

In a Nut Shell:
When you (the generator) are undisciplined, act irresponsibly or allow things to just happen as they may (receptive application), when you have an unclear focus but are accepting and trusting; open and believing (receptive attitude) you have set up conditions where energy is not flowing. You are stuck in the delusion that you can hope, pray or wish your way to abundance without taking responsible action or making any effort.

An example of this would be people who believe that positive thinking, in and of itself, will get them the outcomes they long for. Or of people who believe that God will take care of them even though they are not taking any personal responsibility for their own outcomes. Because this type of person typically has no clearly defined goals and no plans for reaching the fuzzy goals they might have, there is no impetus to provide energy with the boost it needs. Those in this group discount any need to take responsibility for their own lives, preferring to blindly follow some "expert" or a "God will provide" doctrine. They believe that all they have to do to get the outcomes they long for is have faith and everything will turn out fine.

FAITH WITHOUT WORKS

The amusing joke (which is really no joke when you understand the Law of Abundance) that tells of a man stranded on the roof of his house with floodwaters rapidly rising exemplifies the people on the double receptive (-/-) path.

The man is praying to God to save him when a rescue worker appears with a boat and implores him to get in. "No, thank you," the man replies, "God will save me."

Because he refuses to get in, the rescue worker reluctantly leaves. As he continues to pray, a second rescue boat and then a third show up trying to rescue the man and both get the same response as the first. Finally, the waters rise so high, and are so dangerous, that only a helicopter can reach the man and one flies in to rescue him. Again, he refuses the rescue, convinced that God will save him. The man drowns and when he appears before God, he is angry and disappointed. "I trusted in you," the man shouts at God, "and you let me down!" To which God calmly replies, "Not so, my son, I sent you three boats and a helicopter."

On the surface, people on this path appear to be very positive and hopeful. They frequently talk about faith and being receptive to God's plan. They seem to be gentle folks who have genuine faith in God, or positive thinking, or crystals and amulets, or whatever it is that gives them hope. Yet, their *complete* receptiveness is exactly the problem because it sets up a cause and effect pattern where negative things are bound to occur.

THE EASY WAY TO A DIFFICULT LIFE

Those who are receptive on both the application and attitude paths regularly take the easy, but irresponsible way out which, predictably, frequently results in negative outcomes. When people are inundated with negative things, they typically respond with negative feelings (frustration, impatience, irritation, disbelief, disappointment, etc.) no matter what they preach or claim to be feeling.

As these feelings arise, they activate the *attitude* path, which creates conditions for energy to flow *backwards* towards an abundance of things the individual does *not* want. This is usually temporary for people in this group because they work hard at remaining receptive to God's will or positive thinking, or to some other trusted external factor, so will quickly return to the double receptive (-/-) state. Nonetheless, the occasional bouts of resistance keep energy slowly creeping in the wrong direction and things tend to get worse rather than better.

Such people frequently find themselves worrying and wondering when God will start answering their prayers and when life will finally turn a corner and become easier. Those that have reached this point are the ones who fall prey to unscrupulous preachers who promise to intercede for them provided they give money to prove their faith, or to every pill, potion, or product pusher that promises effortless results if the buyer will just consume enough of their products.

They faithfully give the money to the preacher or buy the pills, potions and other products and, when the promised results don't materialize, resistance to not getting the outcome they anticipated activates the negative abundance path and again pushes them backwards so they continue to get more of what they *don't* want.

SOME HABITS DIE HARD

Like the path toward negative abundance, this is a hard path to get off of because it requires that those on it change their behaviors. Those on the (+/+) path only need to change their attitude, which can be difficult enough. But for most people, changing their attitude is much easier than changing ingrained patterns of behavior, and that is exactly what has to happen to shift the energy on the application side of the equation from receptive (-) to active (+).

Those who are prone to moving toward passive faith in the face of difficulties, rather then taking responsibility for their outcomes and meeting their challenges courageously and with disciplined determination, continue to perpetuate the double receptive (-/-) state and to reinforce the receptive (-) application line.

For those on this path, faith is often used an an excuse for being irresponsible and lazy. Blind faith is irresponsible because it leaves all the thinking and knowing to others, who may or may not have your best interests at heart. True faith is responsible. It requires research in order to know. It is believing in something enough to *act on it* and to *keep* acting on it until the goal is realized. In true faith, the application line is active, not receptive.

As long as the application line is receptive, the only other option to being stuck is the path toward negative abundance. As a result, those in this group tend to keep creeping toward more of what they don't want. Most people on this path or on the path of negative abundance cannot successfully make this shift by themselves. They almost always need the help of a good coach or mentor to successfully redirect their lives and outcomes.

PATH 4 – THE PATH OF POSITIVE ABUNDANCE (A LOT OF THE THINGS WE DESIRE)

The final path is the *only one* you want to be on. It is the one path that leads to *positive abundance*, which is an abundance of the things you DO want. For energy to flow toward positive abundance, the application path must be *active* (+) and the *attitude* path must be *receptive* (-). *There is no exception.*

On this path, we are inducing or boosting energy along the *application* line and keeping it active (+) by way of responsible, disciplined, courageous and principled actions. We are sending energy out and allowing it to return to us in full measure by keeping the return line (attitude) *free of resistors*, open, accepting, trusting, allowing, and believing—in other words, being *completely receptive (-) to positive outcomes.*

Illustration 3.04 shows what the positive abundance path looks like. Notice that on this path the receiver (what you are focused upon) is *both clear and positive*.

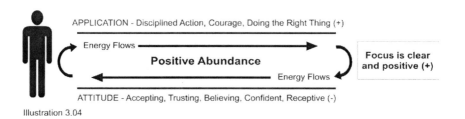

Illustration 3.04

> **In a Nut Shell:**
> When you (the generator) take responsible, disciplined, courageous action (active application) have a clear and positive focus and are confident, accepting, trusting and believing (receptive attitude), you have set up conditions for energy to flow toward an abundance of the things you want.

To have an abundance of the things we want, every part of the abundance formula must be in place and the receiver must be *precisely designed* to accept and appropriately express the energy we send it. If we want 100 watts of light from electricity, for example, we need a bulb designed to deliver 100 watts. If we want a million dollar life, we need a million dollar receiver and we need to know how to build that receiver just as precisely as the manufacturer of that 100-watt bulb knows how to build the light bulb.

People who are fully on this path are personally happy and content, healthy and fit, have great relationships, are financially secure and able to do and have anything they desire.

Unfortunately, most people are not *fully* on this path. Most people who have abundance have it in just a few areas, not across the board. Sometimes it's because they are not as clear or focused in all areas as they are in the few where they are experiencing abundance. Sometimes they don't believe they can or should have it all.

SELECTIVE ABUNDANCE

Guilt over having too much or lack of clarity about what is important prevents many who could have overall abundance from ever getting there. For example, the news is filled with stories of people who have an abundance of talent and plenty of money to go with it, but whose lives are out of control and in ruins.

It is the train wreck lives of these high profile people, who either don't believe they deserve the abundance that has come to them so easily or haven't clarified what they want, that mislead many into believing that wealth comes with a high price and that wealthy people are not happy. But financial wealth is only one aspect of positive abundance and is clearly not the most important aspect. Money is a shallow commodity without an abundance of joy, health, courage, integrity, kindness, contentment, generosity, self-respect, and the love and respect of others.

RARE AND BEAUTIFUL SOULS

Those few rare and beautiful souls who have the whole package are typically financially secure, have great relationships, are fit and healthy, and also live joyous, well-balanced lives. They are sometimes famous, but more often than not, their abundant lives are noticed only by those who have the privilege of knowing them. Even the ones who become famous tend to do it in rather low-key ways.

Speakers/authors Dr. Wayne Dyer, who has authored numerous books from *Pulling Your Own Strings* to *Being in Balance*, and Jack Canfield of *Chicken Soup for the Soul* fame, appear to be among those living healthy, balanced, overall abundant lives. I say, "appear to be" only because I don't know either of these men personally and don't know what their daily lives are like. But I have followed both for years and both seem to have well balanced, healthy lives and relationships and an abundance of all they desire.

Typically, only those who follow the work of people such as these know who they are because they don't do outrageous things to achieve fame. Humility, another component of balanced abundance, precludes their needing the adoration of a lot of fans. Both Dyer and Canfield have a lot of adoring fans, but fame is incidental to their passion for helping others, not a result of their actively seeking fame. This is not to say that fame is bad, just that for the most self-actualized, fame is a *result* of doing something they love and do very well, but not the reason they are doing it.

BALANCED, BOUNTIFUL, GENUINE, AND JOYOUS

What is most notable about people who are walking the positive abundance path in a balanced way is how joyous, humble, responsible, disciplined, courageous, caring and truly genuine they always are. They know and demonstrate that responsible, disciplined, courageous action cannot be an occasional thing and neither can it be something that there is any *resistance* around.

For this group, being responsible, disciplined, and courageous is as natural as breathing. It is an enjoyable part of who they are, not just what they do. They understand the importance of abundance at a collective level and, contrary to what many believe, they are very generous, though selective, with their time, knowledge and money. They are selective, because they have no desire to add to the problems of humanity by enabling weakness and lack of discipline.

Being around fully functioning people is a delightful experience. Others regularly come away from an encounter with a person who is well established on the positive abundance path feeling refreshed, enlightened, energized, and inspired.

REVIEW OF ENERGY FLOW, APPLICATION AND ATTITUDE

The (+/+) and (-/-) paths are not represented in the visual review on page 40 because they do not produce energy flow. Notice that the (+/-) path leads to positive abundance (a lot of what is desirable) where the (-/+) path leads to negative abundance (a lot of what is not desirable).

Notice too that positive thoughts and feelings boost energy toward positive abundance, while negative thoughts and feelings boost energy toward negative abundance. This factor will be explained in greater detail in Chapter 4.

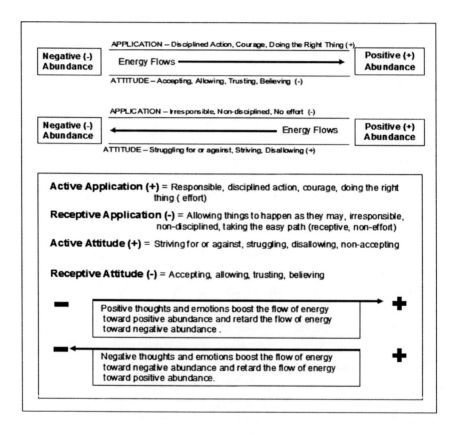

Good thoughts are no better than good dreams
if you don't follow through.

Ralph Waldo Emerson

CHAPTER 4

Begin with Thoughts and Feelings

*The value of a principle is the
number of things it will explain.*
Ralph Waldo Emerson

Since everything is energy and energy has an active (+) and receptive (-) duality, everything in existence, both physical and non-physical, exists along a continuum with either end expressing a duality: positive and negative, darkness and light, good and bad, hot and cold, etc. As we saw in Chapter 3, even abundance itself exists along a continuum with an abundance of undesirable things on one end and an abundance of desirable things on the other. The duality we will be examining in this chapter is that of positive and negative. We will first review these terms as they apply to energy and then examine them as they apply to thoughts, feelings, intent and actions.

As previously mentioned, it's easy to get tripped up on the concept of positive and negative as those terms apply to energy. We have been conditioned to believe that "positive" is good, or synonymous with what is desirable, and "negative" is bad, or synonymous with what is undesirable. But remember, *good and bad do not apply to energy.* In fact, if we consider that positive or active energy (+) on the application side expresses as *effort*, we can readily see that some people might view this as *undesirable*. Being disciplined, responsible, and courageous in order to consistently do the right thing appears to require more effort than many people are willing to exert.

We can also see that certain aspects of negative or receptive (-) energy when applied to the application side, such as doing what is easiest and most expedient in the moment, might be viewed by many as *desirable*, since it is effortless. Be careful not to equate that which is desirable or undesirable with the active (+) and receptive (-) aspects of energy. The active (+) path can bring either positive or negative results, depending on which side of the energy equation it lies on, as can the receptive (-) path.

For example, those who create a *receptive* charge (-) on the *application* side by acting irresponsible, undisciplined, and reticent will get *negative* results. Those who create a *receptive* or non-resistant charge (-) on the *attitude* side by continuing to have faith in their ability to positively impact their future will get *positive* results provided the application side is active and they clearly envision what they expect to reap.

Likewise, those who create an active charge (+) on the *application* side by acting in responsible, disciplined, courageous ways will get *positive* results *provided* they have clear goals and are receptive on the attitude side. Those who create an *active* charge (+) on the *attitude* side by being fearful, worried, closed-minded, non-accepting or who are struggling for or against an outcome, will get *negative* results.

HOW POSITIVE THOUGHTS AND FEELINGS BOOST POSITIVE ABUNDANCE

With positive and negative reframed as active and receptive in relation to energy, let's now look at this dichotomy as it relates to thoughts, feelings, intent, and actions.

As with all other things, *thoughts and feelings are energy*. But unlike the active or receptive factors that influence the application and attitude pathways and express one way or the other in the physical world, thoughts and feelings contain *both* active and receptive energy, which is why thoughts and feelings flow of their own accord.

We can set them in motion if we choose and we can guide and direct them to some extent, but we cannot stop them. We cannot determine *whether* thoughts and feelings flow, only how they flow. We can decide whether we will maintain positive thoughts and feelings or allow negative ones, but we cannot decide whether or not we will think and feel.

Because thoughts and feelings contain both the active and receptive aspects of energy, they can impact energy on both sides of the equation (application and attitude). Because of this, it is at the thoughts and feelings level that we must first apply responsible, disciplined, courageous action. The oft heard advice to monitor and discipline our thoughts is very good council.

Feelings don't seem to be within our control. They continually come and go at will and, while we can suppress one feeling with another one, we can't stop or completely control them. But we can control our thoughts and thoughts influence feelings. The reason we cannot control feelings directly is that feelings are instinctual on a basic level, but they are driven and extended beyond instinct by the thoughts and beliefs we hold. It is our thoughts and beliefs that create our problems, not instinct, so it is these we must control.

Many people think that decisions are made through logic (thinking), but the reality is that we make every decision based on how that decision *feels*. Considerable evidence suggests that feelings run the show more than most people care to admit. We master our lives by mastering our feelings through emotional maturity or what is sometimes called emotional intelligence. Yet the only way to master our feelings is to master our thoughts and beliefs.

Both thoughts and feelings are powerful magnets that speed up, slow down, reverse or otherwise direct the flow of energy and greatly influence our outcomes so managing both will greatly impact results on every level.

Positive thoughts and feelings follow the same path as that of positive abundance. That is, their application requires effort, but there is no resistance to them. Because positive thoughts and feelings are active on the application side, we must purposefully apply them to our lives. Because they are receptive on the attitude side, they never impose themselves upon us. They come only when we allow them to.

We are never happy when we don't want to be, for example, and when we are happy we never wish we weren't.

POSITIVE THINKING

It is because positive thoughts and feelings follow the same path as positive abundance that it can appear that positive thinking produces abundance in and of itself. But positive thinking, even in combination with receptive feeling, will not produce *external results* without *external actions*. The external actions don't necessarily have to be just yours, but you do have to contribute in some way.

Actor and comedian Jim Carrey tells of an incident in which, as a kid, he visualized himself having a new bike after learning about the power of prayer and visualization. His family didn't have the money to buy a bike and his circumstances were such that he had no way of earning the money to buy one. But he kept visualizing, praying, and fully believing he would get the bike, and he actually got one as a result of someone else entering his name in a drawing.

It is incidences such as these that make so many believe that visualization and positive thinking can produce miracles in and of themselves. But a closer look always presents a different picture. Remember, action is an integral part of the abundance equation.

Did Jim Carrey take any action? Of course he did. He let whoever entered his name in that drawing know how much he wanted a bike. He was sufficiently effective at expressing his longing to induce the other person to also take action. Moreover, his previous actions were such that he was deemed lovable and worthy of having a bike by the person that entered his name in the drawing. Had he been a real brat whom no one could stand, it is highly unlikely that anyone would have even thought to enter his name in a drawing, much less have made the effort.

Did the positive thinking and receptivity have anything to do with it? Absolutely! It boosted energy along the positive abundance path toward his clearly defined goal and positive focus and kept him receptive to the possibility of getting a bike. It also provided the faith and enthusiasm that he so effectively expressed. The entire formula for getting what he wanted was in place, including action on his part, whether he realized it or not.

POSITIVE THOUGHTS, FEELINGS, AND INTENT BOOST APPLICATION AND BUILD FAITH

Positive thoughts, feelings, and intent boost energy toward positive outcomes. They influence, and are influenced by, both the active and receptive aspects of energy on the positive abundance path. When applied to an *active* (+) *application* line, positive thoughts, feelings and intent act as *boosters* and help remove resistance from the disciplined, responsible, courageous actions that might otherwise feel effortful. In other words, positive thoughts and feelings increase results by *removing resistance* to being responsible, disciplined, and courageous.

When we have positive thoughts and feelings about the efforts we make to achieve our goals, we have *no resistance* to them. We are receptive to and actually energized by the work we are doing and can work long hours without it feeling like work. Positive thoughts, feelings and intent also add to our levels of trust, acceptance and faith on the attitude line.

NEGATIVE THOUGHTS AND FEELINGS BOOST NEGATIVE ABUNDANCE

Just as positive thoughts and feelings mirror the positive abundance path and act as boosters along both sides of that path, so too do negative thoughts and feelings mirror and boost energy along both sides of the negative abundance path. On the *application* side, negative thoughts and feelings are *receptive* (-). They require no effort on our part. They just show up of their own accord and, if we don't do anything to bring them under control, they get very big, ugly, and unruly.

On the *attitude* side, negative thoughts and feelings are *active* (+). They don't feel good so we try to resist them. But, because they carry an active attitude charge, they *impose* themselves upon us and often won't leave without some intervention on our part. Although we are never happy when we don't want to be, we are often angry, sad, frustrated, or depressed when we don't want to be, and those feelings rarely leave without some form of intervention.

It is precisely because negative thoughts and emotions actively impose themselves upon us and require effort on our part to contain them that they are the most visible and most prevalent in our world. When presented with both positive and negative situations, the negative ones are always the ones that compete for, and usually get, our attention. That's why the news is mostly negative. Positive news makes us feel good and we like hearing it, but it's the negative stuff that rivets our attention, and those who produce the news know that all too well.

The tendency to look for flaws is another example of negativity imposing itself upon us. For example, if we are given a sheet of white paper that is perfectly clean except for a small smudge, it's the smudge that will get our attention. We have to purposefully adjust our focus to see the clean parts of the page even though they occupy most of the surface. The same thing happens when one piece of a thousand-piece puzzle is missing or we see a beautiful face with a blemish on it. We home in on the smudge, the missing piece, the blemish, the problem, the flaw.

NEGATIVE THOUGHTS AND FEELINGS VIE FOR OUR ATTENTION

Life provides us with lots of opportunities to tune in to both positive and negative thoughts and feelings, but negative thoughts and feelings vie for our attention and the positive ones don't.

We are by nature highly receptive to authentically positive thoughts and emotions and always welcome them. The only exception is where early childhood conditioning has built up artificial resistors such that positive thoughts and feelings seem strange. When people have been conditioned to avoid feeling too good about things, or not to expect too much, positive thoughts and feelings can be scary and they are then avoided. On the rare occasions when they are allowed to surface, a person conditioned to reject them will quickly toss them out as invalid, frivolous, or even dangerous.

SELF-SABOTAGE

I recently had a conversation with a man who expressed that he was lonely and wanted to find love. However, he had been hurt in the past and had built up a protective shell around himself which prevented him from getting too close to others, and from letting others get too close to him. When I suggested that he would need to step outside of that shell and open himself up to loving and being loved, he protested that he could never do that because it was too dangerous. Imagine perceiving love as dangerous! But it wasn't really love he was focused on. It was the pain he had experienced in the past. Even knowing that the other option was continued loneliness, the idea of letting down his guard and being vulnerable again was just too scary.

When we have been conditioned to resist positive thoughts and feelings, we, as adults, have the option of letting go of that conditioning or of keeping it. If we choose to keep it, as the man in the previous example did, we are then imposing that condition upon *ourselves*. And often we do that unknowingly.

For example, although positive affirmations are intended to move us forward rather than hold us back, they can set up feelings of resistance when they are inappropriate for us or insincere, or when they are used in an attempt to cover up fears and insecurities. We can fool lots of people, but we cannot fool ourselves. Positive thoughts and feelings cannot be forced or faked. If they are not real and authentic, our internal monitor will give us negative feedback in an attempt to keep us honest.

When positive thoughts and feelings are real and authentic we welcome, appreciate and thoroughly enjoy them and so never resist them. And when we approach them in that natural way, they always boost energy toward positive abundance and we gain immense benefits.

On the other hand, every time someone tunes into a negative thought or allows a negative emotion to continue unchecked, resistance is created in the mind, in the physical body, and in the outer world with detrimental results.

When the *application* side of the energy equation is *receptive* (-), that is, undisciplined and irresponsible, negative thoughts, feelings and intent *boost* the receptivity and shut people down even further. Under the influence of negative thoughts and/or feelings, the irresponsible become even *more* irresponsible, the undisciplined *more* undisciplined, and the fearful become *more* fearful.

On the *attitude* side, energy flows freely only when unencumbered by resistors. And negative thoughts, feelings, and intent *always* act as resistors on the attitude side of the energy equation. The resistance then sets up conditions that move the attitude toward *more* worry, *more* disbelief, *more* non-acceptance, and *more* active resistance (+). Just as positive thoughts and feelings increase our likelihood of getting more of what we want, negative ones increase our likelihood of getting more of what we *don't* want. That is why the wise have paid so much attention to the nature of thoughts and feelings since recorded history.

BEYOND THOUGHTS AND FEELINGS

Thoughts and feelings have power indeed, but don't let that reality lull you into thinking that they are enough. By maintaining positive thoughts and feelings, we can neutralize the *internal* impact of negativity and we can *boost* energy along the positive abundance path, provided the other conditions are met. But remember that only *physical actions* directly impact the external physical world. That's why all the positive thinking in the world will not, in and of itself, get us that dream home, improve our fitness level, or fatten our bank account.

As we saw in Chapter 2, energy attracts *complementary* energy. Therefore, the non-physical nature of thoughts and feelings attract complementary non-physical energy. Positive thoughts can make us feel better about our current circumstances, for example, and make us more appealing to others, but to actually connect with others, or change our physical circumstances, we must *do* something in the external world.

THE HEALTH BENEFITS OF POSITIVE THOUGHTS, FEELINGS, AND INTENT

The health benefits of positive thoughts, feelings, and intent seem, on the surface, to be an exception to this rule, but they are not. The reason positive thinking creates a physical benefit in the body is because it neutralizes the effects of negative thoughts and feelings with positive ones, thereby creating a better balance of energies.

Physical health in the human body is a result of a healthy balance between active and receptive energies and, since we are inundated with negativity in the world we live in, it is easy for the negative influences to create an imbalance in the physical body. A better balance between energies results in better energy flow, which positively affects the immune system. The result may be better physical health, but to get you there, your body did a lot of *physical* work whether you were aware of it or not.

For positive thinking to have *physical* results there must be an *active* (+) *physical* component. The activity inside the human body provides that component for improved health, but it affects only the body. It does not translate to the outer physical world.

Without external action, visualization and receptiveness to having what is visualized—while soothing in the short term—will only result in increased hoping, dreaming and longing in the long term. These eventually lead to resistance, which *diminishes* the flow of energy toward positive abundance.

In effect, sustained positive thinking and expectation, when lacking a complementary active component, generally results in the very *opposite* of what the positive thinker is hoping for.

INSIDE-OUT

Although external action is an essential aspect of the abundance formula, we cannot master the external world and positively impact our future until we have mastered the internal one. We cannot approach the idea of responsible, disciplined, courageous action without resistance until we have found passion and purpose. And we cannot find these in the external world. It is passion that drives us to do whatever it takes to realize the dream—to focus our mental, emotional, physical, and spiritual energies such that we are able to work long hours and perform amazing feats—and love every minute of it. Without passion we are just faking it. And, since we can't fool ourselves or short change the law, if we are trying to build something where no passion exists, we are just wasting time and effort. To recap:

POSITIVE THOUGHTS AND FEELINGS
• Act as boosters to accelerate energy flowing toward positive outcomes and impede negative outcomes.

• Act as resistors to retard energy flowing toward negative outcomes

• Are active on the application side and require effort to sustain

• Are receptive on the attitude side and do not impose themselves upon us

NEGATIVE THOUGHTS AND FEELINGS
• Act as boosters to accelerate energy flowing toward negative outcomes and impede positive outcomes

• Act as resistors to retard energy flowing toward positive outcomes

• Are receptive on the application side and require no effort to sustain

• Are active on the attitude side and impose themselves upon us

CHAPTER 5

The Six Basic Rules of Energy

*To understand energy in its fullest expression
is to understand everything.*
S. D. Buffington

Now that you have a basic grasp of how, when and why energy flows or fails to flow, it will be useful to gain a deeper understanding of the principles of energy. We don't need to be a physicist or an electrician to have a reason to gain an in-depth understanding of the laws and principles of energy and magnetism. All we need is a desire to have abundance. Until we understand these principles, we cannot know how to intentionally apply the Law of Abundance, and without this knowledge, the chances are astronomical that we will apply the law in the wrong way and continue to get *more of what we do not want.*

You have lights in your home that deliver exactly the amount of light you want, a refrigerator and air conditioner that deliver cold where and when you want it, and a stove that delivers heat because the people who build those things understand, and effectively apply, the principles of energy flow. They know how to harness energy so it does exactly what they want it to do. And because energy *always* does exactly the same thing, the builders of homes and the creators of the myriad electrical products can create lots of units with varying features, knowing that every single unit they build using the right design and components will strictly adhere to the principles of energy flow (electricity) and deliver the exact results they intend.

By understanding how, why, when and to where energy flows *without exception*, you will be able to apply the Law of Abundance to your life with the same precision and predictability as a master electrician wires a home or an appliance manufacturer creates a specific product. You will be able to design your life so you can have a lot of one thing and not so much of another, and can determine exactly how each of the things you decide upon will manifest.

ENERGY AND INTELLIGENCE

According to quantum physicists, energy is not just some mindless force that governs the flow of electricity, creates atoms, and attracts them to one another to form matter. Energy has *intelligence* to a far greater degree than was previously thought—the intelligence apparent in universal order and nature, to be sure, but also the intelligence (intentionality, thoughts, feelings and imagination) of people.

That there has ever been a debate as to whether energy has an intelligent component is a mystery to me. The proof of energetic intelligence is everywhere. Without an intelligent component, there would be no precise laws by which everything is governed, and nothing would be predictable. And there would not, *could not*, be human beings.

Humans are intelligent and are one way in which energy expresses. If intelligence were not part of the energy equation, there could be no intelligent beings; *no humans using their intellect to question whether there was an intelligent component to the universe.*

There are six rules of energy that are important to know and remember. This is the stuff life is made of and each rule directly impacts you in some way.

RULE 1 - EVERYTHING IS ENERGY[3]

We typically think of energy as things like sunlight, or electricity, or whatever powers our mind and body, but the mind and body are themselves energy expressing as matter. In fact, as physicist Albert Einstein proved in his $E=mc^2$ formula, virtually *everything* is made up of energy. What we see as mass and what we see as energy are, according to Einstein and a large community of quantum physicists, "different manifestations of the same thing."

Einstein on E=mc^2

"It followed from the special theory of relativity that mass and energy are both but different manifestations of the same thing – a somewhat unfamiliar conception for the average mind. Furthermore, the equation E is equal to mc-squared, in which energy is put equal to mass, multiplied by the square of the velocity of light, showed that very small amounts of mass may be converted into a very large amount of energy and vice versa. The mass and energy were in fact equivalent, according to the formula mentioned above. This was demonstrated by Cockcroft and Walton in 1932 experimentally."

Source: Massachusetts Institute of Technology (MIT)

Why it Matters – Since everything is energy, including us—our bodies, minds, thoughts, feelings, impulses and actions—we are all subject to the rules that govern energy. Einstein's work and that of current quantum physicists have demonstrated that energy and mass are interchangeable; energy can be reduced to mass and mass can be expanded into energy. Knowing precisely how, when and why energy becomes mass and mass becomes energy gives us great power. We can use this power for good or ill, as the creation of the atomic bomb and nuclear reactors demonstrate.

The same principles that have allowed scientists to build nuclear reactors to power cities, and atomic bombs to destroy them are available to all of us. To conform to the Law of Abundance, however, we must learn to apply these principles for constructive, not destructive, purposes.

Imagine what might be possible when we have learned to harness energy constructively, converting matter into energy and energy into matter in wholly useful ways. People the world over would likely experience things more wonderful and amazing than any fairy tale or science fiction novel we could ever dream up.

2. ENERGY IS NEITHER CREATED NOR DESTROYED. IT IS SIMPLY RELEASED (KINETIC ENERGY) OR SUPPRESSED (POTENTIAL ENERGY)[4]

This rule states that energy, no matter what form it takes, is a constant that we can neither create nor destroy. Because it is obvious that we cannot get something from nothing and, since everything is energy, scientists theorize that for anything to exist, energy had to always exist.

Energy can undergo physical or chemical changes, which may create the *appearance* of creation or destruction, but it is simply changing from one form to another. We can throw away or destroy the *form* of things (such as burning them), but the energy still exists. It simply assumes another position or form. Matter is an example of suppressed or potential energy, while the burning of matter is an example of released or kinetic energy.

The bottom line is that nothing is ever destroyed. It just changes from one form of energy to another and very often *people* decide what that form will be.

Why it Matters – When you understand what suppresses energy and what releases it on a human level, you will be able to use it to your advantage. Where you are currently suppressing energy that should be flowing, you will know how to release it to flow toward what you want. Where energy is flowing freely toward what you don't want, you will be able to suppress it to get better results. And, when you realize that you can't get something from nothing, perhaps you won't waste your energy running down that path.

3. POTENTIAL ENERGY, ONCE RELEASED, NEVER RETURNS TO ITS ORIGINAL FORM. IT IS ALWAYS DEGRADED TO A MORE DISPERSED AND LESS USEFUL FORM.[5]

Here is an example of how this rule plays out: When you burn a log in your fireplace, the fire gives off heat. Fire is the means by which the potential energy in the log turns into kinetic energy. Kinetic energy describes the ability of energy to do *useful* work. Scientists tell us that for useful work to occur, energy must flow or move from a level of high quality (more concentrated) energy to a level of lower quality (less concentrated) energy.

Fire is high quality energy which has the ability to do work (warm your body, cook food, boil water, etc), but as the potential energy in the log is burned off and the heat is dissipated into the surroundings, all that is ultimately left is a pile of cold ashes. The high quality energy (fire and intense heat) has now been completely released and has degraded to a more dispersed and less useful form. While the remaining ashes can be returned to the soil and used in their current form, they no longer contain the potential energy of the log and the log cannot be recreated.

Why it Matters – While energy is unlimited in the universe and can recycle over eons of time, it is not unlimited as immediately useful *high quality* energy. As this rule implies, the best application of energy is useful work. When potential energy is squandered, it is sometimes lost for eons and squandered energy absolutely *cannot* lead to abundance.

According to the second rule, we will never run out of energy, but we can certainly run out of *high quality or useful energy* for a very long time and be adversely impacted on personal and global levels.

4. MOST ENERGY EXCHANGE PROCESSES MOVE FROM HIGH QUALITY TO LOW QUALITY ENERGY, WITH TWO VERY IMPORTANT EXCEPTIONS .

Current science teaches that there is just *one* exception to his rule, but the Law of Abundance adds the *human element* to the equation and recognizes *two*. The two exceptions are:

(A) Photosynthesis – The conversion of solar energy to chemical energy by plants and some bacteria. Photosynthesis converts radiant energy (light) from the sun into high-quality chemical energy, which is stored in plants in the form of sugar molecules and low-quality heat energy.

When animals and humans eat plants, the high-quality chemical energy of the plants is transformed within the body to high-quality *mechanical* energy, which is used to perform involuntary life sustaining processes, such as beating your heart, or voluntary processes, such as moving your muscles. Photosynthesis is the means by which all *physical* life is sustained.

(B) Neurosynthesis – The term as applied here refers to the ability of the human mind to synthesize and/or preserve high quality energy. This is not currently recognized by science and, because it has not yet been measured and proven in a lab, some physicists may dismiss it. But there are two ways to test a truth. One is by experiment and the other is by observation. While it may or may not be possible to prove neurosynthesis through experimentation (no one has tried yet to my knowledge), it can certainly be directly observed and it has a long history from which to draw inferences. The term as it applies to the synthesis of high quality energy may be new, but the process is as old as humankind.

In the same way that photosynthesis converts light to high quality energy in plants to feed and sustain us physically, neurosynthesis converts "light" (intelligence, which includes insight, understanding, awareness, creativity and ingenuity) into high quality energy to feed and energize us *non-physically* (mentally, emotionally and spiritually) and to *harness, direct, and conserve* physical energy. The non-physical application of high quality energy is what provides the impetus for the many things that humans create—creations that aid in the sustenance of physical life and the conservation of energy and that stimulate mental, emotional, and spiritual activity.

The wheel, stairs, incline and pulley are a few of the many examples of human inventions designed to *conserve* energy. Everything on the planet that runs on electricity, gasoline, solar, hydro or any other form of power provides examples of human inventions designed to *harness and direct energy.*

Just as plants convert sunlight to sugars, which are then converted to energy when consumed, neurosynthesis converts intelligence and imagination (or creativity) into intentionality. Intentionality stimulates the human mind and emotions and impacts energy in measurable ways, as every invention we use every day proves.

As with physical foods, the products of intelligence and imagination are consumed by the masses and, in both physical and non-physical instances, how this high quality energy expresses depends on how the consumer uses it.

Some people, for example, eat food and use the energy to stay fit, achieve goals, and move toward positive abundance, while others squander their energy by sitting around, complaining and storing up excess energy as fat; energy which will remain in its stored or suppressed form until used. If it is never used in life, it will break down and dissipate as low quality energy after death.

People similarly either utilize or squander the energy produced by neurosynthesis. Those who consume it wisely use neurosynthetic energy to learn and grow and to improve their own condition, as well as the condition of their family, their community, and the planet they live on.

Those who consume it unwisely use it to amuse themselves or escape. They learn and grow very little and add little-to-nothing to the collective pool of creation. They look at the desperation in the world around them and sigh, complain or divert their attention to something more appealing, hoping that "somebody" will eventually do something. Our world would be so much better if these folks would just realize that they *are* somebody.

We must have both photosynthetic and neurosynthetic energy to thrive. Photosynthetic energy sustains our physical body while neurosynthetic energy sustains our mind, emotions and spirit.

Just as plants that are deprived of sunlight (photosynthetic energy) will wither and die sooner than is natural for them, so too do people prematurely wither and die due to insufficient amounts of neurosynthetic energy. Even when the physical body is being sustained through the consumption of photosynthetic energy, if the mind, emotions, and spirit are being deprived, humans gradually (and sometimes rapidly) decline.

Why it Matters – Scientifically, the fourth rule of energy states that the only source of renewable energy is sunlight. The Law of Abundance adds creativity (intelligence plus imagination). Only humans possess neurosynthetic energy, and only neurosynthetic energy can alter physical matter and the world as a whole in *purposeful* ways.

If misapplied or squandered, not only do we suffer on a personal level, but families, communities, societies, countries—indeed the entire planet—suffer as well.

Fuels and foods can be used only once to perform useful work. Once a tank full of gasoline is burned, for example, the *high-quality* energy in that gasoline is lost forever. Once you digest a meal and burn it off as calories, the high quality energy in the food is lost forever. But, cut down a plant and another one grows. Burn a forest and a new one takes its place. Plants are not dependent on the high to low energy cycle. They synthesize their own high quality energy from sunlight. People do the same thing at non-physical levels through intelligence, active imagination, and focused passion, which result in creativity.

Because energy is never lost, we will never destroy it, but we can certainly deplete high quality sources of it, such as oil. In fact, we are depleting that resource at alarming rates, which will require us to eventually turn to new forms of high quality energy.

Neurosynthesis, the ability of humankind to discover and apply new ways of harnessing and directing energy, is what will make that possible.

5. ENERGY TENDS TO CHANGE SPONTANEOUSLY FROM A CONCENTRATED AND ORDERED FORM TO A MORE DISPERSED AND DISORDERED FORM.[6]

Examples of increasing disorder:

a) A glass dish falls to the floor and shatters into pieces, never to return to its original form.

b) Chocolate stirred into milk spreads and becomes dispersed throughout the milk, and does not return to the state of pure chocolate.

c) When plants and animals die, the highly ordered array of cells decay into molecules that become dispersed throughout the environment.

d) A vehicle's exhaust or smoke from a chimney spontaneously disperses to a more random or disordered state in the atmosphere.

e) Pollutants dumped into a river disperse throughout the water.

Why it Matters – On a personal level, we can see the spontaneous flow of energy to a more disordered state by observing that a house left untended becomes increasingly disordered and eventually falls into disrepair, or an untended garden turns to weeds, or the physical body left untended becomes diseased or disabled. And, while these are different phenomena than chocolate stirred into milk or the dispersion of dye into water in that *molecules* are not affected, the result is the same. Molecular dispersion occurs on a micro scale. The tendency to go from ordered to disordered, as we typically observe it, occurs on a macro scale. The macro form of disorder may not impact molecules, but it sure impacts us.

Have you ever wondered why most people get so grumpy and irritable when surrounded by clutter? It's because the natural state of abundance is one of order, not of mayhem, and we instinctively know that clutter breaks up concentration and throws us out of balance and off-course. Just as glass shatters on impact releasing its bond in reaction to physical laws and molecules disperse seeking *equilibrium*, when we feel discomfort in the midst of clutter, we, too, are reacting to physical laws and seeking balance.

Earl Nightingale, personal development pioneer and author of the popular books, *The Strangest Secret* and *Lead the Field*, observed that it was possible to drive through any neighborhood and predict the degree of abundance that the people living in the houses were experiencing. Not just financially, but on every level, especially in their thinking and attitudes. He correctly surmised that it is no coincidence that the homes and yards of those who are living in poverty are almost always cluttered and in need of repair, while the homes and yards of those who are experiencing abundance are almost always well groomed and cared for. It's easy to assume that clutter and disorder are a *result* of poverty, but in fact, they are the *cause*, as Hill correctly stated, and the Law of Abundance makes crystal clear.

An essential component to the flow of positive energy is order. The entire universe shouts this to us, and those who have been listening have responded with responsible, disciplined actions. Those who find discipline and responsible actions distasteful will never experience an abundance of the things they want. They *will* experience abundance because the law works exactly the same for everyone. But, those that are lazy or undisciplined will experience an abundance of things they *do not want* rather than of things they do want. Each of us gets to choose our outcomes.

Through neurosynthesis, humans have the capacity to redirect energy, turning disorder into order and decay into some great new invention. We do that through *attention* and *intention*. We can see a field full of weeds and bramble bushes, for example, and choose to do nothing, or we can turn it into a beautiful garden depending on our attention and intention. We can see a living thing—person, plant or animal—dying of thirst or starvation and choose to allow it to continue to decline, or we can feed, nourish and revive it, again depending on our attention and intention.

When attention and intention are coupled with *passion*, we choose to intervene. Intervention can be positive or negative. When the passion is directed toward positive abundance, the intervention follows the path of responsible, disciplined action and a caring attitude.

ENTROPY

Entropy is a scientific measure of relative randomness or disorder. A random system has high entropy (high disorder), and an orderly system has low entropy (low disorder). The entropy rule states that systems tend to go from higher states of order to disorder when and wherever the useful amount of high quality energy decreases.

When we apply this concept to gardens, homes and physical bodies, for example, it is evident that we either apply high quality energy in the form of purposeful, disciplined action, or all three will entropy (fall into disorder and disrepair). Thus, the systems we regularly interact with will spontaneously tend toward increasing randomness and disorder (or increasing entropy) unless we manage, slow or redirect the process by the *purposeful* input of high quality energy (neurosynthesis).

On a broad scale, we can see the effects of entropy on the overall quality of entire societies and on the global ecological condition. Unlike gravity, which has a singular effect, entropy has a cumulative effect.

When the activities of just a few individuals increase disorder in a community and in the environment, the effect may seem so small and insignificant that we think we can just ignore it. But the cumulative impact can eventually have a very large, negative effect on the quality of life on a personal level, in families, in local communities, throughout nations, and on the entire global ecology.

Consider, for instance, the disorder-producing activities of billions of people who are regularly squandering time, misapplying their energies, following an undisciplined path, and converting more and more of the world's resources to trash and low-quality heat energy. The only way we are going to reverse the ever-increasing entropy we are currently witnessing on a global level is through responsible, disciplined, and courageous actions and the effective application of neurosynthesis or creative intelligence.

EFFORTLESS DISCIPLINE

Don't let the idea that you must be responsible, disciplined, and courageous concern you if you have not been resplendent with those attributes up to this point. When applied according to the Law of Abundance, these are not distasteful things. They are a natural result of the proper use of energy and feel effortless when applied to the right actions. On the path to abundance, discipline and responsible action are *natural and enjoyable* results of learning effective ways to realize your dream and follow your passions. There is *no resistance* or struggle around the efforts connected to the things for which you have real passion.

Although we don't necessarily enjoy some of the things we must do to achieve our goals, if they are part of bringing true passion to fruition, we generally don't mind these activities too much. Where we continue to resist certain aspects of the work required to realize a passionately held goal, it is wise to find ways to change our feelings toward the task, or hire or inspire someone who enjoys that particular task to take it over. Removing ourselves from tasks that produce high and sustained amounts of resistance, and trusting those who don't have resistance to those tasks to handle them, will keep us on the path to positive abundance and everyone will benefit.

Often it is the *perception* of something as being difficult that sets up *resistance* on the *application* side of the energy equation, which results in a *double active* energy combination (+/+), causing energy to cease flowing. If we continue to strive, we become stuck. *To stay on the positive abundance path, there must be no resistance or sense of effort to the actions we take.*

That probably doesn't make a lot of sense until you apply it to something you have a real passion for. When you do, you will realize that there is *no sense of effort* around doing those things. Although you may be working diligently, putting in long hours and disciplining yourself to keep the things you enjoy moving in a predictable (orderly) direction, this activity actually *generates energy*. It does not deplete it. There is no resistance to this type of discipline. Where passion is the driver, effort feels effortless. When we are pursuing a true passion we may be putting in a lot of work, but it doesn't *feel* like work.

RESPONSIBILITY AND COURAGE

Effortless discipline is a result of *focused passion*. Responsibility and courage are a result of *correctly* focused passion. It is passion that drives you forward and motivates you to keep moving toward the desired outcome. However, passion can be properly directed or misdirected. It is the determination to do the right thing and to work as a *generative* force rather than a destructive one, that drives responsibility and courage.

Criminals may be disciplined to get the results they want, for instance. They may work out a plan and follow it to the letter, and because they are working with the Law of Abundance on one level by applying disciplined action (+) toward a result they fully expect to get (-), they can make a fortune being dishonest and destructive. Remember, the Law of Abundance is non-discriminatory. The sun *does* shine on the just and the unjust and rain waters the lawns of criminals as well as those of the virtuous. But criminals do not act responsibly. They don't have the desire or the courage to do the right thing for the common good, so absolute abundance, both internal and external, is not possible.

A good example would be drug lords, who get wealthy by pushing drugs that they know are addictive and destructive. They may amass a lot of money and even gain power in certain circles, but they don't have respect or true peace of mind. And more often than not, this lack of inner peace leads them to get hooked on the very drugs they are pushing to others. They are on a destructive, rather than generative path, which ultimately affects mental, emotional, spiritual, and physical health; eventually, this house of cards has to come tumbling down.

The reason values (such as honesty and integrity) and virtues (such as courage, morality, self-control, generosity, diligence, patience, kindness, compassion, and humility) are so important is because they are *generative* in nature. They activate energy toward positive abundance and confer benefits individually and to the world as a whole.

Lust, greed, gluttony, sloth, wrath, envy, egotism, and selfishness are *destructive* in nature. They are a misuse of energy and, no matter what the short-term gains of those on this destructive path may appear to be, they eventually lead to decline both personally and globally.

6. ALL COMPLEX ORGANISMS AND ECOSYSTEMS ARE OPEN SYSTEMS, NOT CLOSED SYSTEMS, AND MUST BE FUELED BY HIGH QUALITY ENERGY.[7]

Take, for example, the human body. To form and preserve its highly ordered arrangement of molecules and sustain an organized network of precise chemical reactions, we must continually acquire high-quality energy from food. If we don't, our energy is depleted and the body dies and begins to decompose (move to a more dispersed and disordered state).

The same is true for all systems: physical, mental, emotional, and spiritual. The human body does not regenerate its own energy. Neither do high quality thoughts, feelings, attention, and intention. Just like our physical bodies, they need the input of high quality energy.

Physically, the sun powers the maintenance of complexity by providing us and the earth with a constant supply of high-quality energy.

Non-physically, creativity, imagination, and generative values and virtues power the maintenance of high quality energy. Creativity and imagination provide us with a constant flow of ideas that allow us to conserve, harness, direct, and order energy, while values and virtues ensure that the energy we direct is generative rather than destructive.

When energy is applied in destructive ways, high quality energy is depleted, not generated, and since all organisms and ecosystems are open systems, that are also depleted when there is no input of high quality energy, all actions, attitudes, thoughts, feelings and beliefs (which drive values and virtues) directly impact each and every one of us on every level, from personal to global.

In looking at the current state of the world, it is clear that we have not been using energy in ways that are creating a global experience of abundance. It's time we change all that.

KEYS TO UNDERSTANDING

Absorb this chapter before you move on. Understanding the principles of energy is essential for harnessing power, setting the Law of Abundance into motion and cementing in your mind the principles that are essential to getting the results you want.

RECAP OF SIX BASIC RULES

1. **Energy is everything,** including all the physical, mental, emotional, and spiritual components of you and me.

2. **Energy is neither created nor destroyed.** It is simply released as kinetic energy or stored as potential energy.

3. **Potential energy, once released, never returns to its original form.** It degrades to a more dispersed form, moving from high quality energy (that which does useful work) to low quality energy (that which is not capable of doing useful work).

4. **There are two very important exceptions to rule three. Photosynthesis,** which creates high quality energy for physical maintenance, and **neurosynthesis,** which creates high quality energy for non-physical maintenance and for the purposeful harnessing and conservation of physical energy.

5. **Energy tends to flow or change spontaneously from a concentrated and ordered form to a more dispersed and disordered form.** Human attention and intention can alter this effect through responsible, disciplined action.

6. **All organisms and ecosystems are open, not closed systems,**
    and must be fueled by high quality energy. On Earth, high quality
    energy is generated by the Sun (photosynthesis) and creativity
    (neurosynthesis). Humans need both to generate abundance.

*The new source of power is not money
in the hands of the few,
but information in the hands of the many.*

John Naisbitt, Megatrends

PART 2

The Principles of Energy Flow

Everything in nature contains
all the power of nature.

Ralph Waldo Emerson

My own experience about all the blessings in my life is that the more I give away, the more that comes back. That is how life works, and that is how energy works.

Ken Blanchard

CHAPTER 6

The Principles of Energy Flow: Equilibrium

Water which is too pure has no fish.

Ts' ai Ken T'an

Chapter 5 was about principles as they apply to energy in general. The next few chapters are about how and why energy flows or fails to flow. The principles of energy flow are important because how you direct your energy determines what you manifest in your life. These principles apply equally to every arena and at all times. To harness the power that provides us with anything and everything—good and bad, physical and non-physical—it is essential to understand how to direct it toward the good things we want.

As in the previous chapter, examples of how each principle applies to both the physical and the non-physical world in personal and non-personal ways will be presented. Energy is energy no matter how it expresses, and it powers your life just as surely and specifically as it powers the myriad electrical products you use every day. Learning exactly how it works for you personally will allow you to harness it and direct it toward your goals with great precision. This chapter covers the first principle of energy flow: equilibrium.

PRINCIPLE 1 – Energy is always seeking equilibrium[8]

Non-personal example – The reason energy flows is because it is always seeking balance between surplus and deficient factors. Though equilibrium does not exist in open systems where other forces have an effect, energy is still ever seeking to achieve it.

According to physicists, a system that is in equilibrium experiences *no changes* provided it remains *isolated* from its surroundings. In a state of equilibrium, there are no unbalanced potentials, or driving forces within the system. Because physicists can observe energy at perfect rest once equalized in a closed system, and can observe it go into action when outside influences create an imbalance, there is no question that energy flows in an effort to achieve equilibrium.

What we call a "dead" battery is really one in which total equilibrium has been reached in the chemicals that make up the battery. A battery is a closed system, so once it reaches equilibrium, energy no longer flows and the battery no longer does useful work.

It is the constant introduction of variables in an open system that prevents equilibrium from occurring and keeps energy in motion. As you may recall, Rule 6 in Chapter 5 states that all complex organisms and ecosystems are open systems, not closed systems, and equilibrium can be sustained only in a closed system. Life is an open system.

Personal example – Why is any of this important to you? Because, when you realize that energy *seeks* equilibrium, you will know why too much activity and chaos creates anxiety in you and why doing nothing is so hard.

When you understand that perfect equilibrium is not only *impossible* in an open system—which includes us and the world we live in—but is not even desirable, you won't waste energy stressing out over the fact that your life is not always in perfect balance. No open system is ever in perfect balance. Just as the human body, mind, emotions, and chemistry are always adjusting and re-adjusting in an effort to achieve equilibrium, so too is life.

In the human body, it is the constant adjusting and re-adjusting which results in relatively stable conditions in a variable environment, such as body Ph, brain chemistry, temperature, and blood sugar. When the body is healthy, the range of each variable is so consistent as to be highly predictable.

A healthy range for blood sugar, for example, is between 70 and 120. That's a rather wide latitude, but one that is necessary to healthy function. Blood sugar may be around 70 when we have not eaten for a while, for example, and around 120 right after a meal. As long as it stays in the optimal range, all is well. When blood sugar drops too far below 70 or regularly rises too far above 120, however, we have a problem.

LIFE IS A RANGE OF UPS AND DOWNS

Like your body chemistry, life does not exist as a constant, but as an ever-fluctuating range of ups and downs. It is the fluctuation that keeps energy flowing and life vibrant. Those who are functioning from a healthy place recognize life's normal range, allow for the inevitable fluctuations, and are wise enough not to create circumstances that will throw their lives outside the normal range on either side.

There are many ways to create conditions that throw us outside of life's normal range. For example, those who fear change of any kind work very hard at trying to keep everything the same. Though most aren't aware of it, trying to keep things the same requires trying to simulate a closed system. Those who are doing this go through the same routines day after day, varying things as little as possible, moving in a continuous, mindless loop. Their goal is to keep things nice, predictable and balanced, but that is never the result.

Remember the "dead" battery? This is not a life to aspire to. Life is not and cannot be a closed system. It is dynamic. Change and fluctuation are natural parts of life.

When we allow for the fact that we must have the ups and downs to keep life vibrant and dynamic, we won't fall into the trap of fretting when we are experiencing the downs. We won't blame life's fluctuations on ourselves and waste energy wondering what we did wrong to deserve them. Neither will we adopt a Pollyanna attitude that leads us to imagine that, if we think the right thoughts and focus on the right things, we will be exempt from life's down cycles.

NECESSARY ADJUSTMENTS

If we realize that the down cycles are just life making necessary adjustments, much like our bodies adjust our blood sugar, we will be better able to handle life's challenges. We will not be as likely to make down cycles worse by shutting energy down at the very times we need it most.

When we allow down cycles to create resistance in us, we literally slow down the flow of energy. Remember, energy flows to reach equilibrium, which is how we get back to the up side of the life cycle. If we slow the flow by adding resistors, we prolong the very condition we are trying to eliminate. Those who resist and work more diligently to end a down cycle create a double positive (+/+) energy condition that prevents energy from flowing.

The humorous saying "The harder I work the behinder I get" pretty much sums up what happens when we get into a hard-work-plus-resistance routine in response to natural down cycles. There is nothing wrong with applying ourselves diligently to get past down cycles. We just need to do it without resistance so we stay in alignment with energy and keep it flowing in the right direction. Zen masters who teach that a non-resistant attitude should be maintained in every circumstance seem to understand this principle.

THE NATURAL RANGE

Highly unpleasant conditions or unpleasant conditions that *persist* do not fall within the realm of *natural* down cycles. Just as our blood sugar goes up and down within a non-critical range when we are healthy, life also goes up and down within a non-critical range when healthy. When conditions are highly unpleasant or painful, it is either because we have been hit with one of those unexpected "meteors" that temporarily throw us off-track, and don't know how to manage the change, or because we have strayed so far off of our natural path that we have created our own disaster.

Unpleasant conditions do occur within the natural cycle of life, but they do not naturally *persist* over long periods. Under normal conditions, life—like all other energy systems—follows relatively regular cycles, so both pleasant up cycles and unpleasant down cycles are always temporary and manageable unless we do something to throw them outside their natural range.

DYNAMIC APPEAL

The reality is that we need both the up and the down cycles. Even the down cycles are highly beneficial if we handle them properly. Without them life would lose its dynamic appeal. It is in dealing with the temporary down cycles that we become strong and resilient. Down cycles stimulate learning, growth, and innovation.

Virtually everything that we have ever created has been created in an effort to shorten or minimize the down cycles and extend the up cycles. Psychology teaches that we are motivated by only two things: the desire to move away from pain and or toward pleasure. These are simply opposite ends of the same spectrum as are the cycles of life.

Trying to keep things the same actually diminishes life and moves us *below* the normal range. From this place, life feels dull and unexciting. Energy levels are low and resistance is usually relatively high.

We move *above* the normal range by artificially inducing highs. Some people do this through drugs or alcohol. Others use excessive sex, food, partying, and other distractions. Still others use and abuse power, position and money to feed over-grown egos. But, just as our bodies crash when blood sugar takes a dive, those artificially-induced highs come crashing down eventually, and when they do, they result in the lowest of lows.

As you move through life and toward positive abundance, realize that your satisfaction will come, not from avoiding the ups and downs of life, but from seeking a healthy degree of equilibrium. Not like that found in a closed, lifeless system, but such as is found within the normal, beneficial range of all the open systems in the world.

Enjoy the natural highs and let the natural lows enhance your strengths and abilities. From this perspective, the wisdom of "all things in moderation" makes a lot of sense.

> *Because energy is always seeking equilibrium,*
> *once down, it resists going up*
> *and, once up, it resists going down.*
> *This principle applies to more than just*
> *electrical circuits. It applies to your*
> *physical energy, to the accomplishment*
> *of your goals and to the sense of effort*
> *you feel in getting started with new goals.*
> *But remember; once you make a start and*
> *get the energy up, it will also resist*
> *going back down. Make the start.*

CHAPTER 7

The Principles Of Energy Flow:
A Complete Circuit

What lies behind us and what lies before us
are small matters compared to what lies within us.
Henry David Thoreau

PRINCIPLE 2 – To flow, harnessed energy must have a complete circuit.[9]

Non-Personal example – The example of a flashlight works well here. Every part of what makes up a complete circuit, including the energy generator (a battery in this example), the active (+) line, the receptive (-) line, and the receiver (light socket with a bulb), must be present or energy won't flow and there will be no light.

Another example could be applied to radio waves which surround us and exist on a wide range of frequencies, but which can be tapped into only if we have the right senders and receivers to create a complete circuit.

Heinrich Hertz discovered radio frequencies in 1887; frequencies that no one could see or hear and which no one knew existed prior to the creation of senders to boost and direct them, and receivers (radios, televisions, cell phones, satellites, etc.) to put them to work in useful ways.

In order for receivers to make use of the radio waves, there must not only be a sender, but also energy flowing to both the sender and the receiver. For that to happen, there must be an energy source (a battery or generator) to power them, and a complete circuit to keep the power flowing. Until all these elements were in place, all of the amazing things that are possible today through the use of radio waves were only unseen potential.

Personal Example – Our attitudes act like radio waves. They send out messages to self and others non-physically. But unless they have both a sender and a receiver, like radio waves, they are just potential. Energy doesn't need a physical circuit to flow, but it does need a complete circuit.

On a personal level, you are the energy generator. Application represents your line out and attitude represents the return line. Application is what one actually *does* with their thoughts, feelings and intent, while attitude is the *quality* of the thoughts, feelings and intent. The receiver is whatever you are focused upon, and just as radio receivers must be precisely tuned to a particular radio frequency to deliver the sound you want, your personal receiver (focus) must be perfectly attuned to the outcomes you want. Without a clear and precise focus, your receiver will malfunction and you may end up getting a lot of static in your life rather than the beautiful symphony you were hoping for.

Besides lack of a clear focus, a frequent cause of an incomplete human circuit is sending energy toward a receiver that cannot accept it. The best way to demonstrate this is to use another example of electricity. We can hook up active (+) and receptive (-) electrical lines to a battery or electrical outlet and then to a motorless plastic toy, and we can leave it there forever and nothing useful will ever happen. That's because the toy is not designed to accept or receive the current in any useful way.

By the same token, if a person is focused on something that is not designed to accept the energy being directed toward it in any useful way, the energy sent out produces nothing useful. It simply drains away. Wasting time and energy by watching mindless television programs or reading useless gossip magazines are classic examples. They provide nothing useful for improving your life. Think about it. Have you ever gained anything from watching a sticom or reading a gossip magazine article that you were able to apply to your life in any useful way?

DON'T SET YOURSELF UP TO FAIL

Another source of energy drain is continually doing the same thing and expecting a different result. This is a very common way to fail. To demonstrate how futile this is, imagine that you are in your car in the middle of nowhere and you run out of gas. Your engine dies, of course, but you have a fully charged cell phone with you and decide to call someone to come to your aid. You dial a number and the person who answers the phone is not the person you expected. In fact, you don't know this person and they don't speak the same language as you, so you can't even communicate with them. You hang up the phone, dial the *same number* again – and again you get the same person.

This happens several times, so you decide that before you dial again, you will think positive thoughts and start telling yourself that the exact person you want will be on the other end of the line the next time you dial the phone. You repeat to yourself several times the most powerful affirmations you can devise, and then dial the same number again, and again you get the same person. You keep trying different affirmations, different attitudes and say a few prayers, but keep dialing the same number until your cell phone finally runs down and goes dead. So here you are, stuck in the middle of nowhere with no fuel, no energy left in your cell phone, and no means of contacting anyone who can help all because you refused to alter your actions to get a new outcome.

This sounds absurd, but that is exactly what many people do with their lives. They continue taking the same actions day after day and getting frustrated because nothing ever changes. And they can't figure out why they are not getting anywhere.

Those who buy into the idea that simply changing the nature of their thoughts or repeating positive affirmations will get them a different result, even if they don't significantly alter their behaviors, are just as deluded as the person who keeps altering their thinking, but dialing the same phone number.

YOU CANNOT JUST THINK AND GROW RICH

The fact is, you *cannot* just "think and grow rich." You have to *do* the right things or the circuit is incomplete. You also have to be very clear about what it is you want and what specific actions will result in that outcome, or what you get back may not be what you intended. We can't take responsible action or do the right thing unless we know what the right thing is in relation to the outcome we are after. And to know that, we have to do our homework first.

We can't, for example, think about increasing our income substantially and have that occur without a workable plan for making it happen. Once we have a plan, we must know what it will take to implement it. We must also have the information and skills we need to pull it off or find someone who does. We have to develop a strategy for carrying out the plan, and we have to be working with, rather than against, the principles that govern the Law of Abundance.

If we don't plan, things are likely to go awry. If we create a plan, but don't know how to execute it, the plan is of no use. If we know how to execute the plan, but don't take any actions, the vast amount of energy we have available to us is only *potential* energy with no way to express. If we take the wrong actions, the energy is squandered and the outcome will not be what we wanted or expected. If we are working against the Law of Abundance, we will always get a poor result.

Suppose you believed you could think and grow healthy and fit, yet you didn't do anything to make that happen except vividly imagine yourself as fit and healthy. You eat anything you want, including a large dish of ice cream every night before you go to bed and several pastries with coffee every morning, and you never exercise. How quickly do you think you would get the result you were imagining?

WE MUST COMPLETE THE CIRCUIT

We can fool ourselves, but we can't cheat the law. We have to complete the circuit in the right direction, using the right actions in accordance with the Law of Abundance, or we will not have an abundance of the things we desire.

Yet, there is an interesting thing that sometimes happens when someone *regularly* does the work of vividly imagining themselves as fit and healthy or wealthy or whatever. It happens because the discipline of creating clarity and regularly imagining the goal combined with a receptive attitude has all the elements necessary for setting the Law of Abundance into motion. This produces a relatively weak current, however, and progress is typically so imperceptibly slow that most people give up long before they achieve the desired result.

Here's how that plays out for those who persist long enough. Using vividly imagined fitness as an example, if an individual holds that image long enough and clearly enough, eventually energy shifts sufficiently for positive changes to begin to occur. For example, the individual may notice a magazine article that talks about how pastries are mostly fat and sugar; empty calories with no real nutritional value. He reads that pastries do nothing but appease the taste buds for a moment, while adding hundreds of calories to the diet and, worse, up to 70 grams of heart stopping trans-fats.

All of a sudden, morning pastries don't seem quite as appealing and he decides to substitute the pastries with healthier alternatives. He starts losing a little weight and notices that he feels better. Soon he becomes aware that ice cream every evening isn't such a good idea either and he reduces his intake to once a week. More weight comes off. Now he feels even better and decides to take a walk two or three times a week. More weight comes off and energy increases even further. Because he is now applying positive energy *externally* through his actions as well as internally, he progresses at a faster pace.

At some point, a big shift occurs and he discovers that eating the right foods and exercising are actually easier and much more fun than was the old way of doing things and, besides, he looks and feels so much better. He is now firmly on the path to an abundance of what he wants in this area. It all started with just a clearly held vision and a passionately desired goal, but the discipline of regularly holding that image completed the circuit, and as long as there was the disciplined action of maintaining the image (+), and faith (-) directed toward a clear goal, there was energy flowing—however slowly—in the right direction eventually stimulating external action.

Below is a recap of how energy flows through the human circuit. Since it can flow in the right or wrong direction, be sure to keep your actions consistent with the active application path and your attitude consistent with the receptive path so you get an abundance of the things you want.

THE HUMAN CIRCUIT

1. **You** (the energy generator)

2. An active (+) line, which can either be **Active Application** (responsible, disciplined action) or an Active Attitude (striving for or against, struggling)

3. A receptive (-) line, which can either be **Receptive Attitude** (trusting, allowing, accepting, believing) or **Receptive Application** (non-disciplined, irresponsible, taking the easiest path)

4. Your **Focus** (the receiver)

Active Application (+) plus Receptive Attitude (-) flows toward a *positive* outcome (an abundance of desirable things)

Receptive Application (-) plus an Active Attitude (+) flows toward a *negative* outcome (an abundance of undesirable things)

The (+/-) and (-/+) energy circuits as presented in the recap are best compared to *direct current*. The other two combinations (+/+) and (-/-) result in *no energy flow*. If people remained on either non-flowing path consistently, they would remain stuck in one place. But because life is an open system and many things happen to prevent us from remaining static for very long, no one stays on any one path all the time.

ALTERNATING CURRENT

Because of the dynamic nature of life, human energy acts more like an *alternating current* than a direct current. Even those who have learned ways to spend most of their time on the path to positive abundance have times when they are thrown off that well-chosen path by a life circumstance, though usually for only a short time.

Most people spend their life constantly adjusting and re-adjusting trying to meet the demands of changing life circumstances. With each new decision, each different action, attitude, thought or feeling, they move back and forth between two or more of the energy paths. Whether we move toward more or less of what we want, and how rapidly we get there, depends on how much time is spent on the positive side of the fluctuation, how much on the negative side, and how much on one of the non-flowing paths.

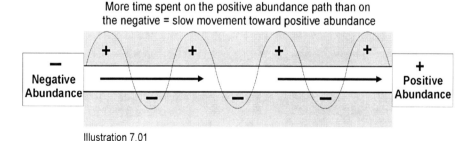

Illustration 7.01

Illustration 7.01 shows how, using more positive than negative decisions, actions, attitudes, thoughts and feelings, results in energy flowing toward positive abundance so we get more of what we want.

Illustration 7.02 shows how, using more negative than positive decisions, actions, attitudes, thoughts and feelings, results in energy flowing toward negative abundance. The result is that we get more of what we *do not* want.

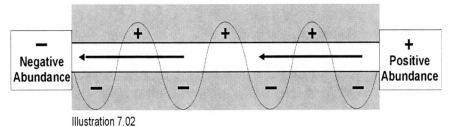

Illustration 7.02

The degree to which energy flows toward positive abundance or away from it depends on the ratio of positive to negative factors and the degree to which we actively apply them to the physical world.

If we tend slightly toward the positive, our condition improves, but very slowly. If we tend strongly toward the positive, our condition improves more rapidly. Likewise, a slight tendency toward the negative results in conditions deteriorating slowly, while a strong tendency toward the negative results in conditions deteriorating more rapidly.

Imagine life as a timed journey that equals your life span. Your life moves toward all that you desire or away from it to the degree that you are in compliance with the Law of Abundance. You are creeping, strolling, walking, jogging, or racing forward or backward at any given time.

Where people continually switch back and forth between positive and negative, as is frequently the case, they are essentially heading toward the desired goal for a while, then turning around and heading in the opposite direction for a while. Whether they are making any progress depends on how far they move forward in relation to how far they move back.

We are moving forward when we are taking responsible, disciplined actions (+) that produce little to no resistance in us (-). We are moving backwards when we are exerting little to no effort (taking the easiest route, being irresponsible and/or undisciplined) (-) and are resistant to our outcomes, attitudes, thoughts or feelings, or those of other people (+). We are stuck and going nowhere when we are on the (+/+) or (-/-) paths. Whether we are moving toward something specific or nothing in particular depends on the clarity and precision of the images we hold, the plans we have laid out, and the goals we have defined.

TO CONTINUE MOVING FORWARD REQUIRES SEVEN VERY SPECIFIC FACTORS:

1. *Active application* (+) which is responsible, disciplined, courageous action
2. *Receptive attitude* (-) which is open, allowing, accepting, believing, receiving, confident
3. Consistently *positive thoughts*
4. Predominantly *positive feelings*
5. Precise and positive *intent* or purpose (being clear about what's important to you)
6. Clearly *defined goals* (defining specifically where you want to be)
7. A *plan* for achieving the goals (the specific steps for getting there)

Illustration 7.03 provides a capsule view of the two energy combinations that result in energy flow. One combination leads to a lot of what we want and one leads to a lot of what we don't want.

The two "stuck" combinations (+/+) and (-/-) are not represented because, on these two paths we are neither moving forward nor falling further behind. Being on one of the stuck paths would be like stopping in the middle of a timed race, thereby losing ground by virtue of allowing time to run out.

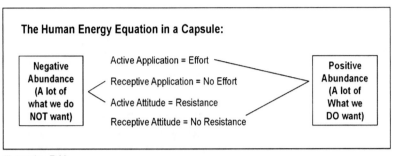

Illustration 7.03

WHAT GOES OUT MUST COME BACK

Energy in the human experience closely mirrors that of electricity. Since it flows in a circuit and is always seeking to return to its source, the energy you send out returns to you in kind on at least one level. We do reap what we sow, but not always in ways that are apparent. The seeds we plant don't always result in externally visible fruits. You can probably think of hundreds of incidences where you or someone else has done something that has had no apparent effect. But the effect is there, whether we see it or not. Let's look at some examples.

EXAMPLE 1

Say you get angry and start screaming and yelling, but there is no one there to hear, except you. The energy you are sending out is not just dissipated as many assume. The receiver in this case is you. Your conscious, active, angry mind sends a message to your receptive subconscious mind which readily receives it and acts upon it. What then comes back to you is fear, anxiety, low self-esteem, high blood pressure, heart problems, or some other physical, mental, or emotional disease.

In this case, you are the one who reaps what you have sown. You have negatively impacted your own energies and your receptive subconscious mind both stores the information for future use and sends the response to the body where, seeking to balance the energy, it is acted upon.

EXAMPLE 2

Now imagine that you make it a practice to repeat positive affirmations every day. You regularly send out positive thoughts, but have no clear goals and take no particular action. Again, the only receiver is you, and again you receive in direct relation to the quality of the thoughts you send out. If the positive thoughts are genuine and create no resistance (such as fear that positive thinking might not work or anxiety because it isn't producing the desired effect fast enough), you will receive the benefit of the thoughts—perhaps as vibrant good health, contentment, or satisfaction—but you won't necessarily reap anything in the outer physical world since there is *no external receiver.*

To expect external results where there is no external receiver is like expecting a downed power line to power your home. It won't. There is a lot of energy in that line, but it is being dissipated into the ground, not directed toward your home. No matter how much energy is flowing through that line, it is not going to produce what you desire. Get too close to that downed line, however, and it will definitely produce a result you don't want because you then become the receiver of the highly charged undirected energy. We can get a similar result from hanging around angry, undisciplined, directionless people.

EXAMPLE 3

Now imagine that you are screaming and yelling at your child, or conversely, that you are telling your child how awesome and loved he or she is. In either case, both you and the child receive the energy you have sent out in the form you sent it and it returns to you in kind. If you send out negative energy, you get negative energy back. If you send out loving energy, you get loving energy back. In this case, you reap what you sow in more ways than one. You may or may not get the energy back from the person to whom you sent it, but you will definitely get it back from yourself. And, since all of our interactions create ripples of energy much like throwing pebbles into a pond, there is a good likelihood that we will get the energy back from the person we impacted, and possibly from the ones they in turn impact as well. This is especially true in families or workplaces where a group of people regularly interact with one another.

EXAMPLE 4

In this example, let's say you are accustomed to helping strangers who you will never see again. As in Example 3, there are two receivers. In this case, the receivers are the stranger and you. But, since the stranger is not in a position to return the energy to you, except perhaps as a thank you, the result is not as direct as it might be from your child. There is evidence in quantum research that suggests it does come back in some way, but probably not directly. As the sender of the kind act, certainly you return the energy to yourself in the form of good feelings, which are known to boost the immune system and add to a sense of well-being and confidence. In this case, you have sent out energy designed to improve the well-being of someone else and you receive well-being back.

Whether internally or externally, we do reap what we sow, so be sure you are sending out exactly what you want to receive back.

> *True happiness . . . is not attained through self-gratification, but through fidelity to a worthy purpose.*
>
> Hellen Keller

CHAPTER 8

The Principles Of Energy Flow: Precision And Predictability

*Statistically, one hundred percent
of the shots you don't take, don't go in.*
Wayne Gretzsky

PRINCIPLE 3 – The flow of energy is precise and absolutely predictable.[10]

Non-Personal Example – It is because the flow of energy is precise and absolutely predictable, that we are able to harness electricity in the way we have. If it weren't, it would not be possible to turn it on or off at will, suppress it, induce it, boost it or direct its flow and intensity in order to precisely power myriad products. We could not wire a house and expect to have energy delivered exactly where we want it, when we want it. And we could not design and build appliances to serve us in specific ways.

Personal Example – The nature of an appliance determines what it delivers. Likewise, the nature of the energy you send out, as well as that of the receiver to which you send it, determines what you will get back. If you build your receiver (focus) with negatively charged thoughts, beliefs and intent, then what manifests will also be negative and you *must* get negative results.

If you build your receiver with positively charged thoughts, beliefs and intent, what manifests will be positive and you *must* get positive results, *provided* you are receptive to them. The degree to which you receive results, positive or negative, depends on the degree to which you have placed boosters on the outbound energy and managed resistors on the return energy.

Positive thoughts, emotions, and intent act as *boosters* to positive outcomes and as *resistors* to negative ones. Negative thoughts, emotions, and intent do the reverse, they act as boosters to negative outcomes and as resistors to positive ones.

Because the nature of thoughts, feelings, and intent strongly influence the direction and flow of energy, it is essential that we apply the abundance formula to our inner selves first and do so in a way that will allow us to direct our thoughts, master our feelings, and purposefully guide our intent. Only then are we able to direct our energy precisely where we want it and get absolutely predictable results.

PREDICTABLE RESULTS

The results we get, though predictable, are not always what we want or expect. For instance, if we are not disciplined, responsible and courageous in the way we manage and master our thoughts, feelings, intentions and actions, they become unruly and we find ourselves on a path we did not intend, dealing with circumstances we don't want.

The opposite is also true. By disciplining our thoughts, feelings, intentions and actions, and behaving in responsible, courageous ways, we find ourselves on the path of our own choosing—one that takes us where we want to go and leads us towards an abundance of the things we desire to whatever degree that we are open to receiving.

As you have likely discovered, thoughts are not easy to monitor, much less master. Yet, because they drive and can exaggerate feelings, those that are emotionally charged always result in an outcome. It is wise then to monitor and manage thoughts.

It isn't necessary to attend to every thought; if we tried, we wouldn't get much else done. But because emotionally charged thoughts direct our energy and our outcomes, we do need to be aware of the thoughts that generate emotions.

THE PERFECT GUIDANCE SYSTEM

Each and every one of us has at our disposal the finest guidance system on the planet. It is as precise as the best navigation tools; a perfect compass. If we let it, this internal guidance system perfectly guides us through life. It is flawless in letting us know when we are on the right path and when we are off, provided we are paying attention to the feedback it continually gives. The problem is that most people don't pay enough attention.

This internal guidance system is considered by some to be the conscience, and certainly, that is a part of it. But it is much more than that. It is the longing you feel to do or be something more. It is the burst of energy and the sense of satisfaction you feel when you are doing something that puts you right in the middle of a natural passion. It is the red flag that goes up in your brain when the wrong person enters your life or when you are about to embark on some questionable activity. It is the intuitive knowing that tells you to take a specific action which turns out to be the perfect thing to have done, and for which you have no logical explanation. It is the knowing that informs you that what you are doing is not the right thing, or conversely, that you are exactly where you should be, doing exactly what you should be doing and all is right in your world.

YOUR INNER COMPASS FUNCTIONS PERFECTLY

Your inner compass is continually sending you signals every moment of every day in the form of feelings. When you are on the right path—the one that will lead you to your perfect place of abundance—the corresponding feelings are those that you interpret as "good." They are pleasant, enjoyable, uplifting, and welcome.

When you are on the wrong path the corresponding feelings are those that you interpret as "bad." They are unpleasant, confounding, draining, fear or anxiety producing, and you resist or try to get rid of them.

We typically interpret good feelings as those that lead to

happiness, contentment, deep satisfaction, joy, love, justice, goodness, peacefulness, and so forth. Bad feelings include fear, anger, irritation, impatience, intolerance, disgust, criticism, injustice, and such.

Though energy is non-discriminatory and flows in any direction we send it, its natural inclination is always toward positive abundance and it is toward that eventual outcome that our inner compass is constantly nudging us. "Divine discontent," that persistent feeling of wanting, longing and needing, is our compass at work.

The aversion to unprincipled, uncaring behaviors on one hand and the lift we get when we are acting in principled, caring, considerate ways on the other, are your compass at work. Longing and positive feelings, as well as resistance and other negative feelings, are signals your compass sends to try to steer you in the right direction. Where negative feelings persist or continue to return, you can bet that you are off your path.

DESTRUCTIVE DISTRACTIONS

Many people have not developed sufficient awareness or effective enough strategies to adjust their actions and attitudes to get better outcomes. Rather than making effective adjustments as their compass registers negative feelings or intense longing, some simply ignore the signals. Others rush down still another wrong path. Still others mask the signals with alcohol and drugs. Many distract themselves with frivolity and a constant stream of fruitless and often meaningless entertainment.

The tendency to distract one's self from bad feelings becomes very apparent during difficult times. It occurred during the great depression when the entertainment industry was one of the few that flourished and the same thing is occurring today. As the pace of life gets more and more hectic and the future more uncertain, forms of entertainment are on the increase.

The great desire of most people to distract themselves when stressed is why singers, actors, and athletes in our society make millions of dollars while police officers, firefighters, teachers, social workers, those in the military, and others who serve humankind in disciplined, responsible, courageous ways often struggle to make ends meet.

Responsible, disciplined folks force us to look at ourselves, which can add to the discomfort of those bent on taking the easy way around their problems. It's much easier to just stay distracted.

Those who mask their feelings or distract themselves believe the measures they are taking actually help. Drinking, drugs, overeating, gambling, and other amusements can temporarily produce what might be interpreted as good feelings. But the feelings are hollow and always temporary. And sustaining them gets more and more difficult and more and more expensive in one way or another. After awhile, it becomes apparent to all but the most deluded that the distractions are simply masks and are not the answer.

Unfortunately, this irresponsible path is one that very few people are able to remove themselves from. It takes responsible, disciplined action and courage to turn the tides, and most that travel this path have not developed these attributes. They lack the skills necessary for coping effectively and don't know how to escape the trap they have built for themselves, so they keep on heading down the path to destruction, and the no-win cycle continues unless someone provides assistance. As many family members and friends of those on this path have discovered, effective intervention usually requires the help of trained professionals. This can be a good therapist or a coach, but even here the individual must be willing to receive the help.

THE PAIN THAT TIME DOES NOT HEAL

Internally generated emotional pain tells us that we are off our natural path—that we are not living in alignment with the Law of Abundance—and unless we recognize that fact and make constructive adjustments, it is inevitable that we eventually slide into greater limitation, greater pain, and for some, destruction.

Internally generated pain is different than pain that arises from external causes, such as the loss of a loved one. *Time does not heal internally generated pain.* In fact, if we don't deal with it, time just *increases* it. Your internal compass will never allow you to have long lasting comfort or joy when you are off your true path. Its goal is to lead you to abundance, so help it do that.

To ensure that you are fully aware of your inner compass and know whether the adjustments you are making are putting you on the path to positive abundance, work through the following exercises.

EXERCISE 1: GETTING FAMILIAR WITH YOUR INNER COMPASS

1. **Begin paying close attention to your feelings.** Realize that authentically good feelings don't have to be constantly fed through external sources. While feelings such as joy, happiness, and contentment can shift up or down depending on what we are dealing with in the outer world and how effectively we are coping, they are not dependent on the outer world. When we are on the path that is right for us, these feelings occur naturally and sustain themselves from within. By noticing when naturally positive feelings occur, and what causes them to diminish or temporarily disappear, you can make purposeful adjustments, alter actions and attitudes and shift your focus to ways to improve the situation.

2. **Keep fine tuning.** The benefits to being on your true path are infinite. Not only will you feel a sense of contentment most of the time, you can know for certain that the path you are on is leading you toward positive abundance. Remember, your compass is flawless. You will maintain good feelings only when you are consistently on your true path. On those occasions when life's events pull you off track, don't allow yourself to stay off-track for long. Use the awareness that you are off-track to examine why and begin making purposeful adjustments.

3. **Know what your true path feels like.** On your true path, life has meaning and purpose. You have a level of passion that creates a natural flow of energy. You have clarity around who you are and where you are headed. There is peacefulness and a

sense of true joy that doesn't exist anywhere else. You are driven in a completely non-resistant and effortless way in a particular direction and you have no doubt that the direction in which you are headed is the right one. Discipline and responsible action occur naturally because your natural drive to realize your purpose continually propels you forward.

4. **Keep a journal in the early stages of developing awareness.** As you begin shifting your awareness and noticing your responses to your inner and outer worlds, the things that throw you off track will become apparent. After awhile, clear patterns will begin to emerge. You will notice that certain circumstances, events, thoughts, actions, attitudes, beliefs, and expectations always produce positive feelings, while certain others always produce negative ones. You will be able to see what pushes your buttons, what kind of thinking, and which beliefs and assumptions are derailing you or keeping you stuck, and which ones propel you forward. When, you know what is preventing you from staying on course, you will be able to create new and better strategies for yourself. You will also become more aware of areas where you need help, and will then have the awareness to enlist the aid of trusted friends or professional coaches to help you past the hurdles.

5. **Be patient with yourself as well as persistent.** We don't all progress rapidly; in fact, most of us don't. That's because shifting our way of being in the world, or altering the way we have been using energy, requires the same initial effort as learning any new skill. How quickly you progress has more to do with the degree of your learning curve than with your ability. We all have the ability to work with the Law of Abundance perfectly, but some of us have farther to go than others. Just as a techie who has spent years learning the workings of a computer would find it easier to learn a new computer program than would someone who had never even seen a computer, there are those who are more experienced in directing their lives than others. But, no matter where you are on the learning curve, if you know where you are headed and are patient with your progress, you *will* arrive.

Realize that when you become impatient with your growth and development or beat yourself up for not getting things right, you are doing two things that you really don't want to be doing: First, you are *strengthening* the factors that are causing the negative responses (thereby getting more of what you do not want). Second, you are delaying or preventing the free flow of energy toward positive abundance by adding resisters thereby shifting your attitude to active (+). Remember, two active energies (+/+) do not produce flow. Be persistent in your efforts (active application), but also be patient (receptive attitude).

6. **Use the Law of Abundance to build trust in your inner compass.** To do that, you must know how your compass expresses. Realize that it *always* expresses as a *feeling* and *not as a thought*. The conscious mind is always looking for solutions and will try to find answers to whatever you are observing. The "answer" always comes up as a thought. When the thought is wrong, as is often the case, the *feeling* in relation to it is usually less than positive. Sometimes misdirected thoughts show up as a vague uncertainty that you can't quite put your finger on. Sometimes they present as indecision, mild anxiety, or some form of fear. If you are paying attention to the feelings, rather than the thoughts, you will be better able to make the correct adjustments, not just to your thoughts, but to your actions and outcomes as well.

The idea that drinking or taking drugs or eating will get rid of emotional pain is an example of how thoughts can lead us astray. The thought is intended to create an instant "solution" to the problem, but if we aren't paying attention to the subtle underlying feeling that tells us it is not the solution, the thought wins out.

You can use the Law of Abundance itself to determine the quality and accuracy of your thoughts and evaluate the intended actions by simply asking yourself two questions: (1) Is this a choice that leads to disciplined, responsible, courageous action? And (2) will this choice lead to increased and sustainable acceptance of self, others, and life, and to increased contentment and satisfaction?

7. **Stay actively aware of what is authentic and what is not until it becomes second nature.** By remaining actively aware, you will learn to trust that your internal compass really is flawless and can guide you to positive abundance if you let it. In time, conscious monitoring won't be necessary. Awareness of your guidance system will become automatic. Once you have developed the ability to be automatically aware of your feeling responses to circumstances, events, thoughts and attitudes, you will no longer have to consciously monitor your feelings. Your compass will be at the forefront of your awareness and will automatically report the feelings to you as they come up. This is the most powerful tool you will ever have. It will keep you headed in the direction of your own "True North" toward the life that for you—and you alone—is perfect abundance.

EXERCISE 2 – CHECKING EMOTIONAL RESPONSE

In their book *The Amazing Power of Deliberate Intent* (Hay House 2006), authors Esther and Jerry Hicks provide a twenty-two point emotional response scale that they call an Emotional Guidance Scale. It is a very good descriptor of the stages we go through as we move from being joyous and fully engaged in life to complete desperation.

As a coach, trainer and psychologist, I have worked with people in the area of emotional responses for over twenty years and find that the Hicks' Emotional Guidance Scale is quite close to what I have observed over the years.

To help you monitor your responses, I have provided an adaptation of their scale (Illustration 8.01). Many of the emotions identified at the top of the scale have been adjusted to better reflect the findings from years of research, and additional descriptors have been added, but the overall credit for the scale belongs to Esther and Jerry Hicks.

You have three goals in this exercise:

1. To learn to recognize the signals your inner compass sends to let you know when you are on or off-track.

2. To discover exactly how far off track you are in any given area.

3. To begin moving up the emotional scale in areas where you are off track, so that the application side of the abundance equation becomes more active and the attitude side becomes more receptive or non-resistant. This ensures that you are better aligned with the energy that leads to positive abundance.

Consult the scale as you focus on the areas within each of the three categories provided in this exercise (relationships, self, and money) so you are able to identify the dominant feeling associated with each area. If your dominant feeling falls below 7 on the scale, there is work to be done in that category.

In examining each of the categories, it will be helpful to first evaluate where you currently are on the Emotional Guidance Scale, and then decide where you want to be.

The numerical distance between where you are now and where you want to be will give you some idea as to how much adjustment will be necessary to have abundance in that particular area.

Say, for example, that in examining the money category, you find that the emotional response to amassing wealth is disappointment and disillusionment (level 13), but you want your response to be that of passion, joy and empowerment (level 1). This means that, where amassing wealth is concerned, you are 12 points below where you want to be.

Then suppose that in checking the category of relationships you find that, in relation to your spouse, you have contentment and satisfaction (7), but not real joy or passion (1). You decide that happiness, enthusiasm, and a form of love that is less intense than passion is more appealing, so you choose level 2 as your goal rather than level 1. In this case, the difference between where you are now and where you want to be is only 5 points.

In comparing the difference between where you are now and where you want to be in the two areas, you can see then that you have a lot more work to do to remove resistors around wealth than you do in that of your spousal relationship.

Emotional Guidance Scale

1. Passion, Joy, Empowerment
2. Happiness, Enthusiasm, Eagerness, Love
3. Appreciation, Gratitude, Freedom
4. Positive Expectation, Belief, Confidence
5. Optimism, Self-assurance
6. Hopefulness, Trust
7. Contentment, Satisfaction, Peace of Mind
8. Complacency, Boredom
9. Pessimism, Skepticism
10. Frustration, Irritation, Impatience
11. Doubt, Distrust, Uncertainty
12. Fear, Worry, Apprehension, Anxiety
13. Disappointment, Disillusionment
14. Discouragement, Dismay, Dejection
15. Overwhelm, Incapacitation
16. Blame, Condemnation, Criticism
17. Anger, Resentment
18. Vengefulness, Bitterness, Malice
19. Hatred, Rage, Fury
20. Jealousy, Envy
21. Insecurity, Guilt, Unworthiness
22. Depression, Despair, Powerlessness, Grief

Illustration 8.01

CATEGORY 1 – RELATIONSHIPS

- Spouse
- Parents
- Extended Family
- Friends
- Coworkers
- Acquaintances
- Unfriendly Strangers
- Children
- Siblings
- A Higher Power
- Neighbors
- Boss
- Friendly Strangers
- Enemies

CATEGORY 2 – SELF

- Awareness
- Ability to Succeed
- Attractiveness
- Charisma
- Self-esteem
- Dependability
- Discipline, Responsibility
- Direction, Purpose
- Health, Fitness
- Intelligence Level
- Self-confidence
- Honesty, Integrity

CATEGORY 3 – MONEY

- Making Money
- Keeping/Saving Money
- Putting Money to Work for You/Investing
- Amassing Wealth
    ~Thousands
    ~Millions
    ~Billions

Add any categories that you consider important.

As you attend to each of the categories, notice your emotional response to each, then ask yourself, *"What must I believe or be telling myself for this emotional response to occur?"*

Examine the thoughts and beliefs that accompany the emotions. Do these serve you? Do they move you in the direction of abundance? What thoughts or beliefs might serve you better? Can you find some evidence to validate the new, more effective thoughts and beliefs? Can you find evidence that will invalidate the perceived correctness of the ineffective ones?

If the thoughts and beliefs are not creating conditions for positive abundance, work on altering them so the emotional response to that category begins moving up the emotional scale. Keep working on the emotional response until your typical response is in the 1 – 7 range on the scale.

KEEPING A JOURNAL

As in exercise 1 (page 92), keeping a journal will be useful to keep you on track now and in the future. Being able to look back and see your progress over time will motivate you to keep improving your outcomes until you get to where you want to be.

As you begin moving up the emotional scale to bring your typical feelings into the range of 7 or above, you may find that it is not possible to take quantum leaps upward—from depression (22) to optimism (5), for example. Most people would have trouble doing that. But it is possible to move from depression to anger (17), which will refocus energies toward action, and then from anger to irritation or impatience (10), which further moves energy in the direction of action and begins shifting your sense of control over your emotions toward empowerment.

From there you can better get to optimism, which removes resistors and adds receptivity to the attitude side of the abundance formula. As you progress up the scale, non-action and high resistance (depression) are altered, first by shifting energy on the application side toward that of action (+), and then by removing resistors on the attitude side so you are more receptive (-) to the outcome you want. When you have managed to shift the application side of the formula to active and the attitude side to receptive, energy begins flowing toward positive abundance and progress gets easier and easier.

Completing this exercise will help you learn to discipline your thoughts and adjust your attitudes and feelings. Please don't avoid doing this step. Remember, it is in disciplining your thoughts and directing your feelings toward positive abundance that you will be able to shift energy toward the realization of everything you desire. It may take some effort, but you are worth it.

For quick reference as you work through the Emotional Guidance exercise, Illustration 8.02 recaps the positive abundance formula.

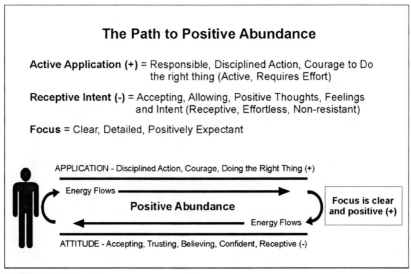

Illustration 8.02

CHAPTER 9

Insulating The Path To Abundance: Faith In Self

Being happy requires that you define your life in your own terms and then throw your whole heart into living your life to the fullest. In a way, happiness requires that you be perfectly selfish in order to develop yourself to a point where you can be unselfish for the rest of your life.
Brian Tracy

When we have spent many years on a negative or non-productive path and have set up a strong energy flow toward outcomes we do not want, and then switch our thinking and actions toward positive outcomes, we initially have energy flowing along at least two paths. One path is a well-entrenched path toward limitation (or negative abundance), and the other is a newly created path toward positive abundance. The majority of people have energy flowing in both directions, to one degree or another, and in different areas of their lives.

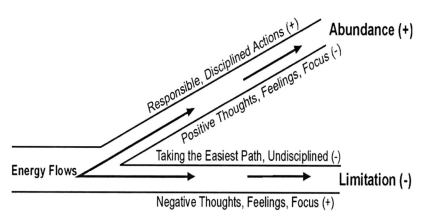

Illustration 9.01

When both paths are flowing, we are receptive to both abundance and limitation (or both positive and negative abundance), but the world we live in tends to reinforce the path toward the negative. As Thoreau pointed out, "the mass of men lead lives of *desperation*," so we have a lot of evidence for negativity and limitation.

It is very easy to look around and see people who are struggling to make ends meet financially, or worse, living in poverty. It is easy to observe those who have no healthy relationships, no love in their life, no focus, and no joy. And, if we allow ourselves to focus on all the negative evidence, we set up conditions that result in a strong magnetic pull in the direction of negative abundance, which can short circuit our efforts to remain on the positive path.

Unless we keep purposefully re-directing our attention and energy to the positive abundance path and make sure it is well insulated, we find ourselves back in the old mindset, doing the same old things we have always done and getting the same limiting results.

In the same way that electricity will form a non-physical bridge and leap from one poorly insulated line to another, so too will energy leap from one poorly insulated path to another in the mind and experience of people.

Illustration 9.02 demonstrates how, without sufficient insulation, negative thoughts, feelings, and a focus on limitations can short circuit the path toward positive abundance and reverse the flow of energy, sending it toward limitation.

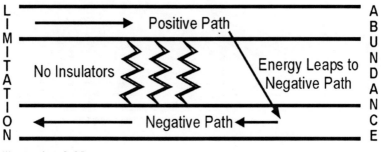

Illustration 9.02

FAITH IS THE INSULATOR

In the case of humans, faith is what acts as the non-conductive "material" to insulate us from the negativity that can short circuit our efforts and cause us to doubt our ability to get the things we desire. I am not talking about blind faith here, but the substantial faith that comes from testing limits, experimenting, exploring possibilities, making keen observations, and from learning and discovery.

Faith that has substance aids us in maintaining positive thoughts, feelings, expectations and intent, and provides us with the impetus to continue working toward our goals without the fears and worries that set up resistance. Faith properly directed strengthens positive thoughts and feelings and *impedes* the flow of energy along the path of negative abundance or limitation and *boosts* energy along the path of positive abundance. In sufficient quantity, faith can even act as a circuit breaker to shut down the flow of energy along the negative abundance or limitation path and prevent it from flowing in that direction.

For the insulation effect to be sufficient, however, we must have faith in three areas: (1) self, (2) others, and (3) a generative force. Not necessarily in that order. All three are equally important, and ultimately, all three are equal, since they are all part of the whole. Faith in self is placed first only because we absolutely *must* have faith in self before we are willing or able to have faith in others. Further, many people must have faith in self, before they are willing to believe they are worthy to be a part of, rather than apart from, a higher power. We must also have faith in self before we will step out boldly, responsibly, and courageously to consistently do the right things and tap into the right energy.

As we examine the three layers of faith, it will become quite clear how and why they act as insulators. Keep in mind that they are ordered by level of difficulty in sustaining that layer of insulation, not by level of importance.

Illustration 9.03 demonstrates how faith acts as layers of insulation, and prevents energy from being short-circuited to the negative path.

We will examine each of the layers separately.

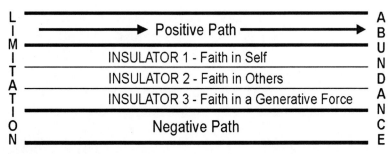

Illustration 9.03

FAITH IN SELF

One would think that faith in self would be the easiest of the three faiths to acquire, but that has not been my experience over the years. Developing faith in self is often difficult because, to have faith in self, we must have true and accurate knowledge of self (natural strengths and abilities, motivators, energizers, limitations, beliefs, blinders, values, etc.) which the majority of people do not have.

We live in a world that encourages us to focus outward and to use external feedback (the opinions of others) to define our worth. We are judged and often judge ourselves by whether we please others consistently, and are acceptable according to what the society we live in tells us is "normal."

Too many people measure their worth by arbitrary things such as the car they drive, the clothes they wear, whether they have the right hair style, smell just right, have the right job, live in the right house, make enough money, and on and on.

The problem is we can't discover who we are by directing our attention "out there." When we do that, the messages are always mixed, and we can never become enough. It is not possible to please all the people all the time, and if our sense of self revolves around other people's opinions, we are doomed to a life of striving.

THE AUTHENTIC SELF

Many people live and die never knowing who they are at an authentic level. Some search throughout their entire life and some just give up in despair. Typically though, the search continues until we either find our true path, or die trying, because that perfectly functioning inner compass, which we all have, continues to tug at us. It keeps telling us that something important is missing; that there is something more that we are capable of, or that the path we are on is not the right one for us. It keeps trying to point us toward that place of joy and contentment that can only be found when we are "home," in that place of complete inner satisfaction and contentment. But those who don't know this, or who avoid the urging for fear of what they might find inside, keep searching in the outer world and so never find the treasure they are looking for—the one they have had inside themselves all along.

Many people never make it "home" because they get too caught up in the easy answers, instant cures and magic pills that promise to relieve them of their distress without their having to do the work or take responsibility for their own outcomes. They don't realize that the irresponsible, undisciplined path is *always* the path to limitation. They have not yet learned that no one will ever get and keep an abundance of the things they most desire on the path of quick fixes. They don't see that taking the easy path now means a difficult path in the future when they will be least able to deal with difficulties. They don't see because they are looking in the wrong places for their truth.

EASE AND EFFORT

Life presents each of us with two application paths and two attitude paths. As you will recall, on the application side of the energy equation, one path is that of responsible, disciplined, courageous action and the other is that of irresponsible, undisciplined, cowardly, or fear-based inaction. In Illustration 9.04 the two application choices are laid out in parallel to one another. The path labeled "Effort" is the responsible, disciplined, courageous path and the path labeled "Ease" is the irresponsible, undisciplined, take-the-easiest-route path.

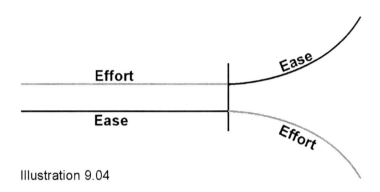

Illustration 9.04

The line that intersects the two paths is the point of no return, which occurs at some point in life for each of us. The point of no return is the place we come to, often later in life, when we simply don't have enough time or resources left to significantly alter the effects of our past.

SOME EXAMPLES OF REACHING A POINT OF NO RETURN WOULD BE:

1. Not taking care of your body, eating unwisely, and not exercising to the point that you end up with clogged arteries, heart damage, a stroke, or some other non-reversible disease and can never regain your health.

2. Treating someone you love so poorly that he or she no longer trusts you, loses respect for you and no longer wants anything to do with you, and then realizing, after the individual has gone out of your life, how important he or she was to you.

3. Not furthering your education either formally or by self-learning so that you have the knowledge and skills to earn a good living, then realizing at 65 that you have no means to retire and no skills to improve your circumstance.

The curved lines that extend past the vertical "point of no return" line in the illustration indicate the end result of our early choices. Those who have chosen the path of responsibility, discipline, and courage early in life, who have expended the effort to eat right, exercise, prepare for their retirement, build healthy relationships and do the right things, eventually find themselves in a place of ease. They have healthy bodies that continue to serve them, they have the financial means and ability to enjoy their retirement, and they have healthy relationships through which they can share their enjoyment.

Those who chose the easy route—who failed to eat right and exercise because it was inconvenient; or who failed to save, invest, and prepare for their retirement because there were just too many things they wanted in the moment for instant gratification; or who failed to build healthy relationships, or to learn, grow and develop themselves in mentally, emotionally, and spiritually healthy ways because that was just too much trouble, at some point find themselves in a place where life is effortful and difficult. This group ends up with insufficient money to enjoy their latter years, or with poor health, or with relationships that are in shambles, or all of these.

WE ALL PAY OUR DUES

Whether we pay our dues is not an option. The only options are *how* and *when*. We can pay them happily or we can pay them begrudgingly. We can pay them up front when we are younger and more capable or we can pay them at the end when we have less time and fewer resources.

When we choose to pay our dues up front, we get to choose how we will invest our time and energy, and how we will shape our future. If we are doing the right things, the responsible, disciplined path doesn't feel like effort at all; we are working with our passions and recruiting or hiring others to do the things that drain us. We expend the energy to stay fit and healthy and include fitness in our daily routines because we know we are worth the effort. We work at our relationships because we know the people we choose to keep in our lives are also worth the effort. We live for the joys of today, but plan and prepare for the future to ensure that the future is just as enjoyable.

When we wait until the end to pay our dues, not only must we endure illness, feebleness, insufficient retirement funds, difficult relationships and a whole host of other problems, we must also endure sadness and regret. Hindsight really is 20/20, and when those who look back over their lives, and realize that they have squandered their potential and no longer have the option of choosing the life they would have preferred, they usually do so with real regret.

THE WISDOM OF OUR ELDERS

During a study I conducted for a psychology project back in the early 1980s, I discovered that when early life choices result in difficult latter years, the primary emotions felt and expressed are sadness, regret, and depression. In that study, I interviewed elderly people, 75 and older, to determine their view of life.

I interviewed those who had lived their lives well, maintained their health, and prepared for their retirement, and those who had failed to do those things. The differences were striking, and—for those who had not prepared—very sad. Those who had lived disciplined lives and responsibly cared for themselves and their relationships, and prepared for their future were healthy and energetic. They reported that they were truly happy and content and it showed in the sparkle in their eyes. They had an abiding wisdom and conveyed a sense of deep contentment. They were truly enjoying their latter years and were delightful to be around.

The second group was a different story. It was heart breaking to see so many basically good people in the depths of desperation in the twilight of their years. Their suffering was physical, mental, and emotional, and in more cases than not, the poor souls had worked hard their entire lives.

Most reported that they had spent most of their adult lives *intending* to find more effective and enjoyable ways to live their lives, but just never managed to get to it. Many reported that they had not known how to get out of the trap they found themselves in as their life spun out of control. By the time they realized they could have done things differently, they reported, making the actual changes was no longer an option. Where the first group was full of life and contentment, this one was full of pain and regret.

Choose right now not to travel your life path to such a sad end. Choose to remove yourself from the hypnotic state induced by marketers who want everyone to believe that instant gratification is the thing to aspire to, and that we need their "stuff" to be somebody. Choose to look inward at your true value and forward to your future.

THE ESSENTIAL FOUR

Faith in self requires four specific attributes. Without these four, we are just faking our way through life and faking just doesn't get it. The four attributes are (1) a clear and accurate sense of self, (2) healthy personal boundaries (3) self-confidence, and (4) a healthy level of self-esteem. All four of these are rooted in *self-knowledge*. If we are focused on the ever-changing outer world, we cannot know the constancy of our authentic self, which resides in the inner world. It is almost impossible to have faith in anything that is unclear to us, including ourselves, so when the truth of who we are is unclear, faith in self is lacking.

We each came into the world with a natural set of traits and abilities that, if allowed to develop fully, perfectly prepare us to live a happy, fulfilled life. But the vast majority of us were born into circumstances that required us to alter our nature in order to be acceptable to our clan (family, school, church, society, culture, or country). During the process of adaption the natural self often gets lost.

A FALSE MASK

When we put on a false mask early in life, in order to fit in and be accepted, we frequently get to adulthood fully invested in that mask and believing that the mask we see is who we really are. But masks are almost always uncomfortable in some way, and as long as we are wearing one, something feels amiss.

Only by recognizing that there *is* a mask—and that the mask is a disguise we are wearing, not who we really are—are we able to remove it and discover our authentic self. Most people don't recognize this fact and so don't take steps to remove the mask, which is a primary cause of personal discomfort. Instead, we put the mask into the properly defined box to keep it safe and intact. For most of us, that box eventually becomes far too small and uncomfortable, and we deal with the discomfort by either distracting ourselves or beginning a search for answers.

Until we remove the mask and get a clear and accurate picture of who we are and what we are about, we can't possibly develop healthy boundaries, self-confidence or high levels of self-esteem. We don't have a clear enough sense of self to insulate ourselves from the negative opinions of others. We can't know what natural attributes we can count on to help us navigate life's storms effectively so we are unable to move courageously into new and unexplored territory, and reach grand goals.

The research my colleagues and I have been doing in this area since 1989 suggests that early conditioning, and/or persistently difficult current circumstances, prevent almost 84% of the population from fully knowing and appreciating themselves, developing their natural strengths and abilities, and realizing their potential. No wonder the masses lead lives of desperation!

WHEN THE ESSENTIAL FOUR ARE LACKING

Self-awareness, healthy boundaries, self-confidence, and self-esteem are essential attributes for faith in self, yet these are the areas the majority of people struggle with most. To the degree that these essential attributes are lacking, faith in self is also lacking.

When we lack faith in ourselves, we are uncomfortable in our own skin and eternally searching for something more. If we fail to find that "something," the searching becomes striving which leads to an actively resistant attitude. The resistance shuts down energy flow, further diminishing faith in self, which creates a downward spiral that results in further erosion of the essential elements.

If you find yourself in this vicious cycle, find a way to get that conditioned mask off and discover your true nature and your natural strengths, passions and energizers. Remember, everything is about energy, and you will have an abundance of it only when you are living authentically.

Everyone loves the self that nature gave them. I have not seen one exception. I can state with absolute confidence that, if you are not thoroughly delighted with who you are, if you don't possess self-confidence and very healthy levels of self-esteem, and if you don't have a deep and abiding faith in yourself and your ability to make good choices for yourself, then you are *not* fully acquainted with your true self and all the potential you possess.

PEOPLE ARE NOT NEGATIVE BY NATURE

People who are negative or problematical, who lack a work ethic or decent values, who are not principled, who are not proud of who they are or how they act, who are not living with absolute integrity, who are just downright difficult and unhappy, are people who don't know and have not sufficiently developed their true self. Such people are often afraid to look inside themselves for fear of what they might see. But they need not be. Such negative behaviors are *always* products of conditioning, not of nature. Nature conforms to the Law of Abundance, so we each come into the world with an abundance of everything we need to become, as well as experience, everything we desire.

Want proof? Go looking for a negative baby. There are babies who cry because they are hungry or uncomfortable, of course (for a baby that is energy rightly used). But I have never personally seen a negative baby and I have been looking for nearly thirty years.

Negativity is a result of conditioning that puts constraints on our natural self; it sets up resistance as a result of our being forced to assume roles that hold us down and prevent us from realizing our true potential. Unfortunately, too many of us have claimed the constraints as our reality and continued to hold onto them long after the external cause has been removed.

THE ROOTS OF EMOTION

We seldom examine the roots of emotions like frustration or anger, for example. We just tell ourselves that we are impatient or we blame other people for making us mad. If we happen to be shy and afraid of people, we assume that's just how we are. We never stop to question whether the anger or impatience or shyness is a learned response rather than a natural inclination.

Emotions like fear, anger, and frustration are perfectly natural when they are *temporary responses* directed toward things that are happening in the world around us. Survival dictates that we respond to our environment appropriately. But long lasting fear, anger, frustration, and negativity are *not* appropriate responses.

Consistent and persistently negative responses are generally directed inwardly at ourselves as much as outwardly at others or at circumstances. They are applied as self-limiting forces rather than used to monitor surroundings or adjust behaviors. *Persistently negative responses are always a result of having lost sight of one's true self.*

A PRIMARY HUMAN NEED

In one scene of the movie, *Shall We Dance?*, the character played by Susan Sarandon is talking to the detective she has hired to follow her husband. She is now dismissing the detective after discovering that her husband is taking dancing lessons rather than having an affair. As they discuss marriage, she tells him that people marry because they need a witness to their lives. How true. The fact is, we form and maintain all kinds of relationships in order to have witnesses to our lives and people who will validate us. This factor can readily be seen in small children before they are taught not to ask for our attention.

Children frequently request an audience; someone to witness their accomplishments and even their play. They regularly make requests such as, "Watch me catch the ball, Mommy" "Look how high I can jump." "Look what I made at school today." "Dad, look how strong I am. I can pick this up all by myself." "Look, I can tie my own shoe!"

A primary human need is to belong to and be accepted and validated by our clan. It is this primary need that drives mental and emotional conditioning and, to have that need met, we must look to others to learn how we are doing. But to get our truth reflected back to us, we must first project it. And to do that we must be clear about what we want those who are witnessing our life to see.

Some questions we should all regularly ask ourselves—and answer—are: Do my actions and attitudes accurately convey what I want others to see in me? Do they build stronger bonds or break them down? Am I presenting to those who witness my life the image I really want them to see? Do I adequately value the people who have willingly agreed to remain a part of my life and be my witnesses? What story am I conveying to them about who I am and what I stand for?

If we aren't showing people who we really are, they cannot reflect our truth back to us. But the fact is, we generally get reflected back exactly what we project, be it truth or fiction. If we are projecting fiction, everything that is reflected back to us feels inauthentic.

We respond to feedback that feels inauthentic in one of two ways:

(1) We take what others reflect back to us and interpret it such that we think the other person is insincere or just plain mean, and we are hurt or angered by the feedback.

(2) We interpret the feedback such that we feel like others are clueless and can't see the truth about us—and wouldn't like us much if they could.

In the first case, the criticisms of others feel unjustified and without merit. We think the people are just out to get us, or they don't understand us and don't care to understand. On the other side of this same coin, compliments feel insincere and we find it hard to be sure that we can trust the positive feedback that other people give us; those who hold to this position usually trust almost no one.

In the second case, compliments feel sincere, but undeserved. Those in this space feel unlovable and are certain that, if others could see what they are really like, they would never want to be around them. They think wearing a mask and putting on a good show is their only option, so that's what they keep doing.

Those in this second group fall between two extremes; on one end, they internally feel and externally appear very insecure. The insecure ones don't think they have much to offer and, in their case, the mask is a protection against feelings of inferiority.

On the other end of the scale is the pompous, arrogant big shot who acts superior to others. Although this person appears overly confident, the problem is still the same; they feel inferior on the inside. They just use a different method to hide it. For them, the mask is to cover up the fact that inside they feel like a fraud.

OTHERS REFLECT WHAT YOU PROJECT

The self you consistently project not only determines what gets reflected back to you, it determines the quality of people you attract into your life, and therefore, the quality of your life. If you project anger and distrust, you attract people who will reflect back to you qualities that promote anger and distrust, and life will present you with more and more opportunities to be angry and distrustful.

If you project shallow, surface traits, you will attract shallow, surface people who live shallow, meaningless lives and present you with lots of opportunities to be shallow.

If you project an unprincipled, undisciplined, irresponsible image, you will attract similar people and your life will grow ever more chaotic.

If you project criticism and harsh judgment, your life will be filled with people and things for you to harshly criticize, and people who will similarly criticize and harshly judge you.

If you project a principled, disciplined, responsible, accepting, non-judgmental, loving, helpful image, you will likewise attract those who validate and share those attributes and who think and act in similar ways. You will attract people who are kinder, gentler, more caring, and accepting; who are happier and more successful in life, and always willing to help.

Those who don't know themselves well enough to project their truth often struggle with life and relationships because they must depend on others to determine and define for them who they are. What they tend to attract are other people who are similarly lost and searching and who cannot give or receive authenticity because they don't have it either. People who don't have a clear picture of who they are often long to have goodness and beauty reflected back to them, but what they keep getting back is whatever false self they are projecting.

REJECTED REFLECTIONS

When the observer fails to receive and reflect back the image the sender instinctively feels is right (but which is not being projected) there is a disconnect between the two. The sender believes the observer does not understand them. The observer does not seem to be witnessing what the sender believes to be true. The validation they were seeking is not there and they resist the feedback. The result is discord, open conflict, or withdrawal. Here one person is trying to accurately witness what he/she is observing, and the other is rejecting the feedback because it fails to match what he/she longs for.

We all build our relationships by attracting and selecting those with whom we are willing and able to relate. We grow relationships or destroy them by what we present to others, what we expect from them, what we give, and what we will accept.

If we don't know who we really are, we have no choice but to accept the opinions of others. When we do that, personal boundaries are almost non-existent and others can easily impose themselves upon us. If their opinions of us are erroneous, because we are reflecting poorly or because they are blind to what we reflect, we get flawed data and generally self-esteem suffers. When we can't show people who we really are, they can't reflect our truth back to us even if they want to. They are forced to make assumptions and often the assumptions are wrong.

In order to build the next level of faith—faith in others—we must know ourselves fully enough to be authentic and project our truth. Only then will we give and receive the kind of feedback that allows us to connect with others in meaningful ways, and only then can we ourselves be fully free.

There is one thing that you can know for certain. You do not need, and are not being served, by whatever masks you don. Your true self is amazing and wonderful and exactly what you need to create the life you long for. Take the time to get to know and appreciate the *real* you. When you do, faith in yourself will not be far behind.

> *There are two great days in a person's life-*
> *the day we are born*
> *and the day we discover why.*
> William Barclay

CHAPTER 10

Insulating The Path To Abundance:
Faith In Others

Take away love and our earth is a tomb.

Robert Browning

To build healthy relationships that promote faith in others, we must create and maintain conditions that lead to positive abundance. Our actions must be responsible, disciplined, and courageous, and our attitude open, accepting, caring and non-resistant. We can't attend to just one part of that equation, either. We must balance both the application and attitude lines and align them with a clear, positive goal.

People who confine themselves to just the correct application path (responsible, disciplined action) become overly rigid and critical. Those who confine themselves to just the correct attitude path (accepting, allowing, trusting, believing, caring, non-resistant) become overly permissive. In both instances, the individual lacks courage. The one confined to disciplined application lacks the courage to trust, to let go, and allow life to unfold. The one confined to a receptive attitude lacks the courage to correct the actions that are creating problems for everyone involved.

In relationships, the goal must always be mutual growth and sustainability. Being overly rigid and critical damages relationships and rarely leads to sustainable growth. Allowing those who are creating problems to continue behaving in ways that are detrimental to themselves and others not only prevents sustainable growth, it diminishes trust and, without trust, damage to the relationship is inevitable. Not only does resistance to the individual who is behaving irresponsibly develop, there is also resistance to those who allow it.

A VICTIM MENTALITY LEADS TO LIMITATION

Consider the victim mentality that is so prevalent in the United States right now. We can't help but feel resistant when those who are leading the country, and making and enforcing the rules (or not), allow obviously ridiculous and irresponsible acts to continue without consequence.

One example is frivolous lawsuits, which occur regularly and without consequence to either the individual who has brought the suit, or the attorney who has accepted it, knowing that it is frivolous and taking it to court is a waste of taxpayer dollars. The man who sued a dry cleaning company for millions of dollars because they lost a pair of slacks is an example of this. If attorneys, who should know better, were held responsible for all costs associated with frivolous lawsuits, they would cease to be brought before the courts.

Irresponsible behavior is so prevalent in the United States that most Americans distrust those in positions of leadership on every level. Polls suggest that the majority of Americans distrust the government, the judicial system and big business—the primary holders of power and positions of leadership. Certainly not all have abused their positions, but all suffer the consequences to some extent when distrust is so widespread, and that is exactly the point. When we allow even a few to act irresponsibly, the whole is adversely impacted.

ENERGY DRAINERS

No matter how hard people try to be positive, energy is depleted and progress greatly slowed when they are in close and frequent association with people who are negative, acting irresponsibly or trying to push their agenda off on those around them.

A common example of this is seen corporations where the majority of people really do want to stay positive and upbeat and do a good job, but their energies are regularly being depleted by those around them who are lazy, irresponsible and/or have bad attitudes. This is true even when the negative ones are in the minority, and is especially true in cultures that are themselves irresponsible and tolerating such employees.

The responsible, self-disciplined people in such an environment will typically report the behaviors of the problem employees to the appropriate source for awhile to try to get something done about them. But if nothing positive happens, the formerly positive employees lose energy and enthusiasm, become disengaged and the entire team becomes less effective. When those who are negative or irresponsible happen to be in positions of authority, the negative effect is greatly magnified.

As a result of the work I have done as a developmental coach and corporate trainer over the years, I have had the opportunity to see the inside workings of many organizations and it is appalling how many of them fail to see how the actions and attitudes of even of a few tolerated negative employees are impacting the people, productivity, and profits of the entire organization. And, because groups of people can shift energy in tidal wave proportions rather than in small currents like an individual might, the direction of a company, and even the economy of a nation, can turn on a dime. I have seen once healthy, productive, profitable organizations fall into ruin in as few as two years as a result of placing an energy drainer in a leadership position. We all witness similar dynamics on a broader scale when we see once healthy economies falter and even fail under poor leaders in whom the people lack trust.

MONEY HAS VERY LITTLE ENERGY

Companies and economies falter and fail because leaders begin focusing on the wrong things. They forget what drives productivity and profitability and mistakenly focus solely on generating profits or building their own empires. But empires cannot exist for long without willing followers; and money, in and of itself, has very little energy to sustain anything. Money is only *potential* energy, and it doesn't even have much of that on its own. Try starting a fire with a few dozen hundred dollar bills and you will see how little real energy money has by itself.

Money's potential is realized only when people put it to good use. And whether it steadily increases or diminishes depends completely on how effectively the people involved are using their own energies. If the culture is one that diminishes positive energy in people, money and profits will diminish. If the culture is one that promotes positive energy in people, money and profits will grow.

Companies such as FedEx, Starbucks and Google, which are very upbeat, positive, and people centered, grew phenomenally and quickly became profitable. These firms are good examples of what can happen when energy dynamics are positive. Their growth and profitability will continue so long as the energy dynamics continue to be positive and their focus remains on people—the people they employ, the customers they serve and the vendors who serve them.

FAMILY DYNAMICS

The same dynamics that can derail an organization or economy can derail a family too, and all it takes is one person acting irresponsibly and/or uncaringly. In any group, when those in authority (the parents in this case) allow negative, undisciplined, irresponsible behaviors to continue, the energies of the rest of the family or group are negatively impacted.

In organizations, people who wish to remain on the positive path leave the company and find a more suitable environment in which to work. Leaving our family isn't quite so easy. We have emotional ties to family that make it hard to completely break off from them the way an employee in a dysfunctional organization can. Yet, I have seen people break off from their entire family or certain members of it physically, mentally and/or emotionally.

Sometimes they just break away mentally or emotionally, and sometimes just physically. The goal is always the same though: to escape the constant pain associated with the family's prevailing negative dynamic. And it is almost always a difficult and initially painful choice.

EVERY RELATIONSHIP IMPACTS US

To keep life flowing toward abundance, we must be responsible and disciplined in the way we live our own lives. We must also be courageous enough to refuse to allow those who insist on being irresponsible, undisciplined, critical, and judgmental to negatively impact us.

Every relationship impacts us in some way. Some propel us forward; others drain or stall our energy and still others divert us to the wrong path where we end up getting a whole lot of what we don't want. The more significant the relationship, the greater the impact.

All relationships in which we must rely on the wisdom, courage, discipline, and responsibility of leadership (parents or other heads of household, bosses, preachers, teachers, government officials, etc.) are significant, because they directly impact our lives.

In the family, the most significant relationships for children are those that exist between them and their parents because the parents are the ones in the leadership role. For the parents, the most significant relationship is the one with the spouse because the nature of leadership, and therefore the future of the entire family, is impacted by that relationship. In any and every relationship, we are impacted for good or ill, and there is no way around that fact.

Say, for example, that you want a happy marriage, but don't believe your spouse is meeting you halfway. You carry your share of the load around the house, sometimes doing even more than your share. You are honest and faithful. You make it a point not to be accusatory or unkind and you try to always be helpful and thoughtful. You are doing everything you believe necessary to build a good, healthy marriage.

On the other hand, your spouse, has not lived up to your idea of what a spouse is supposed to be and do. You resent that fact, though you don't let it show. Your spouse's shortcomings weren't such a big problem early in the marriage, but things just seem to be getting worse and worse, and the harder you try to make them better, the worse they keep getting.

According to the Law of Abundance, this is the only possible outcome until energy shifts somewhere. Why? Because there are two opposing factors bleeding over into the collective pool called marriage. In one case (yours), there is an active application charge (+) since you are working responsibly to do what you think makes a good marriage, as well as an active attitude charge (+) since you are resistant to your spouse's behaviors. Your focus appears to be positive because you are working so hard at doing your part to make the relationship good, but that is the goal, not the focus. The focus is actually on your spouse's shortcomings and is resistant.

In your spouse's case, he/she is adding receptive application (-), to the mix, since he/she is not being responsible or working to keep the marriage healthy, as well as active resistance (+) since he/she is resisting any attempt on your part to get a different outcome. Your +/+ charge in combination with your spouse's -/+ charge is moving the relationship backwards toward negative abundance, or more of what you do not want. In this case, the flow of energy in the marriage is moving the two of you in a sort of spiraling dance that is steadily taking you both in the wrong direction.

THERE ARE ONLY SIX VARIATIONS TO THE RELATIONSHIP DANCE

Energetically speaking, there are only six relationship combinations, and each of them results in an interplay that resembles a dance. In some cases the dancers are not moving because each one is trying to lead. In some cases, they are not moving because neither partner is willing to lead. In others, they are moving around and around one another, spinning in a circle, but getting nowhere. In still others, one is moving toward negativity while the other simply spins, so the dance becomes a slow spiral toward what neither wants. In another, one is spinning as the other moves the two in a slow spiral toward what both prefer. Or each is headed in the same direction and is propelling one another along that path, either positive or negative

The worst combination is the one where both partners are actively moving toward an abundance of negative outcomes. An example of this would be two alcohol or drug addicts who have paired up and are enabling each other's destruction. Relationships in which even one party is on the negative path are never healthy, but this one is especially destructive.

In semi-healthy, relationships one partner is moving toward the positive while the other one is stuck. In this case the dance becomes a slow spiral toward the positive. This relationship can move toward being fully healthy much easier than can the other four unhealthy ones, provided the positive partner does not become resistant to the stuck one and the stuck partner is eventually willing to shift his/her behaviors toward the positive.

In truly healthy relationships, both people are firmly on the path to positive abundance. In this case, the dance is directly toward what is desired. Both are responsible, disciplined, and courageous in their actions and interactions, and both are fully supportive of one another. While they may not always agree with one another, they respect each other's right to have an opinion and neither ever tries to force change on the other. There is overall trust and mutual respect, genuine love, and a deep concern for the good of the other. Both feel truly cherished and empowered in this relationship and believe their spouse is accurately witnessing and reflecting their truth. Sadly, this type of relationship is very rare.

Illustrations 10.01 – 10.06 demonstrate the relationship dance. The zigzag connectors in Illustrations 10.01 – 10.05 represent resistance. In Illustration 10.05, the single zigzag line represents a diminished degree of resistance. There is no resistance in Illustration 10.06, which is the only healthy combination.

STUCK IN A RUT

Illustration 10.01 represents three relationship styles. Though all three result in the relationship being stuck, the cause is different. Where both are functioning from (-/-), they are both irresponsible and undisciplined, and neither is willing to take the lead to change the dynamic. Where both are functioning from (+/+), both are rigid and insistent on their own ways. Both want to lead and neither is willing to relinquish any control to allow the dynamic to change. Where one is (+/+) and the other (-/-), one is being stubborn and resistant and the other is being irresponsible and compliant to his/her own detriment. This latter couple appears to be moving, but they are really just spinning round and round one another and not really getting anywhere. In this combination, the rigid, judgmental (+/+) person is the one that creates resistance, usually by trying to force the irresponsible (-/-) person to conform to his/her rules and being irritated when their partner tries, but fails, to perform "correctly."

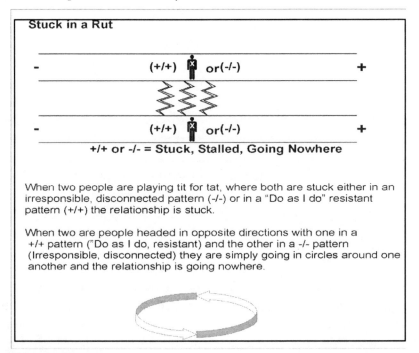

Illustration 10.01

UNSUSTAINABLE

Where two people are moving in opposite directions, relationships are not sustainable. When one person is moving in a positive direction and the other in a negative, something has got to give.

Typically what happens if the positive person tries to maintain the relationship is that he/she begins to feel resistance to the partner's negative behaviors and the resistance causes energy to diminish. Then the positive partner starts moving in a negative direction. As this occurs, there is resistance to this backward movement and the relationship gets worse instead of better. The other response is that the positive person leaves the relationship in order to sustain his/her positive position.

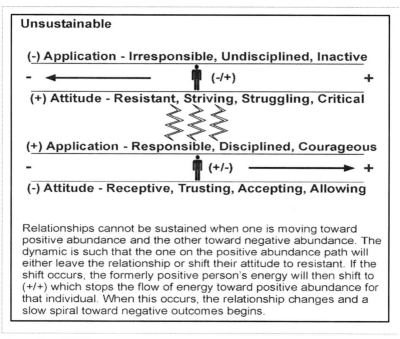

Unsustainable

(-) Application - Irresponsible, Undisciplined, Inactive

-     ⟵───────   (-/+)   +

(+) Attitude - Resistant, Striving, Struggling, Critical

(+) Application - Responsible, Disciplined, Courageous

-                         (+/-) ───────⟶   +

(-) Attitude - Receptive, Trusting, Accepting, Allowing

Relationships cannot be sustained when one is moving toward positive abundance and the other toward negative abundance. The dynamic is such that the one on the positive abundance path will either leave the relationship or shift their attitude to resistant. If the shift occurs, the formerly positive person's energy will then shift to (+/+) which stops the flow of energy toward positive abundance for that individual. When this occurs, the relationship changes and a slow spiral toward negative outcomes begins.

Illustration 10.02

A SLOW SPIRAL TOWARD NEGATIVE OUTCOMES

When one person in a relationship is trying to move in a positive direction and the other is stuck, the typical response is for the more positive person to try to change the stuck one in an effort to get him or her to be more positive. This never works.

Unless the stuck person decides to make changes him/herself, any attempt at inducing or inspiring change only causes more resistance.

The added resistance results in a further slowing of the relationship energies and both people begin a slow spiral towards negative outcomes.

The only way this relationship can improve is for the positive person to become accepting of the behaviors of the stuck one, while modeling positive behaviors, and for the stuck one to decide to adopt the more positive model. This rarely happens because the stuck person is either rigid, regimented and unaccepting of the more positive person's less rigid style (+/+), or is behaving irresponsibly, and is undisciplined and disinterested in changing (-/-).

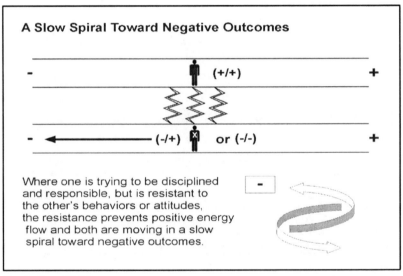

Illustration 10.03

A RUSH TO DESTRUCTION

When both people are irresponsible and undisciplined as well as judgmental of one another and resistant to one another's behaviors, they accelerate each other's negative outcomes. Couples that are both heavy drinkers or drug abusers were mentioned earlier, but this can also be those who verbally, mentally, emotionally or physically abuse one another. In each case they are rushing headlong to destruction.

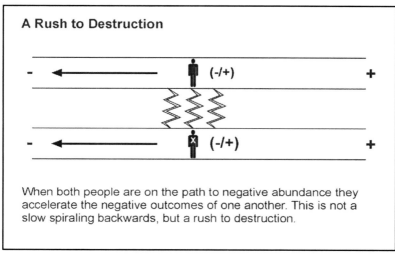

A Rush to Destruction

(-/+)

(-/+)

When both people are on the path to negative abundance they accelerate the negative outcomes of one another. This is not a slow spiraling backwards, but a rush to destruction.

Illustration 10.04

A SLOW SPIRAL TOWARD POSITIVE OUTCOMES

Where one person in a relationship is consistently positive, effectively modeling positive behaviors and attitudes and is tolerant and non-resistant to the stuck person's behaviors and the stuck person is open to growth and change, the positive person can move both of them toward positive abundance, but the movement is very slow and requires a great deal of patience, persistence and willingness to remain non-judgmental on the part of the positive person.

A situation where a responsible, disciplined, courageous, principled person works very hard to support and take care of a hypochondriac spouse who, while stuck in health issues is nonetheless open to learning and adjusting, is one example of this type of relationship.

The relationship survives and conditions improve almost entirely due to the efforts of the positive one and his/her willingness to encourage and praise the spouse's efforts and keep going the extra mile as the hypochondriac is "recovering".

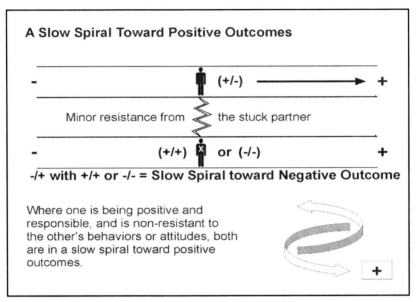

Illustration 10.05

HEALTHY AND GROWING

The positive abundance relationship in Illustration 10.06 is the only one that is not among the resistant combinations, and it can only remain non-resistant so long as both people are fully accepting and supportive of one another.

Being fully accepting and supportive does not mean never disagreeing or having differences of opinion. No two people are going to agree on everything, or want and need the same things all the time. One of the things that keeps a relationship healthy is the freedom to express an opinion or hold a position different from that of the other person without condemnation. People in healthy relationships actually tend to have more debates than those in less healthy relationships because, in healthy ones, each knows that the argument will center on the subject and will not negatively impact the relationship. In healthy relationships disagreement does not result in disapproval so both parties are free to express themselves and communication flows.

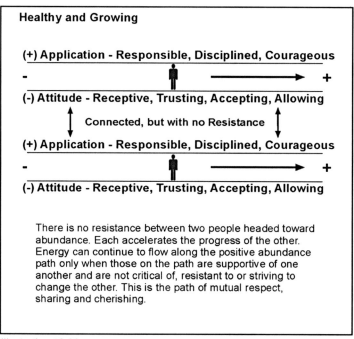

Healthy and Growing

(+) Application - Responsible, Disciplined, Courageous

(-) Attitude - Receptive, Trusting, Accepting, Allowing

Connected, but with no Resistance

(+) Application - Responsible, Disciplined, Courageous

(-) Attitude - Receptive, Trusting, Accepting, Allowing

There is no resistance between two people headed toward abundance. Each accelerates the progress of the other. Energy can continue to flow along the positive abundance path only when those on the path are supportive of one another and are not critical of, resistant to or striving to change the other. This is the path of mutual respect, sharing and cherishing.

Illustration 10.06

ALL RELATIONSHIPS ARE AFFECTED

The minute we become non-accepting toward another person and feel a need to change that person in any way, we have introduced resistors which either slow, stop, or reverse the flow of energy in the relationship. If we maintain the resistance, we then move the relationship into one of the resistant patterns, which are harmful to the relationship, to be sure, but we harm ourselves as well.

Our energies are slowed by the resistance we feel toward the other person and we are no longer flowing as freely toward positive abundance. If the positive energy of one person is regularly being counteracted by the negative energy of another person, progress is invariably slowed or stalled.

Remaining non-resistant to another person does not mean we must accept unkind or inappropriate behaviors. In fact, to remain responsible, disciplined, and courageous, we must stand up for what we believe is right. But we can do that in non-aggressive, non-resistant ways. All great teachers and even all great debaters understand the importance of remaining emotionally neutral while firmly stating one's case.

> All relationships follow one of these six patterns. Just replace the concept of love with that of caring or consideration and you can apply the dynamics to any relationship you have or will ever have and understand why it is unfolding the way it is.

BE DISCERNING ABOUT THE COMPANY YOU KEEP

Whether relationships spiral toward positive or negative outcomes depends on the degree of positive influence in relation to the negative influence. If the negative influence is even slightly greater, the spiral is toward the negative. If the positive influence is slightly greater, the spiral will be toward the positive, but is much harder to sustain because—as you may recall—positive thoughts, feelings and intent do not impose themselves upon us, but negative ones do.

Where negativity exists, it takes more effort on the part of positive people to sustain positive thoughts, feelings, and intent. Also, negative attitudes tend to generate resistance in those who must interact with negative people. The resistance then slows the flow of energy toward positive abundance. The result is that the relationship or the intended outcome (or both) slowly deteriorates.

Because negativity tends to impose itself on everyone, the energy of those who are *actively* working at staying on the path to positive abundance looks a lot like that of what physicists call *pulsating direct current*, especially in relation to other people.

The definition of *pulsating direct current*, according to the online encyclopedia *Wikipedia*, is "A direct current (dc) that changes in value at regular or irregular intervals. A pulsating direct current may change in value, i.e., be always present but at different levels, or it may be a current that is interrupted completely at regular or irregular intervals, but when present, is always moving in the same direction."

People and events may temporarily drag down or even interrupt the energy of those actively working to remain on the positive path, but they never allow that interruption to last for long. They quickly correct the problem, readjust their energies, and continue in the same direction—toward positive abundance.

The recognition that other people have the ability to interrupt the flow of positive energy is the reason that those who teach success and wealth building techniques continually advise us to carefully choose the company we keep. Only people on the path to positive abundance have the ability to significantly speed the progress of another person rather than slow it down or interrupt it.

The reason success-minded people insist on associating primarily with other success-minded people is because they realize that people who are focused upon generating success will speed their progress, while those who focus upon and make excuses for their failures will significantly slow and even interrupt progress.

FACTORS FOR FAITH IN OTHERS

Clearly, we can have greater faith in others when they are propelling us forward rather than when they are dragging us down. So, to build your faith in others, choose your company carefully. The people you associate with will greatly impact your outcomes.

Faith in others can be applied to individuals, or to entire groups of people, such as business associates and co-workers, your community, your country, those who share your culture, social groups, even humanity as a whole. The greater the circle of people you are able to include, the greater that layer of insulation will be. But, to have faith in others requires trust, and to have trust on a broad scale, we must learn to be discerning.

Not all people can be trusted, and if we don't approach others in a responsible, discerning and courageous way, the degree of trust necessary to add this element of insulation will not be possible. We will have too many instances where our faith in others gets dashed to sustain it. As in every other area, to move relationships in the direction of what you want, you need the active (+) charge of responsible, disciplined action and the courage to do the right thing, and you also need the receptive (-) charge of acceptance and trust.

DOING THE RIGHT THING IN RELATIONSHIPS

Doing the right thing includes treating people with respect and dignity, and accepting nothing less from them. It means refusing to deliver or accept negative behaviors, such as unkindness, manipulation, bullying, or dishonesty. It means not pushing your opinions and judgments off on others, and not allowing others to push theirs off on you. It means listening and caring and showing empathy and concern, while at the same time refusing to take part in non-productive, co-dependent behaviors that enable others to be weak rather than strong, victims rather than co-creators, blameless rather than responsible, lazy rather than disciplined, irresponsible rather than responsible, or cowardly rather than courageous. It means refusing to get caught up in the dramas that occur as a result of people projecting the wrong image and then rejecting what is being accurately reflected back to them.

When you enable weakness, lack of discipline, irresponsibility, laziness, delusion, or lack of direction in others, you have done yourself and them a great disservice. You have created circumstances where you cannot trust these people and you have been instrumental in keeping them on the path to limitation. In the process, both you and they have lost opportunities to increase the energy that leads to abundance and to grow and develop in healthy ways.

IT TAKES WISDOM AND COURAGE TO TRUST

In her book, *The Courage to Trust*,[11] Cynthia Wall observes that it takes wisdom to know with whom we can be vulnerable and when vulnerability is appropriate. Wisdom, courage and trust must be developed and these arise from the ability to believe in ourselves and to discern correctly so we can learn to believe in others.

We are not born knowing how to trust. Our ability to trust is largely a result of the many teachers we encounter throughout our lifetime. Everyone we interact with becomes a teacher in some way. Everything we know and believe about ourselves and our relationships has come to us through our interactions with others. Some of the teachers we encounter enhance us, others damage us. But for good or ill, all have taught us something about humanity and impacted us in some way.

Few of us were fortunate enough to have a perfect childhood that left us with a solid base for trusting in ourselves and others. Most of us must learn how to trust as adults and to do that we must first develop the wisdom to be discerning and the courage to explore unknown territory. We are likely to make some mistakes in the process, but wisdom and courage in relating to people can only develop through taking risks. There really is no other way.

Trust is a fragile thing, and like fine china or crystal, we must handle it with care. Wall's work validates how easily thoughtless words and impulsive actions can damage trust and cause people to decide it is unsafe to trust anyone. When we lack trust, we keep our authentic self hidden away so we won't have to suffer rejection or betrayal. But in the process, we often hide our authenticity from ourselves as well. Lack of trust in others sets up lots of conditions for both internal and external struggles, and places us squarely on the path toward an abundance of things we do *not* want.

It takes courage to confide in others, to let down our guard and hope for a caring, compassionate response. Every time we approach someone trustingly, we take the risk that he or she may misinterpret our intent or harshly judge us. When that occurs, there is an emotional shift in our energy pattern, and if we are not careful, the actions of one or two people may cause us to shut down our willingness to trust people in general. We then get caught in a trap of distrust and, unless we know what is creating it, finding our way back to trust can be difficult.

Here are some common traps in which people get caught:

TRUSTING THE WRONG PEOPLE

When we trust the wrong people, or when our attempts at connecting create circumstances that make interacting seem painful or dangerous, we begin to doubt our ability to discern correctly. We begin to believe that we are not capable of making wise relationship decisions and we come to distrust ourselves, in specific, and others in general. Again, if we are not aware that this response is not about other people, but about our current skill level, which we can improve, we will limit how vulnerable and courageous we dare to be in the future.

Confronting the fears that life's experiences have built up around us takes courage and right action, as does refusing to allow those who cannot be trusted to impact our attitude and our outcomes. Avoid getting stuck in self-defeating cycles of fear and distrust. It will impact your ability to have faith in yourself, as well as your ability to have faith in others.

TEACHING PEOPLE THE WRONG LESSONS

If your spouse, children, friends, boss, or co-workers seem to take advantage of you, it's most likely because you have inadvertently taught them that they can treat you that way and gain something of value for themselves. They are getting the outcome they want or they wouldn't continue the behavior.

Work on building stronger personal boundaries. Define who you are and are not, and what you will and will not accept from others. Imagine your personal boundaries as a beautiful bubble of positive energy surrounding your entire being. Become intimately acquainted with the energy inside that bubble and you will know immediately when someone invades that beautiful space.

Work on developing skills on the courage and right action side of the abundance equation (+) and on trusting yourself to know what is best for you (the receptive side).

EXPECTING OTHERS TO READ YOUR MIND

If you fail to ask others for what you want because you believe that they should be able to anticipate your needs without your asking, stop doing that! People cannot read your mind. We have not evolved that far yet.

Examine the possibility that you don't ask for what you want because you don't trust others to listen without criticizing, ridiculing, or rejecting you, or don't believe they will care enough about your outcomes to comply. You will never know unless you ask.

By asking, you have increased your odds of getting what you want by at least 100%, usually more. Work on the courage and right action side of the abundance equation (+) to give you the courage to ask for what you want and, on the receptive attitude side (-), to develop the trust to receive the desired response.

NOT TRUSTING YOUR OWN JUDGMENT

If you stay in relationships, jobs, or even homes or cities that are not satisfying, you may lack trust in your judgment and ability to make important decisions, or to handle the requirements for making big changes on your own. Work on the courage and right action side of the abundance equation (+) to increase your courage to step forth and positively impact your own future, and on the receptive attitude side (-) to allow you to have faith in yourself and your choices.

NOT TRUSTING YOUR ABILITY TO POSITIVELY IMPACT THE FUTURE

If you have a clear vision of your ideal lifestyle, but aren't taking the steps toward making it happen, it could be that you lack faith in yourself, in others, and/or in a generative force, any of which can affect your faith in a positive future. Focus on strengthening the receptive attitude side of the abundance equation (-) in every area where faith and trust are lacking (self, others or a generative force).

On the active (+) side, decide what you want your future to look like, lay out a plan of action and take steps toward getting you to your goal every single day.

In areas where you don't personally have the resources or knowledge to make your dreams a reality, find the people who can help you and partner with them. Good people are always willing to lend a hand to someone who is genuinely committed to improving their lives. Tap into this great pool of knowledge and talent. No big dream has ever come to fruition without the help of a group of committed people.

THE FOUR COMPONENTS OF TRUST

Trust is not possible without four factors: Character, Consideration, Connectivity, and Competence.

CHARACTER

Character includes ethics and values such as integrity, honesty, courage, consistency, kindness, non-judgment, and non-aggression. If we are inconsistent, others will not know what to expect from us. If we are dishonest or in any way lacking in integrity, others will not believe us. If we lack the courage to do what is right, others will not think they can count on us. If we harshly judge others, aggressively push them, or passive-aggressively try to manipulate them into our way of thinking and acting, others will not trust us to be kind or considerate of their thoughts, feelings, opinions or needs.

CONSIDERATION

Consideration includes empathy, thoughtfulness, kindness, caring, contribution, and listening in order to understand feelings and concerns as well as to gather facts. Consideration could be thought of as a part of character, but it is important to separate it out because there are many who have character, but who lack real consideration for others. Often they are not aware that this is lacking, though others can see it.

Take, for example, corporate leaders who act with integrity in their business dealings but are too focused on results to consider their people. They may be consistent in their approach, courageous in the way they present their ideas and beliefs, and solid in holding others to company standards. Their word may be their bond. Yet, if they fail to see and consider the needs of their employees, consideration is likely not a part of their character and trust will suffer.

Those who lack consideration are not attuned to the needs of other people. They may be following their own convictions to the letter and being very true to their own values, but they are not taking the needs of others into account. Even when inconsiderate people appear to be considering others it is usually a planned maneuver designed to get a specific result.

Genuine consideration requires empathy—the ability to put one's self in another person's position, to really feel what the other person is feeling, to understand their position, and to care about their outcomes. Consideration is also the act of choosing to be kind when it is easier, more expedient, or more self-gratifying to do otherwise. Without consideration, there is no way to genuinely connect with others. Where true consideration is lacking, anything that appears to be a connection is just a façade, which brings us to the third factor.

CONNECTIVITY

Connectivity includes communication, listening (in order to understand thoughts, opinions, feelings and concerns), openness, alignment, receptivity, consistency (in order to gain the trust and confidence of others), and discernment (in order to safely extend trust and confidence to others).

Just as your house must be connected to a power source to power your lights and appliances, connectivity is also essential to relationships, and energy must be flowing in both directions. Connectivity cannot occur with energy or intention flowing just one way. There can be no connection, no alignment, and no real communication unless both parties are engaged in the process. One person must start the process, of course, and the better an individual is at building bridges between themselves and others, the more likely it is that connectivity will occur. But it cannot occur without cooperation, which is the cornerstone of connectivity. We cannot trust uncooperative people.

We cannot trust people whose actions are unpredictable or inconsistent. And, typically we neither trust nor understand people with whom we cannot communicate at least on some level.

COMPETENCE

The fourth and final factor is competence. Competence includes responsible, disciplined actions, and the willingness and ability to learn and adjust as necessary to affect good outcomes. It requires a continual quest for excellence, the determination to perform to the best of our abilities, effective self-management and self-confidence, as well as realistic, clear-headed thinking. It also requires refusal to accept sub-standard actions or outcomes in our self or in others. Without competence, we cannot deliver on our promises or perform to the expected standard. It is possible to trust people on all the other levels and still lack trust here.

For example, you may trust someone completely on the levels of character, consideration, and connectivity, and not trust them in a particular area. No responsible person would trust a teenager who has never cared for a child to baby sit their infant, for example. Neither would any sane person be likely to trust a family member with no training to perform an operation on them or fill a tooth. Most people wouldn't be likely to allow a novice to even "operate" on a computer they depend on, much less on any part of their body.

Wherever we doubt that competence exists, we lack trust. Unlike the other three components, competence can be conditional. We can trust someone to be a competent business manager, for example, but not a competent mechanic or computer technician. Such is not the case with character, consideration, or connectivity. These are all encompassing, and to the degree that these are lacking or inconsistent, trust is adversely affected.

Trust is a primary factor for building relationships. Without it, relationships fail to form and those that have formed tend to fall apart once trust is lost. We will not buy anything from those we do not trust; not products or services, not ideas, not claims of sincerity, not words, not anything. Trust is paramount to building and maintaining any kind of relationship.

An excellent book for developing trust is Stephen M.R. Covey's *The Speed of Trust*. Although it was written for the business market, the advice and instructions work equally well on a personal level. In fact, Covey has discovered, as I have, that all trust begins at a personal level and moves outward from there. He describes this outward movement as "waves of trust." His model places self trust first, then relationship trust, then trust at organizational, then market and finally societal levels. The Law of Abundance model takes it out one more level to an all encompassing trust in the generative force.

The Law of Abundance model also places self-trust first, then trust in others, which would include organizations, markets, and for some people, societies. To others, societies—when functioning well—belong in the realm of the third level: trust in a generative force. Societies can indeed be generative when they are working well and supporting the whole of their population in healthy ways.

As you will discover in Chapter 11, however, the generative force extends well beyond societies and impacts much more than what Covey's model identifies. Yet good character—a primary component of trust in both models—is generative in and of itself, so the generative force is present at both the beginning and the end of the trust cycle. Trust is a very important factor and is covered beautifully in Covey's book.

THE GOLDEN AND PLATINUM RULES

Most everyone is familiar with the Golden Rule: Do unto others, as you would have them do unto you. Author and trainer Tony Alessandra took that rule one step further, stating that we should treat others as *they* would like to be treated, not as we would like to be treated. He calls this the *Platinum Rule*. There is a lot of wisdom in this approach because others don't necessarily *want* to be treated the same way we do.

Over the years, I have discovered that, to make the most of relationships, we have to take interactions even further than the Golden and Platinum Rules suggest. There are times, for example, when we need to go beyond doing unto others as they would have us do, because the other person doesn't have any idea what they want or need, or what would help them to get where they want to go in life. If they don't know, and we treat them the way we want to be treated, we are guiding them down our path, not theirs. And more often than not, that is the wrong thing to do too. If we determine to treat them as they would like to be treated and they don't know what that is, we are both stuck.

THE DIAMOND RULE

To ensure that we are instrumental in helping others in the way they need to be helped, we must move beyond the idea of just meeting current needs and include the idea of discovering and facilitating what might enhance the relationship, as well as each person's individual outcomes in the long term. To get there, we must be aware that sometimes neither we nor the other person knows what is necessary to achieve the desired outcome. When they don't know and we don't know, we need to be open to the mutual exploration of options.

To take interactions to the highest level, another dimension must be added. I call this multifaceted approach the *Diamond Rule*. It includes both the Golden Rule and the Platinum Rule and adds a third important element—purposeful application— to ensure positive impact.

The Golden Rule is an important part of the equation because to apply it effectively, we must first have self-awareness, self-love, and self-respect. The Platinum Rule is important because it requires that we understand, honor, and respect the thoughts, ideas, wants, and needs of others.

The third part added by the Diamond Rule is important because it makes us aware of our ability and responsibility to act in purposeful ways such that we positively impact lives—our own and those of others—to improve outcomes and inspire greatness.

Applying the Diamond Rule is analogous to taking diamonds in the rough and bringing out the beauty and shine that has been there all along. Just as a skilled diamond cutter never adds anything to the nature of a diamond that it didn't already have, we never really add anything to our own nature or that of others. The brilliance is already there and has been there all along. We simply find ways to bring out the natural qualities and allow the brilliance to shine through.

The Diamond Rule encourages us to bring out the best in ourselves, and others, by approaching each person, including ourselves, with a firm belief that there exists in each of us true inner beauty and at least one area of brilliance or genius. When we believe it is there, we become willing to look for it until we find it, and to keep patiently and gently polishing until the priceless gem that we know we will find emerges.

The best and most beautiful
things in the world
cannot be seen or even touched.
They must be felt with the heart.

Helen Keller

CHAPTER 11

Insulating the Path to Abundance: Faith in a Generative Force

If we could see the miracle of a single flower clearly,
our whole life would change.

Guatama the Buddha

I use the term "generative force" here because there is no question that a generative force exists in our world. Questions occur only around what that force is. For many people, faith in a generative force means faith in a higher power, but that higher power can also take many forms. Some refer to it as God, some as Allah, Yahweh, Krishna, or some other name that means essentially the same thing. Some see this higher power as the source of all creation and believe it has a direct beneficial effect, but they don't personalize it by giving it a particular name or form. Still others envision it as all encompassing, but simply as a force of nature that is completely neutral and non-personal. The idea of energy, as it is commonly presented by scientists, takes this latter position.

The perceptions and beliefs around the generative force are myriad, and while many people envision some form of creative being when they think of a generative force, it is certainly not necessary to have a personalized point of worship to have faith in this powerful insulator. Nature itself is a generative force, and for those who prefer a non-personalized, non-spiritual approach, belief in the forces of nature appears to be just as effective as any other form of belief. Remember, energy is completely non-biased and non-discriminatory and how you choose to view the generative force is totally irrelevant, so long as you realize it is there and always available to you.

To some degree, we all have faith in the generative force from the perspective of nature. When you cut yourself and expect that the wound will heal, for example, that is faith in nature as a generative force. When you plant seeds and expect them to produce plants, or expect babies to develop in the womb and be born and grow into adults, or even expect that your hair will grow back when you cut it too short, you are demonstrating faith in nature as a generative force.

The faith scientists have in the laws they see repeated again and again in the natural world, even faith in evolution as the movement of living things toward a state of better and better adaptability, is faith in nature as a generative force.

Many people have faith in *both* a personal God and natural forces, and just as your insulation capacity grows as your faith in self and your circle of trusted people grows, so too does belief in the generative force from multiple angles increase its capacity to serve you.

Both science and religion, which have disagreed on the nature of the generative force for centuries, would do well to broaden their perspectives. And no matter which side of that debate you prefer to settle on, realize that, in relation to the Law of Abundance, the broader your perspective and the greater the possibilities you allow, the greater your power to insulate yourself from negative influences and move toward an abundance of the things you want.

According to the Law of Abundance, both the scientific and the religious communities are slowing or stalling their growth by resisting one another's views. Imagine what would happen if traditional scientists broadened their thinking to allow the elements of intelligence, feeling and intention into the energy mix, rather than adhering to the view that energy, while it is all things and the source of all things, lacks these components. That view virtually eliminates *humankind* from the equation. In that humans have intelligence, feelings, goals and intentions, and are certainly part of the whole, the reality of these as naturally expressing attributes of energy is really quite self-evident.

As science delves deeper into the nature of the universe, evidence of the impact of intelligence, feeling, and intent becomes more and more apparent and yet that evidence is still rejected by those scientists who remain too narrowly focused. There is still considerable arguing over the evidence presented by quantum physicists, partly because it's a relatively new science and many of its theories have not been tested rigorously enough to satisfy old school scientists. Further, much of what has come to light suggests that energy does have intelligent, feeling components and an intentionality that impacts the whole, which flies in the face of all that has been taught scientifically over the years.

I find it strange that any scientist would prefer to reject this evidence. Those who do apparently don't see that by rejecting these aspects of nature, they are rejecting their own nature and the nature of every other human being. They are also closing themselves off from the very thing science is supposed to be about; unbiased inquiry.

On the other side of the debate, imagine what might happen if traditional theists broadened their thinking to include the possibility that religion and science actually align when both are properly approached. Imagine what might happen if those who cling to the Bible, or the Koran, or the Kabala (or whatever scriptures they consider to be the only source of spiritual truth), opened themselves to the possibility that God really is everywhere and in all things including you, me, them, and in the minds of the myriad people who continually bless us with wisdom and insights.

To realize abundance, we cannot argue one point of view over another. To do so throws us off the receptive attitude path and shuts down the flow of energy toward our desired outcomes. To remain receptive and open to abundance, we must be perfectly content with allowing others to believe whatever they choose. This can be a challenge when others are trying to force their ideas and opinions on us, and are even legislating our lives according to their own beliefs. But to stay on the path to positive abundance, we must meet that challenge and refuse to allow the opinions and actions of others to throw us off our own path or induce us to argue for our own position.

We can model our own faith wisely, lovingly, and compassionately.

But we must be content to simply model—not argue—and we must let the way others respond to what we model be alright with us. We can share our beliefs with others, but the minute we start resisting their beliefs and insisting that we are right and they are wrong, we have stepped off the path to positive abundance and claimed limitation instead.

Perhaps a better approach would be to simply ask questions and learn all we can about one another's point of view. Then the ignorance that keeps so many separated would no longer limit our thinking or our ability to connect with those whose approach to life is different from our own. In time, we would all be much wiser, and through deeper understanding of one another, kinder.

A SAFE BET?

There is a famous position known as Pascal's Wager[12] that states, "If God doesn't exist and I believe in Him, I've lost nothing. If God does exist and I don't believe in Him, I've lost everything."

This famous wager, like the tree in the forest question, prevents us from asking the right questions or seeking truth broadly enough. It alludes to God as a man. This alone can pull those who have a different view off the path to abundance by creating a need to argue the point. This opinion might even keep very pragmatic people from considering the generative force as a viable source of strength and insulation against negativity.

Pascal's Wager also asserts that lack of faith in a *personalized* God means that we can lose something—in fact, everything. But the Law of Abundance says that everything—you, me, God, Earth, the Universe; even thoughts and feelings—is energy, and energy is never lost.

There is a great deal of evidence that suggests that those who have a concept of the generative force that allows for a personal relationship have better overall outcomes than those who do not, *provided* that relationship doesn't create judgment, resistance to other points of view, or fear of retribution. According to some research, belief in a personal, loving, wise, and beneficial God leads to better health, and helps those who hold this view to cope with adversity better. It is faith in a punitive God or no faith at all that fills psychiatric practices, not faith in God as a generative force.

Evidence suggests that clinging to a *particular* form which God *must* take results in discord, rejection, ridicule, criticism, arguing and even deadly wars. History is full of such accounts and the battles continue to this day.

When the things of spirit get lost in too narrow a religious view, not only do others suffer, the holder of the view suffers as well. A narrow view can actually limit access to generative qualities. When individuals hold the belief that they have been unworthy and that God is not listening or that God is punishing them, for example, they move into a place of fear and guilt. This has the effect of shutting down their energy and limiting their ability to access the generative force that is all around them and that IS them.

No matter who it is or what kind of authority an individual or group claims to possess, if the beliefs held in relation to the generative force limit or in any way cause harm, then that "authority" has turned a naturally beneficial force into a negative and potentially destructive one. And those who participate in that approach would be very wise to rethink their position.

A GAME OF SEMANTICS

Just for fun, let's play a game of semantics and see how close scientific and religious explanations of reality really are. First, read the statement below as it is written, then go back and replace the word "energy" with the word "God" and see what you get.

Everything is energy. Energy is everywhere all the time and all at once; in other words, energy is omnipresent. Energy can neither be created nor destroyed; it is, was, and always will be. Energy manifests in myriad ways and yet it is always energy. Everything is subject to the laws of energy. Energy influences everything in the universe and *is* everything in the universe, therefore energy is omnipotent. Energy follows precise laws that cannot be violated. When someone attempts to violate these laws, there is a consequence.

Did any insights come from the exercise?

A BROADER VIEW

All of this discussion about the generative force is not presented here to convert you to one way of thinking or another, but to expand your thinking so you have more available to you. What you believe will not alter or affect the Law of Abundance one iota, but your beliefs will greatly affect your ability to tap into the law in beneficial ways and will therefore greatly affect your outcomes.

If the belief you hold keeps you primarily in a positive state of mind; if it keeps your emotions positive; if it keeps you acting in disciplined, responsible, and courageous ways; if it compels you to consistently try to do the right thing and to maintain a caring, accepting, non-judgmental attitude toward others and the choices they make for themselves; if it keeps you free of criticism and condemnation then the belief you hold is taking you in the right direction.

It doesn't matter whether or not you believe in a Supreme Being. You can just believe in nature, or science, or luck, or in whatever strengthens and sustains you. And if you believe in a Supreme Being, it doesn't matter whether you address it from it a Christian, Jewish, Muslim, Buddhist, Hindu, Gnostic, or any other perspective; the result will be a good one if all of the elements for abundance are in place. If they aren't, you may want to reconsider what you believe.

RECAP OF FAITH AS AN INSULATOR

The insulators are faith in self, faith in others, and faith in a generative force. When all three of these are strong, the myriad sources of evidence for negative or limited outcomes have less impact on us and we are better able to insulate ourselves from all the negativity that constantly bombards us.

1. Faith in self and others requires trust which has four essential components; the four C's:
   a. Character
   b. Consideration
   c. Connectivity
   d. Competence

2. Unlike lack of faith in self and/or others, which can directly impact their effectiveness, lack of faith in a generative force does not directly impact its effectiveness. Plants grow whether you believe they will or not, for example. What lack of faith in a generative force does, however, is impact an individual's ability to effectively tap into and purposefully use the power and insulating qualities available through this source.

3. In developing strong insulators, begin with yourself. Once you can trust and believe in yourself and your ability to make good decisions and discern properly, begin developing greater trust in those whom you deem to be trustworthy. Know the components of trustworthiness so you are able to discern wisely.

4. Faith in the generative force is already in place for everyone. You can best benefit from it by expanding your awareness of the many ways in which it manifests and by tapping into as many as possible.

TO STAY ON THE PATH TO POSITIVE ABUNDANCE, BE CERTAIN THAT YOU:

1. Keep your **application** path active (*responsible, disciplined, courageous actions*) and directed toward energy rightly used.

2. Keep your **attitude** path receptive (*accepting, open-minded, trusting, allowing, receiving, believing*). Remember that a receptive attitude must be coupled with responsible, disciplined application, in other words, must itself be responsible, disciplined and discriminating. Indiscriminately extending acceptance, faith or trust is foolish and occurs only when we try to take the easiest route.

3. Maintain positive thoughts, feelings, and intent to boost energy along the active (+) application path and keep it flowing toward positive abundance.

4. Avoid negative thoughts, feelings and intent that act as resistors on the receptive (-) attitude path and slow or stop energy from returning to you.

5. Live your own dream and passion, not someone else's.

6. Maintain clear, precise, and positive focus on the things you want so the energy you send out reaches a properly designed receiver and flows back to you in the form you desire.

7. Keep your path well insulated with sufficient faith in self, others, and the generative force.

CHAPTER 12

The Principles of Energy Flow:
Magnetic Pull and Resistance

*"We have it in our power to
create the world all over again".*
Thomas Paine

With the rather extensive subject of faith covered, let's continue through the other five principles of energy flow so that you have a very clear concept of the rules that determine your future and the future of humankind.

So far, we have covered Principles 1 – 3. In Principle 1, we learned that energy is always seeking equilibrium. We saw that when we create conditions that throw us out of balance, the predictable result is anxiety, a form of chaotic energy. We also saw that perfect equilibrium is not possible or even desirable in an open system, and life is an open system. We learned that we should manage change wisely and responsibly since both chaos and the struggle to avoid change are detrimental to energy flow, as well as to the development of outcomes we desire.

In Principle 2, we learned that harnessed energy must have a complete circuit to flow. We saw that a complete circuit for humans consists of self as the energy generator, an application "line" by which we apply or fail to apply ourselves to life (actions, thoughts, beliefs or intent), an attitude "line" which is what we allow into our lives, and a receiver which is made up of the goals we design.

In Principle 3, we learned that the flow of energy is precise and absolutely predictable. We saw that our goals must be specifically designed to deliver the results we want. And we learned that we can know how effective we are at designing our goals by looking at the results we are currently getting.

Principle 4 explains why it is so important to monitor and manage our thoughts, feelings, intentions, and goals.

PRINCIPLE 4 – Energy will always flow in the direction of the greatest magnetic pull or of least resistance.[13]

Non-personal Example – Electromagnetism, a combination of electricity and magnetism, is one of four fundamental forces in the universe. The other three are the strong nuclear force, the weak nuclear force, and gravity. Only gravity and electromagnetism have long-range effects. And only electromagnetism has both attraction and repulsion components, which is why it is the force that drives energy and the one you need to be most familiar with.

The Law of Abundance operates within this force. Atoms form through electromagnetism. The flow and direction of energy and the formation of matter are governed by it. This force is responsible for practically all of the phenomena we encounter in our daily lives.

Electromagnetism is the force that directs, redirects, and reverses energy flow and makes everything we use possible, including every convenience you enjoy, the air you breathe, the water you drink, the earth you walk on, the sun that warms you and the stars into which you gaze. Even the brain activity and the light waves that are allowing you to read these words are dependent on electromagnetism.

Personal Example – Just as the flow and direction of energy can be controlled through electromagnetism in motors and other receivers, the flow and direction of energy is controlled in humans through the strength of their focus, thoughts, feelings and intent, which combine to create a strong magnetic pull toward the charge associated with that cluster.

If thoughts, feelings, intent, and focus are all negative, for example, the natural flow of energy toward positive abundance is reversed; energy then flows *backwards* toward limitation or negative abundance, which, you will recall, is an abundance of things we *don't* want.

Even if the intent is positive, but the focus is unclear or fuzzy and thoughts and feelings are more negative than positive, the flow of energy is reversed or slowed to a stop, and the result is limitation, or more of what we do not want (*see Illustration 12.01*).

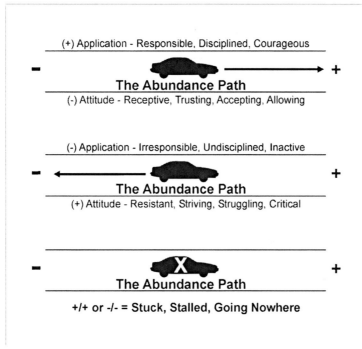

Illustration 12.01

Imagine yourself, your business, your community, your nation and the world as vehicles, all having the equivalent of an electric motor driving them along a roadway that leads toward or away from an abundance of good things. As long as the energy is flowing in the right direction (active application and receptive attitude), the motor will run in the proper direction and propel the vehicle forward toward positive abundance.

The path *away* from abundance leads to less and less of what we want, and to more and more of what we do not want. The farther away from the positive end we travel, the greater our loss. And if the energy powering the motor is running backwards (receptive application and active attitude), the vehicle can only go one way: backwards toward negative abundance. If the motor is hooked up wrong (+/+) or (-/-), it doesn't run and the vehicle is stalled, going nowhere.

INTENT, ATTENTION AND CHOICE

Intent is a state of mind that acts like an electromagnet to direct our energy. Intent can be defined as a determination toward a certain purpose, aim, objective, or goal. Intent is much more than mere dreaming and hoping. It determines the general direction our life will take. It is a driving force that influences what holds our attention, and what drives our decisions along the way.

Many people claim that their intent is to have an abundant life, but where they place their attention, the choices they make, and their actions say otherwise. Anyone who insists that their intent is to have an abundant life is not being honest with themselves if their attention is always on the easy way out or they regularly choose convenience over responsibility. These people may dream of having an abundant life and wish for it, but they don't really *intend* it.

What those who take the easy route *intend* is a life of ease. They dream of having abundance and imagine that abundance will provide them with a life of ease, and they are right. But the Law of Abundance makes it very clear that we cannot achieve abundance if the application path is the path of least resistance. Non-resistance must occur on the *attitude side*, not the application side.

Interestingly, everyone I have ever interviewed who is taking the most expedient route through life to their detriment feels some degree of resistance to their outcomes. Resistance to boredom or guilt shifts energy to active (+) on the attitude side, and the (-/+) combination then results in energy flowing backwards toward negative outcomes.

REALIZING GOALS

To realize any goal, we must *intend* that goal to the extent that we are actually taking the steps to reach it, and making choices that keep us taking the necessary steps *without resistance*. To be certain that energy is flowing in the direction you want, be sure that your *intent is clear*, your *attention is focused* on the right things, and your choices keep your feet firmly planted on the path you desire.

Often people are not really aware of where they are placing their attention and directing their energy. The results they get, therefore, are not what they want or what they think they intend.

If, for example, you *don't want* limitation more than you *do want* abundance, your attention is on limitation, and the greatest amount of energy is flowing toward *limitation* rather than abundance. You are attending to limitation even though your desire is abundance. The speed with which the unwanted outcomes materialize depends on the amount of attention you give to what you don't want in relation to the degree to which you have *already taken ownership* of the things you do want.

This may sound strange and many think it is backwards, but *until we take mental and emotional ownership of what we want, we have chosen to claim ownership only to what we already have*. And if what we claim ownership to is less than what we want, that is what we manifest—less than what we want.

So, how do you take ownership of abundance when the life you are living doesn't yet match your idea of abundance? You lay out a path to a clearly defined goal, claim that goal as yours *right now*, decide what steps you will take to claim the abundance that is *already yours*, and choose to take those steps. Your choices will determine the direction you take at every juncture and where your path ultimately leads.

Before you can have abundance to the extent you can envision it, you must have energy *already* moving toward positive abundance. You put energy in motion by taking ownership of what you have determined is your piece of the universal pie. Not at some point in the future, but right now.

A HUNDRED MILLION DOLLARS

Imagine that you were informed that you had a hundred million dollars in a bank account in Switzerland and there was no question that this was an absolute fact. The money is there and it's already yours, but before you can have it, you have to get to Switzerland and claim it in person. No one else can do it for you. How intent would you be on getting there? Even if you didn't have a dime to your name in your current situation, you would find a way to get to that bank in Switzerland. Your attention would be wholly focused on trying to figure out a way to either earn the money or convince someone to loan you the money to get you there. You would probably be willing to handsomely repay anyone who helped you get there once you were able to claim your money. Every choice you made and every action you took would be to get you closer to that account.

The truth is, you do have a bank account, and it is as large or small as you decide it will be. It is *already yours*, but you do have to claim it in person. No one else can do it for you. Like the bank account in Switzerland, you may not be able to put your hands on it right now, but it is already yours, nonetheless. Decide what that account looks like, take ownership of it, and set out right now to get it.

CLARITY IS A CHECK WAITING TO BE CASHED

Comedian and actor Jim Carrey tells of writing a check to himself for ten million dollars back when he was an unknown and living near poverty. He put a date on the check to indicate when he would be able to cash it and stuck it in his wallet. He regularly took that check out, looked at it, claimed that money as his own, and would then put it back in his wallet. He said that the very year he put on that check as a cash date, he made his first ten million dollars for a film he starred in. By the pre-determined date he actually had the money that would allow him to "cash" that check.

Taking ownership of what you determine is already yours will focus your attention and dictate your choices, just as it did for Jim Carrey. Although the date on the ten million dollar check was a date in the future, Carrey's *claim to it* was not in the future. He claimed it the minute he wrote himself that check and determined to do whatever it took to be able to cash it.

Placing the realization of your goals in the future *keeps them in the future.* As long as your goals are seen as a future reality, there is no urgency to take the steps that make the goal possible. The demands of the day hold your attention, and the choices you make are those that will simply get you through the day.

HAPPINESS AND SURVIVAL

Your subconscious mind has two goals for you—just two. It wants your happiness and it wants your survival. Period. Happiness to the subconscious mind is mental and emotional survival, which actually take precedence over physical survival. The importance of happiness over physical survival is why people are able to commit suicide.

To ensure your happiness and survival, your subconscious mind attends to what you believe is most important and most urgent. There is no urgency to do anything until the time to do it actually arrives, so anything placed as a future goal has no urgency, and attention to that future goal is deferred until the time arrives. The problem is that the future *never* arrives.

GRATITUDE

One way to grow your awareness of having abundance right now, no matter how far you might be from your ultimate goal, is to spend some time each day focusing your attention on the abundance that you are experiencing right now, and expanding your awareness of abundance. By attaching a feeling of deep gratitude to each and every thing you can claim in your current experience, you focus your attention on the attitude of abundance, which removes any resistance to the idea of already having an abundant life and allows energy to move more freely in that direction. If you don't already do this on a regular basis, you will be surprised at how many things you have to be grateful for.

For example, do you have eyes with which to see? Ears with which to hear? Do you have the senses of taste, touch, and smell? Does your mind allow you to think, read, and learn? Do you have health? Does your heart keep blood flowing through your veins? Do you have people who love you and who you love? Do you have food to eat? Clothes to wear? Feet and legs upon which to walk? Can you behold the beauty of nature, of smiling faces, of children at play?

Realize that everything your eyes can behold, or your ears can hear; everything any of your senses can take in is already yours. Not yours to hoard to yourself, but surely yours to enjoy. The earth, the trees, the grass, the sky, the sunshine, the moon, the stars, the sound of laughter, the song of birds—all of this and so much more is yours. You can claim them and add them to your awareness of abundance or not. But the more you claim now, the more you will have to claim.

If properly approached, being grateful for the many things you already have will expand your consciousness and boost energy toward positive abundance. Gratitude for what you already have should not minimize the importance of your goals. It should expand your awareness of ownership and keep you focused on positive abundance as your reality.

When you combine gratitude for what you already have with a clear vision of where you intend to go, you have essentially laid out a circuit that defines the path along which energy will flow in your life. And by claiming that life path as yours right now, you set energy into motion toward that end.

Energy flows freely in whatever direction we provide an open channel. If we are focused on avoiding or eliminating the conditions we don't want, our attention and, therefore, our energy is focused on what we don't want. If we are focused on growing the conditions we do want, that is where our attention and energy are.

MORE THAN POSITIVE THINKING

Focus, intent, attention, and choice all proceed from thought, so the importance that has been placed on monitoring one's thoughts is surely valid. If how we use our thoughts determines what we give energy to, and it does, disciplining our thoughts and applying them responsibly is certainly sage advice. But, as you know by now, that is just one part of the formula. Still, many people insist that all they did to attract everything they wanted to their life was change their way of thinking.

Positive thinking and the Law of Attraction as it is generally presented (positive focus, thoughts, feelings and intent plus a clear vision of what you want) seems to work well for some people, poorly for others, and not at all for many. Curious as to why, I began observing and interviewing people who fit into all three categories. I wanted to know what the successful group was doing that the unsuccessful ones were not.

THE HIGHLY SUCCESSFUL

What I discovered is that the successful ones dedicated a portion of each day to meditating on their desired outcomes. They took the time and effort to clarify their visions and claimed them to such an extent that what they envisioned felt real enough that they were able to take complete ownership of it. Many in this group reported that their goals were so real to them that they could see, hear, taste, smell, and touch them. Their goals were specific, written down, and reviewed regularly. They had laid out their plans right down to the daily steps that they regularly took for the realization of their goals.

None of this seemed like work to this group because they knew with certainty where they wanted to end up. They had a passion for the course they had set for themselves and it was *their* course, not someone else's. The lack of effort had caused many of them to discount the fact that they had developed *disciplines* that had activated the application side of the abundance equation.

Until it was pointed out, many in this group hadn't even considered that what they were doing was a discipline, and often didn't equate their actions with courage, though much of what they did was quite courageous. They generally knew they were being responsible, but didn't see that as the result of any particular effort either. Many reported that they had always had a sense of responsibility, even before they began using positive thinking or the Law of Attraction to become more successful. In every case, whether they realized it or not, this group had created conditions that ensured that both application and attitude were flowing in the right direction. They had the entire abundance formula in place.

THE SLIGHTLY SUCCESSFUL

Those for whom the formula worked, but poorly, stated that they meditated on their desired outcomes, and while they hadn't disciplined themselves to meditating regularly, they did try to do it two or three times a week. This group had taken the time to clarify their visions and had laid out goals, but they were not nearly as specific as those of the first group, and the goals were not so clear that this group was actually able to experience them in the here and now. They took steps toward the realization of their goals whenever they got the chance, but not every day, and the steps they took sometimes felt like work. They believed that if they stayed with it, they would eventually get over the "hump" and the goal steps would get easier to do.

Most felt a passion for the direction they had set for themselves, but many stated that they had passions in other areas as well. They had chosen the one they were working on because it seemed to be the quickest route to realizing their goals. The individuals in this group had developed some disciplines and were acting responsibly much of the time, but some of the discipline felt like work, so there was some resistance around it and they didn't do things they knew they should, and actually wanted to do, consistently.

Their determination to exert the effort had activated the application side, and their receptivity to reaching their goal had activated the attitude side. However, the effort they felt in taking the steps to achieve their goals and the resulting resistance had (1) diminished their activity on the application side of the abundance equation, and (2) placed resistors on the attitude side so energy was not flowing freely in either direction.

THE UNSUCCESSFUL

Those who were not getting the results they wanted at all reported that they focused on their desired outcomes and recited positive affirmations, but rather irregularly. They had general—but not very specific—goals and, because they had not clarified the goals and laid out a plan yet, they were not taking regular steps toward the realization of goals. They did not feel a complete sense of ownership of the future they envisioned, but thought they would when they were able to clarify their goals better.

Most were unable to state with certainty when they would be able to do that or, conversely, stated grand goals that they knew were not possible in the time frame they had allowed. They generally believed, however, that continuing to focus on positive thoughts and repeat the positive affirmations would eventually help them gain the clarity, reach the goals and realize their dreams. In other words, individuals in this group were doing a lot of positive thinking and giving themselves a lot of personal pep talks, but they were not applying any real discipline, so the application side of the abundance equation was not being activated. Moreover, this group envisioned having abundance *in the future* and many protested that it was not possible to believe they already had abundance, because they didn't.

KNOW WHAT YOU WANT AND CLAIM IT NOW

To ensure that abundance is your outcome, claim it now and then regularly check the relative strength of your "want/don't want" and "now/future" spectrums to ensure that your attention is on the right things. Be sure that *wanting abundance* has the greater strength, and having it is a *now* awareness. Keeping the right focus occurs when we consciously monitor what we are attending to, and make new and better choices as necessary.

You will learn more about making effective adjustments in

Chapter 17. For now, follow the guidelines in Illustration 12.02 to do a
quick check on your current focus and the energies that are connected
to it.

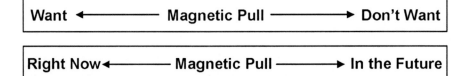

| Want ◄————— Magnetic Pull —————► Don't Want |

| Right Now◄——— Magnetic Pull ———► In the Future |

Checks and Balances

Check the relative strength of what you want compared to what you don't
want by noticing the clarity around each condition and the strength of the
energetic charge connected to each.   Once what you want has greater
clarity and energy, check the strength of your ownership of that goal now as
compared to in the future. If there is not a greater clarity and energy around
what you want, and having it right now, consciously shift your focus and
your energies in that direction. Your goal is to be completely *receptive* to
the idea that you already own everything you want.

Illustration 12.02

PURPOSEFULLY DIRECTING ENERGY

If you went through the checks and balances exercise, you may
have noticed that your experiences accurately reflect where you
have been placing your attention and allowing energy to flow.
Whether you are headed toward ruin or a rich, fulfilling life
depends in very large measure on the choices you make from moment
to moment.

Where we place our attention is a choice, and as soon as we choose
to shift our focus and expectations, our energy shifts right along with
it. You can actually feel this happening by shifting your focus back and
forth between something negative and its positive opposite—between
a life of poverty and pain and one of abundance and joy, for example:
or between a close encounter with someone you consider difficult
to be around, versus a close encounter with someone you consider a
complete delight.

Only humans have the capacity to significantly alter nature in purposeful ways, even working against it if they choose to. We alone can choose our actions to the point of brilliant innovation or total destruction. Although there are animals that create things (for example, birds build nests, ants build colonies, and beavers build dams) animals do not have the capacity to innovate or to choose significant change.

Ornithologists, those who study birds, can tell a wren's nest from that of a robin's, because all wrens and all robins build similar nests. They don't change their behaviors, innovate, and decide to build something brand new and different. Beavers don't suddenly get flashes of inspiration and start building more stable and longer lasting dams out of rocks rather than wood. They can't conceive of cement and then create it to build grand dams like the Hoover Dam in Nevada. Only humans have that degree of intelligence, creativity, and insight, as well as the ability to choose whether or not to use these great attributes.

Our ability to choose allows us to separate ourselves from the masses or remain a part of them. Unlike the ants in their highly structured colonies, we are not born to our position in life. Certain babies are not born to be workers, others as nursemaids, and still others as royalty, as are ants and bees. Although some cultures try to force people into molds and some are successful at it, we know that what babies become has far more to do with the choices they make throughout life than with their biology.

Although biology has great influence on our outcomes, and to a large degree determines the path we find appealing, it does not compel us to follow any specific path. Once we reach adulthood and have the capacity to think and act independently, we can choose the path we will travel. And the path we are traveling right now is the result of the choices we have made from moment to moment and from day to day up to this point.

CHOOSING THE ROAD LESS TRAVELED

In his poem, *The Road Not Taken*, Robert Frost speaks of the choices that regularly confront us, and how the right choices can "make all the difference." Indeed, they do. There are those who were born with every biological advantage—a healthy body, an intelligent mind, and plenty of natural talents—who choose to take the path that is the easiest, least responsible and least productive. These people squander their talents and abilities through the choices they make and the beliefs they choose to hold. And because they do, they share that most traveled path with the masses who Thoreau observed were living "lives of quiet desperation."

Sometimes the beliefs people hold to, and which impact their choices, were created very early in life. They developed as a result of difficult circumstances, which the child had to endure at the hands of inept or cruel parents, teachers, and/or other influential people. When conditioning begins very early in life, people may get to adulthood and not even know at a conscious level that they have greater abilities than they are now expressing, and greater potentials which they have yet to explore and tap into.

Yet, there are those who have come from similar circumstances who have met with some event or catalyst that has induced them to reexamine themselves and choose a different, more beneficial path; to do the work to discover and claim everything nature gave them; to choose a new, less traveled, more abundant path. There are even those, such as Helen Keller who was blind and deaf, who have done amazing things with their lives in spite of their challenges.

The internal compass that let's us know when we are on the right path and when we are not, and the choice to listen to and heed the urging of that compass, or not, is always available. But taking the less traveled road, the one that leads to positive abundance, takes awareness and courage. And when we have been on the more traveled road since childhood, moving to the less traveled one also takes a lot of initial work and dedication. And it takes believing that we are worth the effort.

There are several oft-repeated analogies that point to what happens for many people who seem to be in a life-trance induced by early conditioning, and the beliefs that arise about their abilities.

One is of elephants that are chained by one leg to trees when they are babies. They soon learn that pulling and tugging on the chain only causes them pain, and eventually they quit trying to pull free. By the time they reach adulthood, they can be chained to a small stake, which they could easily pull out of the ground, but because of the earlier conditioning, they never try.

Another analogy, which seems to point to biology more than conditioning, is of a type of caterpillar called Hemileuca Maia that is biologically programmed to follow the leader under every circumstance. In this analogy, the caterpillars are put onto the rim of a pot where each follows the other round and round until they starve to death and die.

Unlike elephants and caterpillars, we have the ability to reassess our circumstances and to make new and different choices. We can, choose to eliminate the negative affects of our conditioning and direct, to a very large degree, our biology. Those who allow themselves to become victims are not victims of their conditioning and/or biology so much as they are victims of their own choices.

We may not always get to choose the events that occur in life from moment to moment, but we do get to choose our overall direction in life and how we will travel the path we have chosen. At any given moment, we can choose to be miserable or joyous. We can choose to focus on the beautiful and amazing parts of life, or the ugly and unseemly parts. We can defer our happiness until some unknown future time, or we can have it right now. Since the Law of Abundance does not discriminate, every option is available to us in great abundance. It's up to each of us to decide which ones we will tap into.

MIND OVER BIOLOGY

The degree to which we experience positive abundance depends largely on the choices we make. Those who choose to be responsible, disciplined, courageous, and generally positive in their actions, focus, intent, thoughts and feelings, are using energy correctly. Because they are on the right path, they are able to tap into endless opportunities in far more tangible ways than many imagine.

An article in *Parade Magazine* (March 18, 2007) reported the results of research done by Dr. Henry S. Lodge of Columbia Medical School, which suggests that we even choose how we will age. The article stated, "From your body's point of view 'normal' aging isn't normal at all. It's a choice you make by the way you live your life." It goes on to state that "True biological aging is a surprisingly slow and graceful process. You can live out your life in a powerful, healthy body if you are willing to do the work."

The body is constantly renewing itself, and how that process proceeds depends almost entirely on the choices we make along the way. According to Dr. Lodge, we choose whether the new cells our body creates come in stronger or weaker. "You choose whether they grow or decay," he states. "Your cells don't care which choice you make. They just follow the directions you send." So too does all of life. Like the cells in your body (which are energy in specific expression), energy doesn't care which choices you make. It just follows the directions you send.

But does the Universe actually orchestrate such things? It does seem that way to many people. Stories about seemingly miraculous events probably number in the billions. You have probably experienced something akin to divine intervention yourself. I know I have on many occasions. But in a world directed toward abundance, what we see as divine intervention or a miracle cannot be occasional things. They must be there every minute of every day so that we are all free to tap into them.

Our only duty is to be prepared to receive what is so abundantly available. The energy that makes up our abundant universe knows no limitation and continually lays opportunities at our feet. What is limited is our attention to the many opportunities, our willingness to claim the ones that will best serve our purposes and to make the right choices.

THE POWER OF CHOICE

At any moment, we can choose whether we will be responsible and disciplined or irresponsible and undisciplined. We can choose to be courageous or to be cowardly, and under which circumstances. We can choose whether we will be joyous, content, loving, kind, tolerant, accepting, and generally positive; or whether we will be miserable, discontent, anxious, unkind, intolerant, or generally negative. No one makes us be or do any of these things. We alone choose our responses, and how we choose to respond determines our outcomes.

All personal change occurs as a result of the choices we make, and in the end, each of us must choose for ourselves. We can offer new choices to others, but we cannot require them to choose our offerings short of using force. The minute we use force, however, we have inadvertently chosen to step off the path to abundance and squarely onto one of limitation, or worse, a lot of trouble. If people realized this more fully, they would probably be less likely to waste their time and energy trying to change the thoughts, opinions, ideas, and actions of other people.

No matter how "off-base" we think another person is, trying to change him or her is a waste of energy and a choice for limitation. Energy is far better used when we are directing our own thoughts and actions.

Ultimately, the choices we make determine the kind of life we experience. Our choices direct more than just our thoughts, feelings, and actions. They direct energy, and therefore, the very essence of life. We are all on our particular path as a result of the choices we have made. So if the path you find yourself on is not exactly the one you want, realize that only you can change it, and then make new choices.

"There is a tide in the affairs of men,
which taken at the flood, leads on to fortune.
Omitted, all the voyage of their life is bound
in shallows and in miseries. On such a full
sea are we now afloat. And we must take the
current when it serves, or lose our ventures."
William Shakespeare

Put more simply . . .

"Even if you're on the right track
you'll get run over if you just sit there."
Will Rogers

CHAPTER 13

The Principles of Energy Flow: Non-discrimination

"I'll go anywhere as long as it's forward".
David Livingstone

PRINCIPLE 5 – Energy is non-discriminatory. It will follow any and every pathway available to it and will produce any result, provided sufficient energy is generated, and the receiver is properly designed to receive it.[14]

Non-personal Example – When an electrician wires a house, the house can have as many light fixtures and electrical outlets as the builder wants it to have. No matter how many complete circuits the electrician builds into the house, electricity will flow through them. You can plug appliances into the outlets and run as many as you want to, provided the house has sufficient energy (amps) flowing to it. Electricity does not discriminate between a washer, a toaster, a lamp, a computer, a television, or whatever else you want it to power, so long as the voltage is compatible.

In America, most household appliances run on 110 volts, and the energy entering a house is regulated so that it delivers energy within that general range. So you can hook up myriad appliances designed to run on 110 volts anywhere in your house, and the electricity delivers indiscriminately to every one of them in the exact way the receiver (appliance) is designed to receive it. You only run into problems when you try to run more appliances than the power to the house can sustain. Then you trip the main breaker.

Personal Example – In humans, the goals we focus upon and the visions we maintain are the many receivers. The way the goal or vision is *designed* is what determines how the energy expresses when it arrives. Whatever we envision expresses in exactly the way we envision it *energy-wise*, but its manifestation may *not* be exactly what we envision at the physical level. The reason is because, while we are an integral part of the energy pool, we are not able to alter *potential* energy unless and until we or some other force acts upon it in the right way, freeing it to become kinetic (or useful) energy.

It is kinetic energy acting upon potential energy that creates our experiences in the *physical* world. All physical matter is *potential energy*. We can impact potential energy or matter through potential energy (other physical matter) or kinetic energy (our thoughts and actions), but we attract it only through *kinetic energy*, not through other potential energy.

For example, as was explained earlier, money is physical matter that has very little potential energy in and of itself. We can burn paper money and release what little energy it has, thereby impacting it. Or, by using the kinetic energy generated by our thoughts and actions, we can put the money to use and accomplish all kinds of things with it, thereby impacting *and* attracting it.

We cannot put several one hundred dollar bills together, stash them in a drawer, and have them multiply or accomplish anything at all. The money, as potential energy, would have no impact on the potential energy of the other money in the drawer. Only through applying kinetic energy (thoughts and actions) can we release the potential energy of money, and if we do it in the right way, the money will grow and multiply. Likewise, we can realize our goals and visions only through the actions and interactions of released (kinetic) energy. Potential energy is just that—only potential until acted upon.

We can't see far enough ahead to predict what kinds of potential energy (people and other physical resources) the goal we are focused upon, and the energy we send out, will attract and act upon. Neither can we know how the kinetic energy we send out will interact with other kinetic energy in the bigger scheme of things. We can only send the energy we have released through active application (+) and receptive attitude (-) toward a clearly defined goal and trust it to express in the most beneficial way.

THE WAY ENERGY EXPRESSES WILL DEPEND ON:

1. How the energy we send out combines with complementary energies.

2. The strength and endurance of the energy we send out.

3. The clarity and quality of the receiver (goal or intent) toward which we send it.

4. How receptive we are to what comes back to us.

What we receive back will exactly match the conditions we have created, in the exact proportions we determine, by the amount and quality of energy we generate, send out, and are open to receiving back. Let me reiterate that it will exactly match the *conditions we create*, not necessarily the image we hold.

THIS OR SOMETHING BETTER

There is a sage bit of advice that suggests that when we envision what we want, we send it out into the energy pool as "this or something better." That's good advice because we can't know what potential energies might be released beyond what we can envision. If we are open to what we envision or *something better*, we aren't as likely to miss opportunities that show up looking different from what we envisioned, as they often do. Sometimes what shows up is more than we anticipated, sometimes less, and often different, but it always matches the *conditions* we have created in the sending and receiving.

On the application side of the equation, the quality of the energy we send out will greatly impact our outcomes. We affect the quality of energy by our degree of responsibility, discipline and courage, and the clarity and precision of our goal (or lack thereof). Often, it is the clarity of the goal and our faith in our ability to affect the desired outcome that allows us to keep the return line open and receptive.

Almost all advice on creating success emphasizes the need to have *clear and specific goals*. But there is a lot more to "clear and specific" than many of us have imagined. Not only do we need to know precisely what we want, we must know precisely how to manage the energy we send toward those goals and receive back.

You may have heard the maxim "be careful what you wish for because you just might get it." Too much energy can be directed toward a receiver and create results we don't really want (rather like a sunburn instead of a lovely tan), or we can send too little energy or focus it too narrowly, creating an imbalance. We need to be very specific when creating goals so energy flows to *all* of the important areas of our life to the degree that we want it to express in each area. People who don't do this may find they have an over abundance of things manifesting in one area of their life and far too little in another.

For example, workaholics who are so focused on their work and making money that they neglect their health and their relationships, and often end up with neither. What good is achieving work and income goals if health fails and relationships fall apart?

On the other hand, those who appear to be workaholics to people who prefer not to work so hard, but who love what they are doing and still live healthy, balanced lives, may simply be following their passion. It is not uncommon for those who love what they do to spend a lot of time doing it, and there is nothing wrong with that so long as the passion doesn't override wisdom and balance.

The other factor that determines how our goals manifest is the degree and quality of the energy that comes back to us. Any resistors that we place on the receptive side of the abundance equation in the way of fear, anxiety, worrying about the outcome, or any other negative thoughts and feelings, will diminish the amount of energy that gets back to us, thereby altering our outcomes. Resistors can come from outside us as well as from the inside. Indiscriminate associations with people who regularly express negative thoughts and feelings, for example, will create resistance in our experience as well as in theirs.

RESISTORS – IMPEDING THE FLOW OF ENERGY

Where magnetism propels energy along, resistance impedes it. Illustration 13.01 demonstrates how energy flows freely along the positive abundance path when the application line maintains an active (+) charge through responsible, disciplined, courageous action, and the attitude line remains receptive (-) through being open, accepting, trusting and non-resistant.

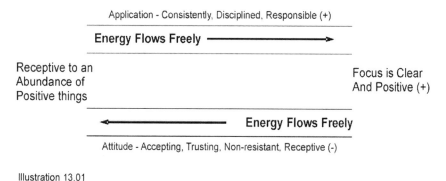

Illustration 13.01

Illustration 13.02 shows the effect of resistance on the attitude line. Notice how each resistor reduces the amount of energy that is allowed to flow back to the energy source.

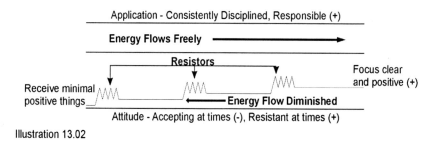

Illustration 13.02

In Illustration 13.01, there are no resistors on the attitude path, so energy flows unimpeded in both directions. In this instance, you receive back a full measure of the energy you send out.

In Illustration 13.02, some negative attitude, such as fear, doubt, concern, irritation, or anger, has created resistance and reduced the amount of energy returning to you. In this instance, the energy you are sending out is not returning to you in full measure.

Say, for example, that your vision and focus is a well balanced, abundant life that includes time to enjoy your family, stay healthy and fit, and have sufficient leisure time to travel. It also includes growing a successful company and amassing wealth. In the first scenario (Illustration 13.01), your actions would be such that you feel you have, or are moving steadily toward, the balance you seek, so there is no resistance or negative responses to your outcomes or daily experiences.

In the second scenario (Illustration 13.02), either your actions fail to produce the desired balance or your expectations of how life should unfold are unrealistic. Say, for example, that, although your goal is a well balanced life, you think you need to grow your business and wealth first and then you will have time to spend with family, get fit, and enjoy leisure activities. In this case, you are holding a vision of a balanced, healthy life, but your actions, while responsible and disciplined in growing your business, are sending your energy in just one direction, which does not allow the other areas to develop.

Your family wants your time and attention, and although you want to give it, you don't believe you have sufficient wealth to take time away from work. You feel frustrated because you can't spend the time with your family, and impatient to get the business to that envisioned place of success. The result is resistance.

Say you also want to exercise to keep fit, but don't feel like you can take the time right now. So rather than staying fit, you begin putting on weight, and now your stamina isn't what it used to be. You look at the condition of your body and feel worried and frustrated—resistance increases.

Add to that the fact that you haven't had a real vacation in two years, and want to take your children to Disneyland while they are still young enough to really enjoy it, but the time is not right. The business needs attention—resistance increases even more.

Each of these factors slows the energy returning to you, such that the goals you have set will each take far longer than you had hoped. As resistance continues to build and energy continues to decline, the realization of the goals gets farther and farther away. The result is that you keep working harder and harder but make very little progress and may have no idea why.

Holding a dream or vision to which we are not being true, is bound to create resistors, reduce the flow of energy, and set us up to eventually fail.

You are probably already aware of how your energies are being directed and whether there are imbalances that need correcting, but awareness is not enough. To be certain that you are not shutting down energy where you don't intend to, take the time to check your values in relation to the way you are using your energy. There is an exercise in Chapter 23 that will help you do that.

What this power is, I cannot say. All I know is that it exists and becomes available only when you are in that state of mind in which you know EXACTLY what you want and are fully determined not to quit until you get it.

Alexander Graham Bell

CHAPTER 14

The Principles of Energy Flow: Compatibility

*Failure is more frequently from want
of energy than want of capital.*

Daniel Webster

PRINCIPLE 6 – **The flow of energy must be compatible with the receiver or the effect will not be as intended.**[15]

Non-personal Example – A 100-watt light bulb requires between 110 and 120 volts of electricity. If it receives that amount, it will properly deliver 100 watts of light. Any more than that and the bulb will burn out quickly. Any less, and the bulb won't deliver 100 watts of light. A rheostat, which allows you to brighten and dim lights, does so by controlling the energy that reaches the receiver.

Personal Example – Imagine that you have a lot of hopes and dreams and spend a lot of time imagining what life would be like if all those dreams came true, but you don't do much (provide a sufficient amount of energy) to turn the dreams into reality. Often this is a result of too many hopes, dreams and desires and too few real, concrete goals and actions. In this case, the line you have laid is insufficient to carry the energy and power your dreams.

Trying to focus on too many goals simultaneously scatters energy and is another way in which the energy that arrives at the intended destination is too diminished to power the goal. Say, for example, that you want a new car, but you like five different ones and can't decide which one you like best. As a result, your thought energy is scattered in five different directions and no one source (vehicle) is receiving enough energy to draw you to it or it to you. The longer you remain undecided, the more anxious you become. The anxiety acts as resistors, further slowing energy and your ability to achieve the goal. Until you decide on the car you want, the anxiety will continue to mount, resistance will continue to build, and the energy you are generating will be too weak and dissipated to allow you to get *any* of the vehicles. You have to make a decision (properly channel your energy) to get a result.

An even more extreme example would be someone with a dozen interests who is unwilling to let go of any of them. This is like trying to chase twelve rabbits at the same time and wanting them all so much that you can't choose any one of them, so end up with none.

To ensure that the energy that reaches each of your goals is compatible with the goals, determine the amount of energy necessary to achieve each one. There is no problem with having multiple goals as long as they are not in conflict with one another, don't require you to run in opposing directions, and are prioritized so you know how to budget your time and energy wisely and well.

KNOW, FIRST AND FOREMOST, WHAT IS MOST IMPORTANT TO YOU

Put the most important item at the top of your list and give those top items a sufficient dose of high quality energy. If you squander energy on the less important things (the busy work that just keeps piling up or the fires that need fighting) you will not have enough to deliver to the things that are important. When you can't get to what is really important, your frustration over that fact sets up resistance and diminishes your available energy, and everything suffers.

Let's see how that plays out. Suppose that spending time with your family is a high priority for you, yet your job is so demanding that you often work 10-hour days, and sometimes even bring work home with you. Because the work needs to be done, you have dinner sitting at your desk rather than with the family, and on those nights, you are lucky if you have time to give your children a hug and a kiss before they go to bed.

You would also love to start a home-based business that would give you more freedom and flexibility, but you just don't have the time to do the research and put a plan together.

What typically happens in a situation like this is that in the early days of the demanding job you have enough energy to pull off the hours and spend time with your family too. But when the demands don't let up, your resentment and frustration set up resistors that diminish your energy, so you have less and less energy left over to give to your family. In time, you have no energy for your family or yourself and too little to meet the demands of the job. You are experiencing what is appropriately called burnout.

Just like the light bulb that burns out too quickly because of an energy overload, so too will people burn out when they are sending too much energy to a demanding job, a demanding spouse, a demanding child, or whatever. Burnout occurs most often when the thing demanding our time and attention is either not a top priority, or is not the only priority, but is requiring time and energy as though it was.

Burnout usually occurs as a result of resistors that build up and shut down energy flow. As energy diminishes, what started out seeming like a doable thing gets harder and harder to sustain and eventually something has to give. Investing too much energy in any one thing to the detriment of other things that are important to you will never bring you the results you want.

Choose not to let the priorities of others, or one interest or need, cause you to send too much energy to one place such that there is too little left over for other things that are important to you. If you do, the energy that arrives at every source will be incompatible with that source and what you will end up getting is definitely not what you want.

PRINCIPLE 7 – **Energy can be harnessed, altered, and directed by altering the factors that release or suppress it.**[16] Each of the factors below is a means by which energy is altered or directed. Each applies to the human experience just as it does to electricity.

Conductors – In electricity, conductors are any material or substance that allows an electric current to flow (such as metals, the earth, or water).

In human experience, attitude and intent are the conductors. Attitude determines the degree to which we are willing to develop responsible, disciplined, courageous actions, and stay open and receptive to positive abundance. Intent drives the behaviors that attitude determines.

Insulators – In electricity, insulators are materials that do not allow an electric current to flow. Insulators are used to either prevent energy flow or to channel it, and prevent the arcing or bridging of electricity from one line to another.

In human experience, insulators are faith in self, others, and a generative force.

Transformers – In electricity, there are two types of transformers: (1) step-up transformers, which boost the flow of electricity, and (2) step-down transformers, which retard the flow.

In human terms, the most powerful step-up transformer (booster) is *passion*. Passion is a natural motivator that drives energy forward and seems to multiply it. Positive thoughts, feelings and intent, and working with, rather than against, your nature, also act as step-up transformers to *boost* energy toward *positive* abundance and as step-down transformers to *retard* energy along the *negative* abundance path.

Things like fear, doubt, distrust, criticism, and working against, rather than with your nature, act as step-up transformers that *boost* energy along the *negative* abundance path, and as step-down transformers *retarding* energy along the *positive* abundance path.

Resistors – Resistors slow, stop, or control the flow of energy. This can be purposeful, to help control the amount of energy that arrives at a particular destination, or it can be unintentional.

In human terms, it is *attention* that directs energy, but it is the *quality of attention* that either keeps energy flowing or sets up resistors. What we fail to attend to has very little, if any, energy flowing toward it. What we choose or are required to attend to has energy flowing toward it, but the quality of our attention determines how freely it flows.

Positive attention allows energy to flow freely along the positive abundance path, where negative attention creates resistance and causes energy to slow down, come to a halt, or be redirected away from what is desired, which means we get less of what we want. On the negative abundance path, positive attention acts as a resistor that slows, halts, or redirects energy flowing toward negative outcomes, thereby increasing our ability to have more of what we want.

Increased resistance results in a *decrease* of energy flow. For example, when we are required to attend to something we don't like doing, the quality of our attention determines our result. If we focus on the negative aspects of the chore, the quality of the attention we give it is negative, so there is *resistance* to the chore and our energy is quickly drained. If we focus our attention on the positive aspects of the chore, we still may not enjoy it, but there is *less resistance* to it and our energy in performing the task won't be as depleted.

There are many people who don't necessarily enjoy their jobs, for instance, but those who stay focused upon, and attend to the negative aspects of the job, are the ones that live for weekends. And they are often too drained to enjoy it when it finally arrives. The condition known as "burnout" occurs as a result of constantly attending to things around which there is a lot of resistance. It's the same principle that causes an extension cord, which has a certain load capacity, to heat up and burn out when it is overloaded. Too great a load (too much attention), combined with resistance, equals burnout.

Impedance – In electricity, impedance is opposition to current flow in an alternating current circuit and is made up of two components: resistance and reactance. In human terms, impedance describes essentially the same things: the two components that act on energy to slow or impede its flow are resistance and reactance.

To prevent energy from flowing toward negative outcomes, for example, we must impede negative thoughts, feelings, and actions. We do that by reacting to the thoughts, feelings, and actions that have created the unwanted results such that we build resistance to them. In other words, by purposefully impeding the things we don't want. *Discipline is purposeful impedance to unruly thoughts, feelings, and/or actions, for example. Responsibility is purposeful impedance to irresponsible actions. Courage is purposeful impedance to fear.*

Inductance – Inductance describes the conditions under which the natural flow of energy is reversed. In electricity, this is done by introducing an electromagnetic force strong enough to oppose the natural magnetic force, thereby reversing the poles and the natural flow of energy from clockwise to counterclockwise. Inductance occurs when the electrical and magnetic forces interact in such a way as to reverse the natural flow of energy.

Just as the natural flow of energy in electricity is clockwise, the natural flow of energy in human experience is *toward positive abundance*. Inductance on a human level is the means by which we reverse the natural direction of energy in our lives, and rather than allowing energy to naturally flow toward abundance, we redirect it toward limitation and negative outcomes. We do that by failing to discipline unruly thoughts, feelings, and actions, by observing and responding to the negativity around us, and by buying into the concept of limitation.

Switches – We are all familiar with switches, and the fact that we can use them to direct or eliminate the flow of electricity. We also have switches to direct or eliminate the flow of energy at a human level.

In human experience, the most effective switches are the choices we make. They act as mental monitors that redirect thoughts and determine what we focus upon. We can use these mental switches to shut down either the positive or the negative path, depending on the nature of the thoughts and decisions.

*The highest possible stage
in moral culture is when we
recognize that we ought to
control our thoughts.*

Charles Darwin

Freedom is actually a bigger game than power.
Power is about what you can control.
Freedom is about what you can unleash.

Harriet Rubin

CHAPTER 15

The Principles of Energy Flow:
Design

Go confidently in the direction of your dreams.
Live the life you have imagined.
Henry David Thoreau

PRINCIPLE 8 – The nature of the receiver determines how energy will express.[17]

Non-personal Example – A freezer delivers cold, an oven delivers heat, and a radio or telephone delivers sound waves. These are examples of energy expressing in specific ways, according to the design of the receiver. A downed power line, on the other hand, results in energy arriving at a non-specific destination, and because the receiver has no specific purpose or design, all that energy is dissipated into the ground, which renders it useless or destructive.

Personal Example – Clearly defined, specific goals act as receivers for people, and the clearer they are, the better the result. A life without design is generally a life of wasted energy and disappointing results. People who decide they want something more, but who have no clear picture of what that is, are misdirecting energy in much the same way as a downed power line. They may send a lot of energy toward hopes, wishes, vague dreams and desires, but much of the energy is wasted and the little that returns almost never comes back in the form hoped for.

The human mind is always in search of understanding so it directs its energy toward whatever has the greatest clarity. If there is greater clarity around what we don't want than what we do want, that is where the energy flows and what is experienced in life.

Each area of life has an active receiver, but most people are not aware of the nature of these receivers. For humans, receivers are whatever we give *attention or intention* to. We pay attention to lots of things we don't really want, and we have intentions that we are not consciously aware of.

For example, if we say we want to be a multi-millionaire and dream of being one, but never do anything to make it happen, we may have our attention on the *idea* of wealth, but our *intention* is to take the *easiest route* through life. Our real attention, therefore, is on finding the easiest way, and the easiest way is to entertain ourselves and soothe our longings. It is a lot easier to hold to the *idea* of wealth, than to work for it so we hold onto the idea and add it to our other easy routines.

When poorly designed receivers return undesirable conditions, most people change their actions in an effort to get a different result rather than changing the nature of the receiver. But, altering actions, while continuing to maintain the same focus, intent and beliefs, guarantees the same undesirable results because energy can only express in the way the receiver determines.

When the receiver continues to faithfully deliver the same results over and over again, and nothing the person does changes the outcome, many come to believe that life just happens to them; that they have no control over it. These people have no idea why they keep getting the same poor results even though they are taking different actions. But *different actions will not bring different results as long as the nature of the receiver remains the same,* because the nature of the receiver is what determines how energy expresses.

Examples of this would be people who want to lose weight and keep trying different diets and different weight loss products, but continue to hold onto, and at the same time rail against, the image they see reflected back to them in the mirror. Or, those who have difficult, unhappy relationships with lovers or spouses and keep changing partners, hoping they will finally find the right one, while at the same time holding to the belief that relationships are difficult, thereby creating a self-fulfilling prophecy. In each new relationship, they ignore areas of compatibility and look for areas of difficulty, and they find exactly what they expect to find. The new partner perfectly matches the details of the image being held (the receiver).

To change an outcome, we must *change the nature of the receiver,* and to do that, we must examine the receiver closely enough to determine whether it is likely to deliver the desired results. To get exactly what we want, every aspect of the receiver must be designed to receive and send exactly what we want.

Many of our receivers were designed so early in life that we sometimes don't know what their design is or even that they exist. And not knowing, we don't realize that we have the option of redesigning the receiver if it isn't delivering the results we want. When receivers were formed early in life, and we have no awareness of them, we can at least be aware of the result and, based on the result, can do some reverse engineering and come to some conclusions about the nature of the design. Once we are aware of its nature, we can then work on redesigning it to get a different outcome if we choose.

Sometimes those early designs serve us very well and sometimes not so well. Here are some examples from my own life of how early designs can help us or hinder us, and will surely determine our outcomes unless we choose to redesign them.

EXAMPLE 1 – POSITIVE ABUNDANCE

I was blessed with a mother who gave me an abundance of love. As a result, I never questioned whether I was loved or lovable and I never had any resistance to loving and being loved. My mother modeled love as open and active expressions of affection, appreciation, and gratitude, and I followed that model, which gave me the formula for abundance in the area of love. I have a clear picture of what love looks like, a workable model to emulate, and there is no resistance to the idea of loving and being loved. Long before I ever experienced abundance in any other area of my life, I had an abundance of love. I still do. I am surrounded by love from family and friends. There is even a sense of love for and from many of my business associates. I can honestly say that I don't have an enemy on earth. I don't assume that everyone who knows me loves me and never has a problem with me, but I can honestly say that every one of my relationships are positive and in some way beneficial.

The design of this receiver has always served me well, and I have no need or desire to change it. However, I didn't always allow it to express fully when I was younger. I was prone to ending difficult relationships without trying to understand or correct the dynamic, for example. Mostly because I lacked understanding and skills. Although there was always a great receiver there, I was able to take full advantage of it only after I learned to use it effectively.

Many people don't take full advantage of the models they have available to them for the same reason; they haven't learned to use them effectively. Like a great computer program, no matter how many features it has or how user friendly it may be, until we have learned how to use it effectively, its many features will remain under-utilized.

EXAMPLE 2 – LIMITATION

Although I had plenty of love, my family of origin had very little money. There were seven children, and my father, who was the sole source of income, was self-employed and somewhat of a free spirit. We never went hungry, but money was always in short supply. My early experiences with money taught me that it was very limited and that I should not ask for it unless there was just no other option.

For example, going to my father to ask for the money for school supplies was a traumatic event and I hated doing that. Therefore, I would borrow paper and pencils from friends until they got mad at me and told me to buy my own. To manage without money, I learned ingenuity, great problem-solving skills, and how to work hard, but because I never had a positive model of financial abundance, I didn't learn to expect to receive money for my efforts. In fact, I had learned not to expect it and not to ask.

As an adult, I worked hard, came up with some pretty ingenious things, and helped a lot of people solve their problems, but I continued to struggle with money. No matter how hard I worked or how often I changed my tactics, my financial condition did not improve. It was not until I changed my relationship with money and my view of it that things began to shift. Now, understanding how the Law of Abundance works, the reason is perfectly clear.

Where unconsciously keeping the model of loving and being loved served me well, unconsciously keeping the model of money certainly did not. Here I had set up the perfect path for staying stuck. I used the positive attributes of ingenuity and problem-solving, I disciplined myself to work hard and responsibly, I stepped into unknown territory courageously, and I was dedicated to doing the right thing (+). But I was also struggling to escape the limitation model I had grown up with, and was actively resisting it (+). Besides the (+/+) energy combination that prevented energy from flowing, the only clear picture I had, the only model or receiver, was that of limitation and scarcity. That's what had clarity and that's where my energy was focused. Because I was focused on limitation, whenever conditions were right for energy to flow, it flowed toward what I was focused on—limitation and scarcity.

In understanding the Law of Abundance, the importance of how energy is directed and the importance of the receiver's design, I did a clarity check in each area of my life: family, finances, friends, fitness, career, leisure, personal growth, and so on. Although I had done a lot of work over the years and made great strides in the area of money, there was no question that there was still greater clarity around the limitation model than around abundance. I could see that I had certainly made progress, but what I had laid claim to was only moderate amounts of money, not significant amounts.

Once I understood where my energies were being directed and what they were being directed toward, I was able to begin redesigning my money model. Since I have done that, more and more opportunities have opened up for me. By altering the nature of my receiver, I have forever altered my results and I know that if I want even better results, I need to keep improving on the design of the receiver.

As you begin examining the receivers in every area of your life. You may be amazed, as I was, at the lack of clarity in the areas you are still struggling with. Without clarity, you have a better chance of winning the lottery than of arriving at a place of positive abundance. The examples that follow demonstrate why the clearer and more precise the receiver, the better our chances of getting the results we want.

THE CLARITY TEST

Just as a telephone is specifically designed to send and receive frequencies and has a specific frequency which is defined by a particular number, so too does each of your receivers, both conscious and unconscious, have a very specific frequency. Telephone frequencies are so specific and yet so all encompassing that you can be driving down a highway in California with a cell phone and call the cell phone of someone driving down a city street in New York and reach that person.

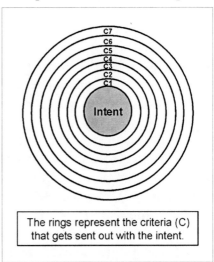

The frequencies of your goals and intentions are just as specific and all encompassing. It doesn't matter that you are in one place and the object of your intent is in another or that you are headed in different directions, those two frequencies are going to find one another and connect, provided conditions allow them to.

The rings represent the criteria (C) that gets sent out with the intent.

Illustration 15.01

Radio waves are just one aspect of the wide electromagnetic frequency range that exists everywhere and at all times in our atmosphere. They spread out in every direction, as is demonstrated in Illustration 15.01, and can travel for millions of miles. Everything is subject to energy frequencies, including people.

Like telephones, radios, televisions and other sending and receiving devices, people both send and receive frequencies. This is evidenced by the often-unexplainable results people get when they set specific goals and lay out a plan with a specific design. Accounts of inexplicably attracting people and conditions that help fulfill clearly held goals are so common as to be cliché. But as with other sender/receivers, for people to get the desired results, the frequency sent out must be *very* specific.

AN EXERCISE IN FUTILITY

Let's use the analogy of dialing a telephone to further clarify this. If your phone number is 321-4567, I must dial those exact numbers in that exact order to reach you. If I have five of the seven numbers in the proper sequence, but must choose the last two at random, the odds of my reaching you are pretty slim. If I have all of the numbers, but don't know the order they go in my odds are even slimmer. If I am missing even one number and don't know the order, my odds of reaching you are next to none.

Intention works the same way. Every call (intention) you send out has criteria and the only way that "call" can be answered is for the criteria to match the goal. Let's look at the intent to achieve financial wealth and apply criteria in the way that it is typically applied by those seeking the wealth. We will use the phone number example given above as our representative number (321-4567) for the frequency of the intent.

When the criteria for goal achievement are not specific enough, the result is the equivalent of a rolling number. Rolling numbers come up randomly, which makes getting the right numbers in the right combination nearly impossible. If you have ever purchased a lottery ticket, you know that the odds of winning are several million to one and you don't even have to choose lottery numbers in the right order. Even if we assume that a particular sequence is not necessary for goal achievement, the "numbers" that define the frequency still need to be exact. The following examples might help to explain why non-specific goals have worse odds of getting us the results we want than buying a lottery ticket might.

Criteria	Non-specific Application of Criteria	Numerical Equivalent
What?	More money	Rolling Number (0 – 9)
By when?	This year	Rolling Number (0 – 9)
How?	Through increased business	Rolling Number (0 – 9)
From what source?	New customers	Rolling Number (0 – 9)
As a result of what?	Sales of my products/ services	Rolling Number (0 – 9)
By what application?	Hard work, responsible action	Rolling Number (+)
What attitude?	Worry, doubt, struggle	Rolling Number (+)

Though attitude is not a part of the plan, it influences energy flow and impacts the plan's outcome. Random numbers combined with the (+/+) energy combination results in no energy flow. This is equivalent to a lottery ticket with no chance of winning.

Criteria	Alternate Application of Criteria #1	Numerical Equivalent
What?	$120,000	Numerical value 3
By when?	December 31, of this year	Numerical value 2
How?	Through increased business	Rolling Number (0 – 9)
From what source?	New customers	Rolling Number (0 – 9)
As a result of what?	Sales of my products/services	Rolling Number (0 – 9)
By what application?	Hard work, responsible action (+)	Rolling Number (+)
What attitude?	Faith, receptiveness (-)	Rolling Number (-)

This approach results in 5 random numbers combined with a (+/-) energy combination. Here energy flows, but without clear goals, the odds of getting the intended result are about the same as buying a lottery ticket with almost no chance of winning

Criteria	Alternate Application of Criteria #2	Numerical Equivalent
What?	$120,000.	Numerical value 3
By when?	December 31, this year	Numerical value 2
How?	Sell X amount of Y product to customers A, B, and C	Numerical value 1
From what source?	Product X, Y and Z Service X, Y and Z Specific to customer's need	Numerical value 4
As a result of what?	Contacting each, building good relationships, providing what they want/need	Numerical value 5
By what application?	Responsible/disciplined action (+) (Make X calls per day, keep in touch, apply good selling and negotiation skills)	Numerical value 6 (+)
What attitude?	I will approach 15 customers per week, and hope they will be receptive. I need to improve my ability to be persuasive and to effectively sell . I'm not very good at that. (Here faith in self, and to some extent, in others is lacking. There is fear, doubt and worry)	Numerical value 7(+)

Specific numbers with NO energy flow (+/+) = Correct frequency to specific receiver, but no energy to return the desired results. We keep "calling the number" we know to be correct, but get no answer. In this case, persistence keeps us stuck because, although we the right "number", we are not providing an open channel for the frequencies we send out to return to us.

Criteria	Alternate Application of Criteria #2 Numerical Equivalent
	(Same formula as #2, but with a different attitude)

Criteria		
What?	$120,000.	Numerical value 3
By when?	December 31, (year)	Numerical value 2
How?	Sell X amount of Y product	
	to customers A, B, and C	Numerical value 1
From what source?	Product X, Y and/or Z	
	Service X, Y and/or Z	
	Specific to customer's need	Numerical value 4
As a result of what?	Contacting each, building	
	good relationships, providing	
	what they want/need	Numerical value 5
By what application?	Responsible/disciplined action (+)	
	(Make X Calls per day,	
	keep in touch, learn good selling	
	and negotiation skills)	Numerical value 6 (+)
What attitude?	I have faith in my ability to provide	
	customers with what they want	
	and need, and I have faith that the	
	customer will be responsive to my	
	products and services because they	
	fill a need. I also have faith in the Law	
	of Abundance to bring specific results	
	when I am properly applying the law	
	(confidence, receptiveness, trust)	Numerical value 7 (-)

Specific numbers with energy flow (+/-) = Correct frequency sent to a specific receiver and combined with an open channel for clear reception. Exactly when the "call" will be answered cannot be predicted precisely, but as with dialing the right number when making a telephone call, positive expectation, and persistence increase our odds of achieving the goal sooner. In this case, persistence pays because we have the right number and are applying it in the correct way.

These same principles hold true for everything you will ever want. If you apply them to happy, healthy relationships, for example, the clearer you are on what criteria constitutes a good relationship, and the more responsible, disciplined and courageous you are in ensuring that the criteria are in place. And the more open, receptive, allowing, trusting, principled and non-resistant you are, the better your chances of having good, healthy relationships.

We cannot just hope things will work out, and we cannot force our wants, needs, and opinions on another person and expect good results because, in both cases, we are working against the Law of Abundance. It doesn't matter what you apply the principles to; they always work in exactly the same way every time and all the time.

RESISTANCE ON A POTENTIALLY POSITIVE LINE

Another thing that can go wrong in moving toward goals is in believing we are doing all the right things (disciplined, responsible, courageous action coupled with receptiveness and faith), yet not realizing that thoughts and feelings can set up resistors that slow or stop the flow of energy. Using the telephone number example again, you may be "dialing the right number" but resisting the results. Say, for example, that you expect the call to be answered right away, and when it isn't, you become impatient, irritated, or disappointed. Each of these emotions becomes a resistor.

If after calling four or five times, you begin to get really upset and think that the intended receiver should be more available than that, the thought adds another resistor. If the expected result is not forthcoming in what you think is a reasonable time, you may go one step further and begin to question your ability to ever get the result you want. Now you have entirely changed the receptive path to an active (resistant) one, so energy is not flowing at all, and you stop calling.

Another example of having the right "number" but getting the wrong result occurs at the expectation level, which is often under our radar screen unless we are checking for it.

Example of a resistant expectation – You maintain that people should understand what you are trying to convey to them, but they just don't seem to get it. In this case, you expect others to be a problem.

Example of a non-resistant expectation – You understand that some people don't seem to be getting the message you are trying to convey, so you keep changing your message and connecting with people until you find the right one. You get feedback from others to determine the clarity and quality of the message so you can perfect it and find the right people to receive it. In this case, you expect others to help you find the solution.

Monitor your expectations to see if they are tripping you up. You may be surprised at how many you find that you were totally unaware of having. Work at replacing any that feel negative with positive ones.

Expectations Exploration – *Mark where you think you fall on each of the following scales.*

I Am Completely Incapable	————————————————	I Am Completely Capable
People are Completely Undependable	————————————————	People are Completely Dependable
People are Always Inconsiderate	————————————————	People are Always Considerate
The World is Completely Dangerous	————————————————	The World is Completely Safe
I Feel Completely Limited	————————————————	I Feel Completely Abundant

The expectations on the left side of the scale are fear inducing and lead to distrust, while those on the right side are confidence or faith inducing. Look at where you placed yourself on the expectations scales and explore the beliefs and expectations that led you to place yourself at that particular place on each scale. Examine your beliefs and expectations from *both ends* of the scale.

For example, on the capable/incapable scale, no matter where you placed yourself, you will want to explore the areas in which you feel completely capable and why that is true. You will also want to explore any areas where you feel incapable, and why that is true.

Knowing why and where you feel capable or incapable, why and when you trust or don't trust people, why and when the world feels safe or dangerous, and why and when you feel abundant or limited, will bring many insights into what you need to adjust to get and stay on the path to positive abundance.

Argue for your limitations,
and sure enough, they're yours.

Richard Bach, Illusions

All change is a miracle to contemplate;
but it is a miracle which is
taking place every instant.

Henry David Thoreau

PART 3

Applying the Principles
of Abundance

*"Abundance is not something we
acquire. It's something we tune into."*
Wayne Dyer

Excellence is an art won by habituation.
We are what we repeatedly do.
Excellence then is not an act, but a habit.
Aristotle 384-327 BCE

CHAPTER 16

Applying Abundance Principles to Everyday Actions

You are never given a wish without also being given the power to make it come true. You may have to work for it, however.
Richard Bach

We have all heard the hypothetical question "Is the glass half empty or half full?" Some will say it's just semantics, but it is far more than that. Ultimately, how you see that glass determines whether it gets filled, emptied, or remains at the same level. You know from what you have learned so far that the Law of Abundance is such that you can't just sit there and hope, wish, or positive think the glass full. It cannot and will not fill itself. Neither can you always sit there wishing and hoping for more water and have someone else conveniently show up to fill the glass for you. At times, it appears that way, but the glass always gets filled because *someone* (you, a waiter, a friend, or a family member) had an *intention* and *took action*. The rules of abundance make it clear that you (or someone else) must *do* something specific as well as expect something specific to get a result. Besides having the clear goal of having the glass filled, there must be positive application (+) as well as a receptive attitude (-) on someone's part.

To get that glass filled, you or someone else has to take responsible action. Unless you are in a situation where someone is anticipating your needs and intends to meet them, either you must ask someone to fill your glass for you, or you must get up and fill it yourself. But before you will take responsible action, four things have to occur: (1) you have to want the water, (2) you have to want water *specifically*, (3) you have to believe that there is water to get, and (4) you have to believe that you have the ability to get it through the actions you take.

If you don't want the water, you won't bother. If you want something besides water, you won't ask for, or go seeking, water. If you don't think there is any water available, you won't bother to ask for it or look for it. If you want water and know there is water available, but don't think you are capable of getting it, you won't even try. You will just sit there and fret because your water glass is not full. Your idea of being capable of getting the water can include physical capabilities as well as mental and emotional capabilities.

Many people fail to get the things they want in life, not because they are physically incapable, but because their thoughts, feelings, and beliefs lead them to conclude that they are incapable. If, for example, you expect people to be upset, put off, or inconvenienced by your asking for water and you have an aversion to creating those perceived outcomes, you won't ask. If you are afraid that asking might call attention to yourself and you find attention uncomfortable, you won't ask. These are conceptual limitations, not physical ones, but it doesn't much matter because the results are the same.

ASSERTIVENESS

Studies suggest that approximately 88% of the American population will not negotiate or assert their rights unless they are forced to. If these studies are right, only 12% of the population comes anywhere close to getting the things they want in life. The ability to act assertively requires faith in both self and others. We have to believe that we are capable of saying and doing the right things, and we have to believe that others are considerate and/or wise enough to respond to our requests appropriately.

Assertiveness requires that we take responsibility for the outcomes of all our interactions, have the discipline not to react when other people try to push our buttons, and the courage to act in the right way and do the right thing to ensure the best outcome for all concerned. It also requires being caring enough to consider the impact that our actions and requests will have on self and others, now and in the long-term. It requires the wisdom to see beyond the moment and understand what we are teaching other people, and to consider whether we are teaching the right things.

In every interaction, we are teaching people how to treat us and others. If we allow people to get positive results from negative behaviors, we are teaching them that there is a benefit to acting that way, and everyone who they encounter will have to endure the negative behaviors.

If we refuse to accept difficult or unreasonable behaviors, we teach those who try to bully their way through life that there is no benefit to acting that way, at least sometimes, and not with us. If enough people are courageous enough to send the same message, those who would bully and abuse others will have to learn better ways to interact if they are to get a good result.

Say, for example, that you are treated rudely by a co-worker. The easiest route in the short-term, and in the external world, would be to say nothing and just avoid that person as much as possible. That is not the easiest route *internally* because it leaves you feeling violated and resentful. It isn't the easiest route externally either in the long run, because avoiding a difficult co-worker drains off a lot of otherwise useful energy. Plus, with the recurrence of such incidences, you come to believe that you can't trust yourself to stand your ground and can't trust others not to treat you poorly.

If the co-worker gets by with acting rudely most of the time, he learns that rude behavior gets him the outcome he wants and doesn't result in a consequence, so he continues and perhaps escalates the behavior. Only by taking responsible, courageous action and disciplining ourselves to respond appropriately, can we counter aggression, build trust in our own abilities, and teach others better ways of interacting.

We get what we want out of life far more easily when we can trust ourselves to respond to situations appropriately. It is through self-trust that self-confidence grows, and through self-confidence, that self-esteem grows. Without self-esteem, we don't believe we are worthy of the effort it takes to have a happy, healthy, abundant life. Abundance always begins with a sense of confidence and self-worth.

SELF-TALK

Self-talk begins with an emotion—a subtle and often undetectable feeling about something. Once we begin the self-talk in response to the emotion, the self-talk drives our thinking and thinking in turn intensifies the emotions to the point that we are more aware of them. The emotions drive our actions, and our actions determine our outcomes. Often, the dialogue we carry on with our self is intended to direct our actions or motivate us in some way. Yet far too often, that is not the result we get. To understand the importance of self-talk, let's apply some examples to the Law of Abundance.

EXAMPLE   1

I have GOT to stop over-eating.

The intent here is clearly to stop doing something that is not producing the desired outcome. But the self-talk is not going to produce the desired result because it creates a response that sets energy in motion in the wrong direction.

Here's how that statement impacts energy:

The focus: over-eating.

The application: the thought of action, but no immediate responsible, disciplined action (-). The receptive application in combination with a focus on what is not wanted creates an attraction toward the negative.

The attitude: self-criticism, striving against being overweight (+). We now have the perfect formula for the flow of abundance toward a negative outcome: a backward (-/+) energy combination and focus on what is not wanted.

The result: *more* over-eating and *more* weight. In other words, *more* of what is not wanted.

EXAMPLE 2

I have GOT to start exercising more.

Although this statement appears to be positive in that it appears to be focused on exercise, the effect is exactly the same as the over-eating statement. Why? Because the focus is still on the condition that set the thought and emotion in action: lack of fitness. The nature of the thought and emotion is that of striving toward a more fit body, and working harder toward a result.

Here's how this one plays out.

The focus: lack of fitness.

The application: the *thought* of action, but no immediate responsible, disciplined action (-).

The attitude: irritation and impatience with self, striving toward (+).

The result: a (-/+) energy path and focus on what is not wanted = *more* lack of fitness.

Understanding how our self-talk impacts energy flow allows us to formulate statements that flow in the direction we intend. We can change the above two statements, for example, such that they evoke very different emotions and set up the right conditions for energy to flow toward what we do want, rather than toward what we don't want.

A word of caution here: for affirmations or declarations to have a positive effect, *they must encourage the right focus and evoke the right emotions and actions.* We may be able to fool our conscious mind into thinking that positive affirmations are getting us somewhere, but we cannot fool our subconscious mind or the laws of the universe. Our words must create a response that results in the right attitude *and* the right application or we are wasting our time and energy.

A BETTER WAY TO STATE EXAMPLE 1 – LOSING WEIGHT

I love how I feel when I exercise and eat the right portions of healthy foods so that my weight stays within two pounds of my 137-pound ideal.

The focus: your weight at a specific ideal and within a specific acceptable range.

The application: self-encouragement, which creates an active charge (+). The active charge will be further enhanced by taking immediate responsible action: eating the right portions of healthy foods and exercising even if this action is minor. These positives create a strong attraction toward more of what is desired.

The attitude: allowing, being receptive (-) to the positive image of your ideal weight, and the positive feeling of enjoying the *result* of exercise and eating healthy foods.

This combination sets up the correct (+/-) conditions for energy to flow toward a positive and clearly defined goal (a specific weight). We now have the perfect formula for the flow of abundance toward a positive outcome.

The result: *more* enjoyment around eating healthy foods in the right portions, *more* enjoyment of exercise, *more* of the actions that lead to the desired weight and *more* energy flowing in the direction of the ideal body image.

Caveat – The words you use will *not* produce the results you want if there is resistance to the current body image or a negative view of self. For energy to flow along the receptive path, there must be *no resistance* to the current body image. And this is the snag for most people who are trying to get in shape.

Resistance to the current body image keeps the focus stuck on the *current image*, so that is what has the strongest pull and what remains the reality. When a negative body image is held, even when through extreme dieting, the individual is able to lose weight, the weight eventually returns to its original level, and if this fact causes even greater self-recrimination, additional weight is added; we get *more* of what we don't want.

To achieve an ideal weight and fitness level, the place to start is always on the *attitude side*. If those who desire a more fit body are not accepting of their body right now, or if they are struggling against a body image that they just can't find anything worth loving and accepting, they cannot sustain the efforts necessary for changing the current reality. Even if people think they are focused on the body image they want, but are not accepting of their current self, they are simply spinning their wheels.

Before we can consistently apply the discipline to eat properly and exercise in order to remain healthy, we have to have a sufficient degree of self-esteem to believe we are worth the effort. If we don't believe we are worth the effort, the necessary discipline becomes a struggle that we are unable to sustain so we have two active charges (+/+) keeping us stuck right where we are and draining energy.

It isn't necessary to love the way we look with the weight. If we loved that part of ourselves, we wouldn't have the impetus to change it unless our health was at stake. But it is necessary to love and accept ourselves *apart from* the weight.

We are not just a body. We have hearts, souls, and minds that make up far more of who we really are than the body does (in spite of what advertisers would have us believe). We must love and accept and stay focused upon all these other wonderful parts. It is self-acceptance and self-esteem that keep energy flowing toward the desired goal and that allows us to maintain a clear and realistic focus on a healthy body image, and eventually realize the goal.

Self-acceptance puts us in a receptive state (-). When combined with the disciplined action (+) that occurs as a result of knowing we are worth the effort, along with a clear and specific body image, we now have the formula for an abundance of physical fitness success.

A BETTER WAY TO STATE EXAMPLE 2 – EXERCISING

Exercising is a great use of my time. It keeps my energy high and my body healthy and fit. Early morning is a good time for me to exercise because it energizes me for the day.

Focus 1: a healthy, fit body with lots of energy.

Focus 2: exercising early in the morning and being energized.

Application: self-encouragement, which sets up an active charge (+), and is further enhanced by taking immediate responsible action (incorporating a morning exercise routine into your day). This need not be elaborate; 5 or 10 minutes in the beginning will start the energy flowing along the right path. The positive focus combined with positive application drive enjoyment and what started out as a five minute routine eventually expands into a full-fledged, healthy workout.

The attitude: allowing, accepting, and being receptive to the positive images of yourself exercising, being fit, and feeling energized (-).

The result: *more* exercising, *more* fitness, and *more* energy.

Here again, we have the perfect (+/-) formula for the flow of abundance toward a positive outcome. As with weight loss, however, there must be total acceptance of self (non-resistance) for this to result in more of what you want.

CHAPTER 17

Right Action

Right action tends to be defined in terms of individual rights and standards that have been critically examined and agreed upon by the whole society.
Lawrence Kohlberg

The concept of right action presents us with a big question: exactly what is right action? If it is something that preserves individual rights and upon which we all agree, as the Kohlberg quote above suggests, how do we get to that place of agreement? That question is most easily answered by continuing to refer to the rules of the Law of Abundance. If the action is to lead to an abundance of beneficial outcomes, individually and collectively, it must be both responsible (+) *and* well received (-), disciplined (+) *and* adaptive (-), and both courageous (+) *and* accepting (-).

Clearly, things like laziness, slovenliness, and rigid perfectionism are not right actions. But what about the actions that arise from religious, academic or cultural zeal? Surely such individuals believe they are taking the right actions when they insist that those who are not following "the right way" (their particular version of right action) are foolish, deluded, "sinning" or misguided and need to alter their thinking, mend their ways or correct their course. Surely, they feel fully justified and correct in defending their beliefs and traditions, even if it means actively opposing those who disagree. But when we consider right action according to the Law of Abundance, it is clear that these are *not* right actions, no matter what those who perform and perpetuate them believe.

Just as sitting around lazily and hoping or praying for deliverance is a formula for failure, so too is trying to force people to your way of thinking or believing to *any* degree, much less to the point of arguing and violence. There is absolutely no way that responsible, disciplined, courageous action *combined* with a receptive, adaptive and accepting attitude could result in hatred and violence, or even in the levels of intolerance we are witnessing on so many levels and in so many arenas today. If everyone obeyed the Law of Abundance, there could be no wars, no crime, no hate, and no intolerance.

Throughout the ages, philosophers and spiritual teachers have taught non-resistance in one form or another. Many have not clarified this concept, however, so the idea of non-resistance is often misunderstood. For abundance to flow in the right direction, non-resistance has to be on the *attitude* side of the energy equation, not on the application side. Yet there are teachings that suggest it should be applied to *both* sides in some instances and to *neither* side in others.

On the application side of the abundance equation, receptivity to whatever happens is irresponsible. Allowing other individuals to bully us, or even allowing them to decide how we should live or what we should think, robs us of the power to create abundance, certainly internally and often externally as well.

An example of misunderstanding and misapplying the concept of non-resistance is in the way some people approach the Biblical advice to "turn the other cheek." That advice was likely intended for the attitude side of the equation and given as a metaphor to explain the attitude one should assume in the face of anger. It has been interpreted to mean non-action, however, instead of non-aggression.

An *essential* piece of the abundance equation is a*ction rightly taken* and few would assume that complacently taking a beating from a bully constitutes right action on our part. Counter-aggression is not the answer either, which is likely why the advice was given in the first place.

If we apply this scenario to the flow of energy, we can see that the *right action* is firm, courageous resistance (+), and the *right attitude* is keeping a calm, cool head (-) which keeps energy flowing in the right direction.

Right action requires us to act with courage and strive to do the right thing. As mentioned in the section on assertiveness, we teach people how to treat us, and if we allow a bully to abuse us we are not only teaching him that it is alright to bully us, we are teaching him that bullying people in general gets him the outcome he wants. This lesson does not lead us, or the bully, to abundance.

WRONG USE OF ENERGY

On the other side of the coin, arguing or fighting back demonstrates, and therefore teaches, that we are justified in rejecting those whose actions we don't like or with whom we disagree. We teach that we have a right to react harshly or to judge or criticize others, or that it's alright to push our own agenda off on others if we don't like their approach. Whenever we actively apply ourselves to trying to make other people think or act our way, even in response to an aggression, we create conditions where what we get is not what we want.

The fact is, meeting aggression with passivity *or* aggression conflicts with the Law of Abundance and shuts down energy flow. Rejecting, judging, and criticizing create an *active* charge on the *attitude* line (+) and actively working to change those who don't share our way of thinking or behaving creates an active charge on the *application* line (+). The result is that energy does not flow. It becomes static and is squandered away, and our result is that we get nowhere.

Few of us imagine that we can squander our time and resources and achieve any degree of abundance. Most everyone is aware that wasting time and energy is not the right use of these precious commodities. But what many do not seem to realize is that right use of energy requires more than just managing the flow. It also requires that we plan ahead, determine where we want to go, lay out a map to that place, and learn what we must learn to be better prepared for life on planet Earth.

We can't just plunge headlong into one new venture after another without first having done our homework, and expect life to flow smoothly. It is life without a plan that gets most of us into trouble. Working hard on the wrong things, struggling to do what we have been told we should, even if it drains us of energy and joy, or just stumbling through life trying to figure it out on the fly, is definitely *not* energy rightly used.

Many people who jump into things enthusiastically may give the appearance of working hard. But plunging ahead without a clear vision and a well thought out plan for reaching the goal actually places people squarely on the receptive *application* path (taking the easy way out), which, as you know by now, is the path to limitation or worse, an abundance of the things we don't want.

Here's an example of that approach. A man named Bert, while watching television late one night, ran across an infomercial about real estate investing. He wanted to be his own boss and thought that might be the way to do it. The infomercial promised lots of money and lots of free time to sail around on the yacht the ad promised Bert would soon be able to buy.

Bert talked a friend into investing $30,000 in a property with the understanding that, if the friend put up the money, Bert would do the renovations and they would split the profits 50/50. Bert estimated the cost of renovations at $5,000, the time to complete the work at 30 days and the profit from flipping the property in 60 days at $70,000. He quit his $38,000 a year job and went to work on the renovations, certain he would quadruple his old salary that year. Six months and $49,000 later, the house was finally ready to sell. The actual profit on the house was only $19,000 and he had to split that with his partner. Bert's total income for six months of hard labor and way too many unpleasant surprises: $9,500.

Bert thought he was on the path to abundance. He had a clear vision of himself running his own business and being his own boss. He could clearly see himself on that yacht sipping Piña Coladas. He was thinking positively (at least for the first 60 days) and had positive expectations going into the business. So positive, in fact, that he was able to sell his friend on financing the start up. Needless to say, the business didn't last long. Bert had to find a job and go back to work to make ends meet.

What went wrong? On the surface, all of the elements seemed to be in place for abundance to flow, but only on the surface. Although Bert thought he had a clear vision of the goal and positive expectations for reaching it, what he really had was a pipe dream with no research or experience to back it up. He estimated costs and time requirements unrealistically and seriously over-estimated his ability to renovate a fixer-upper without help. He had no idea what to look for when buying a property to remodel and was blind-sided by a rash of problems he hadn't anticipated.

In no way were his energy and resources rightly used. Conservation of energy in the world of humans requires that we think ahead and plan for the things we might encounter on the path we have chosen. We must factor for the likelihood that things will go awry occasionally, or that some of the people we encounter will have their own agendas that might conflict with our own. We must proceed with wisdom.

PLANNING TO SUCCEED

Let me use a simple example to demonstrate how a little advance planning can help us get better outcomes. Imagine that you are on your way to work one morning. It is pouring rain and a tire on your car goes flat. If you haven't planned for such an event, you may or may not have an inflated tire, and you may or may not have a working jack.

If you have both the tire and the jack, but you are in business attire, you will still have to get out in the rain and fix the tire. Or, you could wait for the rain to stop before you get out (which might be hours or days). Or, you could wait for some good Samaritan to come along and do the job for you. But, in this scenario, it is the morning rush hour and everyone is trying to get to work just like you are, and it is pouring rain. Under these conditions, the likelihood of someone stopping to help is slim, though it could happen—in time.

If, on the other hand, you realize that flat tires do occur and you have planned ahead for such an event, you know when the tire goes flat that you have an inflated tire in the trunk and you know the jack works. But as a really good planner, one who is working with the Law of Abundance, you also have bought a membership in an auto club that is known for fast, reliable service. And you have a charged cell phone with you. You even have the number of your auto club programmed into your phone. So all you have to do is select the number and request assistance. You don't fret and you don't get wet.

That is wise conservation of your energy. The flat tire still happened, but the outcome with and without having taken responsible action *before* the problem occurred is what made all the difference. To assume that the Law of Abundance or any other natural law will bring us supernatural results, like positive thinking our way out of having a flat tire, is just foolish. Yet some people waste a great deal of time and energy and deal with a lot of disappointments doing the equivalent of just that.

The terrible disaster that befell New Orleans in 2005 ,when Hurricane Katrina hit, is a classic example of hoping your way into a disaster. Levees were built to protect the below-sea-level parts of the city, but engineers had known since the levees were built that they would not hold up to a category 5 hurricane. They informed city managers of this fact, but the city managers ignored the warning, went ahead with the below standard levees, and allowed homes and businesses to be built in the low-lying areas anyway.

The attitude seemed to be that, although a disaster was possible, it couldn't happen to *them*. Maybe to some future generation, but not to them. Their wishful thinking did nothing to protect the city when Hurricane Katrina hit. Moreover, although the city managers knew a disaster was possible, they didn't have a plan in place or resources allocated should such an event occur.

We all watched the result of hope without action as the city fell to ruin and thousands of people were stranded for days amidst appalling conditions. As people died on the streets, a fleet of school buses that could have carried them out of the city and to safety sat submerged in floodwaters unused and now in ruin.

Even the federal government was unprepared to handle the scope of the disaster. Many millions of dollars were wasted on resources—such as food, water, ice, medical supplies and temporary housing—that never reached those who needed them.

At the same time, credit cards for large sums of money were issued to people who were unaccustomed to managing such sums and spending ran rampant. While thousands were struggling to get destroyed homes and businesses functional again, thousands more were squandering taxpayer dollars on entertainment, jewelry, and fancy clothes.

Because both the local and federal governments acted irresponsibly and failed to correct their course effectively, more than two years later the low-lying neighborhoods were still in shambles, with no clear plan for recovery in place.

As the New Orleans example readily demonstrates, we cannot hope, dream, wish, or think our way to an abundance of the things we desire. The path to an abundance of things we don't want is an easy path to follow, but a hard pill to swallow. By following the exact path of the energy generated by those who made decisions for New Orleans, we can see how the only possible outcome was one of eventual disaster.

HERE'S HOW IT PLAYED OUT:

- The levees were built to less than adequate standards to save money and the problem was repeatedly and almost completely ignored, which falls into the category of irresponsible action (-).

- There was resistance to the warnings of impending disaster—resistance to investing the money, to taking the right action, to having a workable plan, and to taking the steps necessary to be prepared for such a disaster—which falls into the active attitude category (+)

Their receptive (-) application combined with active (+) attitude literally guaranteed that the city would eventually end up with a whole lot of what no one wanted. Now the state and federal governments will have to spend many times more money than they would have, had they not resisted spending to prevent the disaster in the first place (responsible action).

To correct the problems that now exist in New Orleans the people there will need to reverse the flow of energy. This means they must collectively take responsible, disciplined, courageous actions (positive application), trust that the city can and will be rebuilt (receptive attitude), have a clear picture of what the rebuilt city will look like (clear focus), and provide the energy (money, human resources and ingenuity) to complete the "circuit" toward a positive outcome.

SENDING OUT A WORKING NUMBER

As we saw in Chapter 15, goals are frequently not achieved because individuals, families, communities, and countries send out the equivalent of rolling numbers, rather than specific ones. There are literally millions of examples at every level of human existence, but one should do to make the point. A study done on the numbers of people who make New Years resolutions shows that less than 3% actually keep them. That 3% number seems to hold in many studies.

One study conducted back in the 1980s that followed 100 Harvard graduates from graduation to retirement found that only 3% were highly successful. It was discovered that what this 3% had done better than the other 97% was to set clear, specific goals, lay out a life plan, and follow it.

A study my company, NaviCore International, conducted in 2006 found that 2.8% of the population had done the work of developing themselves to the healthy, effective levels that ensure success and satisfaction in life. The other 97.2% still had some work to do. It is no coincidence that around 3% of the world population is highly successful, and about the same percentage has clarity around who they are, where they are headed and what they want out of life.

Until we have clarity, we cannot know what the right action is. When we cannot discern which actions will lead to right or wrong outcomes, we stay stuck in uncertainty and cannot move forward courageously.

There are many ways to fall short of our dreams and ideals and only *one way* to achieve them. The laws that govern energy, and therefore outcomes, are exact; the formula must be followed exactly or we cannot get the results we want.

Part of that formula is clarity of purpose, and there is no way to eliminate that piece from the equation. Energy is ever willing and able to serve each of us, but we must provide the blueprint. *We* must design the circuits along which it can flow.

Remember that energy will follow any and every path laid out for it. Energy is non-discerning, which means discernment on our part is essential.

The price of greatness is responsibility.
Winston Churchill

*The greatest good
we can do for others
is not to share our riches,
but to reveal theirs.*

Author Unknown

CHAPTER 18

Grace, Awareness, And Wisdom

By three methods we may learn wisdom:
First, by reflection, which is noblest;
Second, by imitation, which is easiest; and
third by experience, which is the bitterest.
Confucius

GRACE

What exactly is the role of grace as it applies the Law of Abundance? What exactly is grace? As applied to the Law of Abundance, grace is the state of peacefulness that allows us to move through life responsibly and courageously, unruffled by the people, circumstances, and events that surround us. It is what keeps us doing the right things ourselves and flowing in harmony with the Law of Abundance. It allows us to avoid becoming resistant when others make different choices than we might have, or when the world around us seems limited or chaotic. In short, grace is the ability to unconditionally accept life as it unfolds and others, wherever they are on their journey.

Unconditional acceptance does not mean that we must agree with or condone the way others conduct their lives. It does not mean that we must allow behaviors that offend or harm us. Neither does it mean that we should allow those who present danger to others to proceed unchecked. Allowing those who do harm to run amuck is clearly not responsible or courageous.

Grace simply means that we respect the right of others to have their own thoughts, opinions, values and beliefs. And to conduct their lives in ways consistent with their values and beliefs so long as their behaviors do not have a direct negative impact on others. *Direct negative impact* would include things such as murder, rape, theft, and vandalism. It does *not* include lifestyles or opinions and beliefs that are different from our own, but which have no *direct* affect on our lives.

Our attitude toward something does *not* constitute direct affect. Each individual is wholly responsible for his or her own attitude. And those who have small children are also responsible for the attitudes of their children until the children are old enough to reason on their own. Once they are old enough, the parents are then responsible for stepping aside and allowing the young adults the privilege of developing their own reasoning abilities and opinions.

Grace is acceptance, combined with awareness of what actions or avoidances lead to abundance, and the wisdom to consistently take the right actions. It provides us with the courage and insights to not only walk a positive path ourselves, but to gently and lovingly encourage others toward right actions by our example. We have a duty to set a good example, but that never gives us the right to force or coerce change.

The founders of the United States understood this concept and built it into the constitution in many ways. The right to life, liberty and the pursuit of happiness, the right to worship as we see fit, the right to free speech, the right to defend ourselves. All of these mandate *mutual respect*, which is the essence of grace. People with agendas frequently distort the original intent, but clearly, the founding fathers intended that American citizens proceed responsibly and with grace.

Even when we look at the Law of Abundance on a universal level, we can see that grace is an integral part of the equation. For example, the physical matter within Earth's atmosphere is encouraged toward earth through gravity. The Earth and other planets in this and other solar systems are encouraged into orbit.

There is wisdom in this, since physical objects just floating around the Earth randomly or heavenly bodies randomly wandering in space would mean disaster. Yet if we look at the nature of this precise order, we can also see that it is only *encouraged*, not compelled. The order can be interrupted on Earth and in space, though not without some unusual event or effort intervening and often not without consequence. For instance, stray meteors can and do enter the orbit of planets and hit them, and NASA can create a weightless environment where the laws of gravity do not seem to apply. If adherence to natural laws was compulsory, such things could not occur.

To tap into the many benefits that a state of grace provides, we must likewise encourage without compulsion. Create your world the way you want it to be, and allow the world others have created for themselves to be alright with you. Give love, give acceptance, give encouragement, give hope, give instruction, but demand nothing.

> **The Essence of Grace**
> *There is only abundance.* You are free to allow it or to resist it. If you choose to allow it, you get to choose how it will manifest.

COMPLETE AWARENESS AND WISDOM

To properly direct our time and energy, we must be fully aware of ourselves, others, and our life purpose. We must know who we are, where we are headed, why we are headed there, and how we will arrive. We must also know who we can depend upon to champion us along the way, who and what might trip us up, and how each person we have chosen to allow into our life fits into the overall scheme of things.

To be fully aware, we need full understanding. To fully understand, we need knowledge that has been validated by our own experience. The greater our level of knowledge about any given thing and the greater our experience of it, the clearer we can be about it. Clarity leads to confidence and confidence leads to courage. With clarity and courage, we are far more capable of consistently choosing the right action. And right action leads to wisdom. There is great peace in deep awareness and great awareness in wisdom.

The Law of Abundance gives us clear guidelines for knowing what the right thing is. We know that we must always follow the path of positive application and receptive attitude, for example. But knowing this intellectually is very different from having a deep awareness of it.

For example, you can know and agree that it is a good thing to be responsible, disciplined, and courageous, without actually being that way. When you experience yourself *being* responsible, disciplined, and courageous on a consistent basis, it is no longer just an idea. Your awareness becomes deep and complete.

Rather than seeing yourself as *doing* something responsible or *acting* in disciplined or courageous ways, you become aware that you *are* responsible. You *are* disciplined. You *are* courageous. This is not just the way you act, it's *who you are*.

The minute you decide this is *who you are*, the need to make future decisions as to whether you will or will not walk this path is no longer necessary. You are firmly on the *positive application path* to abundance. You don't just decide from moment to moment where and when these attributes are necessary. When they represent who you are, you *live* responsibly, courageously and with discipline in order to remain in integrity with yourself.

Regarding the attitude path, you can know and fully agree with the concept that kindness, generosity, non-judgment, acceptance, and non-resistance to positive and beneficial outcomes are desirable states, but until you experience yourself *being* kind, *being* generous, *being* non-judgmental, *being* accepting and non-resistant, these are only nice ideas. Being requires us to *live* the attributes and consistently model them to others. Only then are we firmly on the *receptive attitude path* to positive abundance.

Being and knowing are clearly not the same things. We can have encyclopedic knowledge without having wisdom, and we can have wisdom with little-to-no formal education. We move from knowing to being only through experiences that lead to integrated awareness and true clarity.

Most negative emotions (fear, anxiety, anger, frustration, hate, etc.) are a result of lack of information or skills; of not knowing. If we fear our "enemies," it is because we don't know and understand them, or they don't know and understand us, or both. If we fear our future, it is because we don't (and can't) know what the future holds *and* we don't have sufficient faith in ourselves, others and the generative force to believe we can affect our future in positive ways.

We lack faith in ourselves to the degree that we lack awareness of our strengths and capabilities. We lack faith in others to the degree that we lack sufficient knowledge or understanding of them. And this applies to family, friends and co-workers as well as to strangers and enemies.

For example, when we are unable to determine what will inspire irresponsible or dishonest people to greater levels of responsibility and trustworthiness, or when we cannot know what to expect from them, faith in them is diminished whether or not we are familiar with the individual. But, wherever faith is lacking, it is certain that we, they, or both, lack awareness and/or wisdom in some area.

The first right action we each need to take, then, is that of gaining awareness and wisdom—first in our own lives, then in relationships, and finally in the actions and attitudes necessary for getting and staying on the path to abundance.

No one else can know and understand who we are and what we need to have the kind of abundance we desire better than we can. It follows then, that abundance must always begin with self and expand from there.

The people who get on in this world are the people who get up and look for the circumstances they want and, if they don't find them, make them.

George Bernard Shaw

CHAPTER 19

Choose Your Path

Two roads diverged in a wood and I –
I took the one less traveled by, and that
has made all the difference.
Robert Frost

To stay on the path to an abundance of the things you desire, you need to be intimately familiar with how and why energy flows or fails to flow along each potential path. Only then can you know what to adjust to get the outcomes you desire. To keep you tracking, we will revisit the four energy paths and explore means for getting off the wrong paths and staying on the right one.

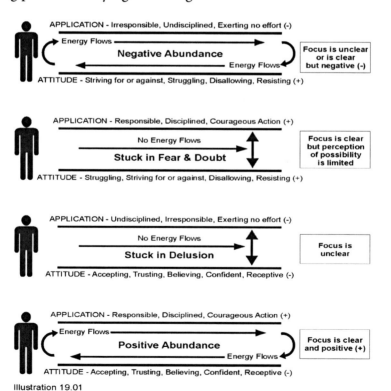

Illustration 19.01

THE PATH TO NEGATIVE ABUNDANCE -
THE IRRESPONSIBLE AND RESISTANT PATH

As before, we will begin our exploration of the four paths with the least desirable one, the path that leads to a lot of things we don't want.

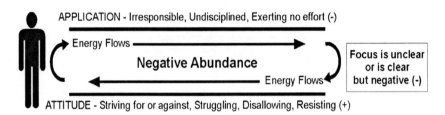

Illustration 19.02

Though this is the path to steer clear of, it is a well traveled road. This is the path traveled by those with a victim mentality combined with resistance to their results. Their lives are heavily punctuated by struggle, worry, fear, frustration, anger and disappointment. When people believe that they have no control over what happens in their life and relationships, on the job, in the country in which they live, or in the world, they seldom try to affect change. They just take the easiest, most expedient route (receptive application – allowing things to happen), while at the same time longing for better outcomes and struggling against the very lack and limitation they are creating (active attitude).

There are millions of people who go to work every day to a job they don't like, for example, mostly because they don't know how to effectively change their circumstance, and don't take the initiative to find out. They come home in the evening so exhausted from a day of what feels like (and may be) hard labor that all they want to do is relax and escape their misery. They turn on the television and watch actors pretending to live the life they wish they could live. The hours pass and they drag themselves to bed only to get up the next day and do the same things all over again. They live for the weekend, but are often so weary by the time it arrives that they can't enjoy it.

A recent Gallop poll (2004) found that 74% of American employees are disengaged from their jobs to some extent. Disengaged employees are those that just show up and do what is required of them. They have no real passion for their job or the work they are contributing to their employer. Often they cannot see how what they are doing is providing anything other than profits to the company they work for, and they are not too motivated by that notion. They remain in the job because they need a paycheck, not because they see any value to the work they are doing. In every case, however, there is some value to the end product or service, or no one would buy it.

An equally high number of people report relationship problems, and the majority of these people are doing the same things in their relationships as unhappy employees are doing on the job, struggling with the discomfort, but not doing anything about it, mostly because they don't know what to do and are not willing to exert the effort to find out.

But relationships are so essential to happiness and a sense of well being, that most people state that they would be willing to try other approaches if they just knew what to do. For those firmly entrenched on the path to negative abundance, this seems to be all talk however. No matter how much help is extended or advice offered, they will typically come up with a thousand reasons why any new approach won't work, but will not actually make any attempt to find out.

When people think they are doing all they can do and the relationship continues to be difficult, the easiest thing to do is blame the other person and that's what most people do. It's much easier to focus on another person's flaws and shortcomings than find solutions, and the people on this path are quick to take the easiest route. They tend to take the position that things would be better if the *other person* would just change. Even if they consider their own part in the drama, they rarely consider taking responsibility for changing the dynamic.

They don't understand that they are fueling the very fire they want to extinguish. People who feel misunderstood or who are belittled or devalued come to resent the one who fails to see value in them. Those who feel understood, seek to understand and come to cherish the one who so honors them. We each decide moment by moment whether we will devalue or cherish, and we each reap the results of our choices.

In every relationship the choices we make have far more to do with us than with the other person. If being right is more important than being kind and loving, we devalue. If being kind and loving is more important than being right, we cherish.

The Law of Abundance always flows in a complete circuit so the energy we send out always returns to us in kind. Those who have good relationships have them because they consistently send good things toward others. Those who have bad relationships have them because they send bad things and, in this case, the sending doesn't have to be consistent. Intermittent negative signals are usually sufficient to cause other people not to trust our intentions toward them.

We instinctively know that those who truly cherish us do so all the time, not just when we are behaving the way they want us to. Those who choose to cherish may not always like what the beloved one does, but where there is cause for disapproval or disappointment, the focus is always on the *action*, not on the individual. We can effectively fix actions, and the Law of Abundance tells us we should, so long as we go about it in a responsible and loving (accepting of the other person) way. We cannot fix *people*, no matter how much we try. And all we get when we do try is resistance, which sets up conditions that *must* lead either to a stalemate, or to more of what we do not want.

Another place where negative abundance is commonly seen is in the area of self-care. It is estimated that 7 in 10 adults in America are overweight (70%), and a high percentage of those are obese. Most people don't exercise regularly or eat right, even though they know they should. Lifestyle diseases, such as type II diabetes and high blood pressure, are rampant and the problems are growing annually. Here, as in other areas of life, when a victim mentality is adopted (it isn't my fault, it's in my genes), we set ourselves up for more of what we do not want, such as more weight and more disease.

At home, in the workplace, physically, mentally, and emotionally, a very large percentage of the population, and indeed of the world, is trudging along this wide path to destruction, and it manifests in myriad ways and along broad spectrums. While some are struggling in jobs they don't like, others are struggling to find a job. While some are greedily struggling to get more and more material wealth, others are struggling with abject poverty. While some are struggling to gain control of their relationships, others are struggling with loneliness. While some are struggling to lose excess weight, others are struggling with starvation.

When we are in a position to make choices, and certainly most adults in developed nations are, the conditions we find ourselves in are almost always those we have created for ourselves or which we have failed to take steps to remedy.

WHAT TO ADJUST TO GET OFF THE PATH TO NEGATIVE ABUNDANCE

This is the most difficult path to remove ourselves from, because on this path, we are misapplying energy in every way. Where we should be taking responsibility for our outcomes and moving toward specific goals, those on this path are taking on the role of victim. Because they see life as out of their control and believe that their only recourse is just to let life happen to them, that's what they typically do.

Where we should be receptive, open to possibility, trusting, believing, non-judgmental, and non-resistant to achieving desired goals, those who are on this path are striving, struggling, fearful, judgmental of self and/or others, doubtful of positive outcomes, resentful, and resistant to change.

Getting off this path is critical on a personal level, in relationships, in communities, nationally and globally. We cannot afford to continue the march down this path. To understand how very essential it is that we remove ourselves from this path as early as possible, take a look at the matrix in Illustration 19.03. It demonstrates the degree of effort necessary to remove ourselves from the path of negative abundance (destruction) and get on the path to positive abundance.

The "birth" designation on the graph can refer to the birth of an individual, a family, a business, a culture or a nation.

The farther down the path to negative abundance an individual, family, business, culture, or nation moves, the greater the effort and the longer it must be sustained to get to positive abundance.

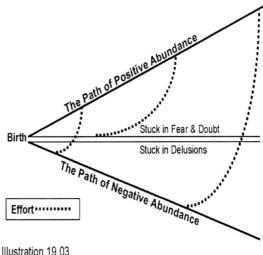

Illustration 19.03

In time, the effort becomes so great that we just don't have the energy to make the necessary corrections. This has likely happened numerous times throughout history, which could be what resulted in the demise of many once great civilizations.

Change is rarely easy, but the sooner we start making adjustments, the shorter our journey to an abundance of the things we want, and the better our odds of sustaining a satisfying and even joyful existence. Once on the path to positive abundance, negative events may cause us to dip toward the negative temporarily. But once there is momentum in the direction of positive abundance, getting back on track is far easier than moving from a less desirable track.

If you are on the negative path, or even one of the stuck paths, be willing to exert the initial effort, knowing that once you have momentum going in the right direction, you will begin experiencing greater abundance. In time, sustaining the momentum will be much easier than dealing with whatever you are experiencing now.

Just as the current of a river assists a rafter who is flowing with the current, and hinders one that paddles upriver against the current, the energy that directs you toward abundance will be activated and will assist you once you create the initial momentum. You will then be flowing with life rather than struggling against it and everything will become easier and more enjoyable.

HERE ARE SOME SPECIFIC STEPS YOU CAN TAKE:

1. **Take responsibility.** The first thing you must do is take responsibility for your own outcomes. All of them—at work, at home, in relationships, physically, mentally, emotionally, and spiritually. Only you can determine your life path and the health of your body, mind, emotions, relationships and finances.

   In relation to your livelihood, only you can decide whether you will find your right work, how rewarding it will be, and the reason it has meaning and significance. You decide because it is never really about the work itself. It's about your attitude toward the work, and whether you see any value in it. You can be completely happy being a janitor or a garbage collector when you are doing your right work and know that what you do contributes in some meaningful way.

   There are garbage collectors, for example, who love the work they do because they know that they are keeping communities clean and safe from garbage borne diseases. They are providing a service that allows the rest of us to be free of worrying about what to do with the tons of garbage we generate—and they get to work outdoors.

   Every job has a purpose or it wouldn't exist. And every single one is honorable and valuable in that it serves a purpose. Rather than looking down on those who are willing to do the really dirty jobs, we should be honoring them. Without their willingness to do those jobs, where would we all be?

   The way you see the work you or anyone else does is all a matter of perspective, and you get to choose your perspective. You also get to choose how your relationships, your health and every other part of your life will unfold provided you take responsibility for it.

   You get to determine how healthy and fit you will be when

you decide whether you will eat wisely, exercise, and take care of yourself, for example because, in spite of what some claim, we are not slaves to our genes. It is actually the other way around. Our genes are slaves, and willingly so, to our visions, and there is a great deal of research to back this up.

In a 1986 paper, for example, Dr. George Solomon and Dr. Rudolph H. Moos of Stanford University School of Medicine reported on a study in which they found that people who are emotionally healthy but predisposed to arthritis are able to divert the disease. On the other hand, those who tend to be anxious, depressed, or suffer some other emotional upset, are at highest risk for the disease.[18]

More recently, Dr. Bruce Lipton, in his book, The Biology of Belief (Elite Books, 2005), presents considerable research that provides strong links between the nature and quality of thoughts and emotions, and overall health. He states, "Epigenetics, which literally translates as 'control above the genes,' is a newly recognized second genetic code that controls the activity and programming of an organism's DNA. This hereditary mechanism reveals how behavior and gene activity are controlled by an organism's perception of its environment. The fundamental difference between the old DNA genetic code and the new epigenetics is that the former notion endorses genetic determinism—the belief that genes predetermine and control our physiological and behavioral traits—while epigenetics recognizes that our perceptions of the environment, including our consciousness, actively control our genes. Through epigenetic mechanisms, applied consciousness can be used to shape our biology and make us masters of our own lives."[19]

The conclusion of many researchers is that the majority of our genes provide possibilities. We determine whether those possibilities are activated, or remain dormant, by the chemicals we release or suppress through our thoughts, feelings, intent, focus and lifestyle.

You alone are responsible for what you think, feel, and believe.

Only you can decide whether you will stay stuck in ignorance or expand yourself by exploring new information. You alone have control over your emotions and your beliefs. You alone can claim or abdicate personal power. You alone decide the quality of your life.

2. **Determine exactly what you want your life to look like.** Once you have taken full responsibility for your life and your outcomes, design the life you want and lay out an exact blueprint. Write out the specifics for how you want to develop yourself, connect with others, make money, and live your life in general. Cut out pictures that match your vision and put them where you will see them often. Be sure to include personal and relationship factors (health, happiness, and general well-being), as well as financial and life-style factors. Include sight, sound, taste, smell, and touch wherever possible. Breathe life into your vision so that it becomes very real for you. Your design needs to be as precise as the design for a perfect product would be. You are, in fact, designing the most important product of all—your life.

3. **Use the checks and balances procedure.** Once you have a clear picture of the life and relationships you want, check the strength and clarity of the vision you have created against the strength and clarity of your current situation. If the current situation appears clearer and has more energy around it, add more details to your vision, and then recheck. Continue using the checks and balances procedure and adjusting until the energy flowing to your new vision is greater than the energy flowing toward the life you now have. Keep adjusting until the life you desire has greater clarity and strength.

4. **Stay open to something different than you have imagined.** When you are open to receiving what you are imagining or something better, you don't get stuck on one possibility and miss opportunities that show up in a form different than you imagined.

5. **Claim it now.** Once you are very clear on what abundance looks like for you, claim it as yours right here and right now. This is an

important step because of how the subconscious mind works. It is very literal in the way it translates things, and as long as you place things away from yourself in time or space, the subconscious mind treats it like a future event and waits until the future arrives. As long as you keep it separated from yourself, it remains in the future, no matter how close it appears. Don't just hold your vision close; own it.

I once heard a man who had a lot of wealth in assets, but little cash flow at the time, state that he was broke (meaning that he had no cash to work with at the time). He then immediately commented with a smile, "But I'm not poor. There's a lot of difference between being broke and being poor."

Indeed there is! Those who feel they are poor, feel powerless and without hope. Those who feel they are only temporarily broke, but have access to wealth, are empowered to change their current condition. This is the mindset I am talking about. Maintain the mindset that, although you can't get your hands on everything you want right now, it is already yours and all you have to do is figure out a way to get to it.

6. **Trust yourself.** There is no one else on earth that is better suited to determining your ideal and making it happen than you. By trusting yourself to make good decisions, or to readily correct bad ones, you will be more open to making good decisions and taking essential risks.

The only way to build complete trust in yourself is to truly know who you are, and to believe that the authentic self you will discover beneath all the negative conditioning is truly amazing.

Remember, the nature of the universe is to be abundant and you came into the world abundantly equipped to be happy, joyous, and completely fulfilled. If you haven't already discovered that part of yourself, all you need to do is uncover it. You don't need to *create* anything. You only need to discover and claim what is already yours.

7. **Seek out others you can trust to help you achieve your goals.** Nothing grand has ever happened without the help and support of a group of dedicated people. We need the help of other people to realize almost any dream, indirectly if not directly. The way to get the support of others is to convey your vision to them with passion and clarity, and show them that you are responsibly doing your part to make the dream come true. Few people are willing to invest much time in those who will not help themselves. The most effective and successful people, those who can really make things happen, usually have very keen antennas for slackers and won't suffer them at all.

Successful people are in the best position to help others succeed, and they are almost always willing to help those who are serious about getting ahead. Unsuccessful people are often willing to rush down any path with perceived promise, and so will be quite willing to jump on your band wagon, but all too often they do so without considering the qualities and capabilities necessary to be successful, so they can waste a lot of your time and energy. Rarely are unsuccessful people in a position to be of any real help.

First, prove yourself worthy of quality help. Then, choose those who are already successful to help you grow your support network. I am not talking about just success in terms of money, either. If your goal is to build healthy relationships, someone with a lot of money, but with poor relationships, would be a poor mentor. If your goal is good health, someone with good relationships and/or a lot of money, but who is in poor health, would be a poor mentor. Fill your network with the people who already have what you want and need, and learn from them. If you can't find a good mentor, a good coach, trained to assist in the area where you need help, can be priceless.

8. **Use the techniques in chapters 26-29** to release any negative energy that may be keeping you stuck or headed down the wrong path.

*No power is strong enough to be lasting
if it labors under the weight of fear.*

Cicero

CHAPTER 20

Stuck In Fear Or Delusion

What if I should fall right through the center of the earth . . . oh, and come out the other side, where people walk upside down.
Lewis Carrol, Alice in Wonderland

STUCK IN FEAR – THE PATH OF TOIL AND STRUGGLE

Most of the people trying to improve their outcomes fall into this category. They work very hard to get ahead, take responsibility for their outcomes and are willing to discipline themselves. They are courageous and caring enough to take the right actions. They continue to learn new ways to move ahead and are willing to try many avenues. They do the work recommended by the experts. They are frequently good, responsible family members, employees, friends, and citizens.

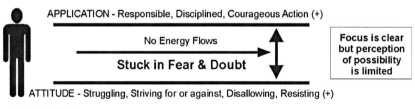

APPLICATION - Responsible, Disciplined, Courageous Action (+)

No Energy Flows

Stuck in Fear & Doubt

Focus is clear but perception of possibility is limited

ATTITUDE - Struggling, Striving for or against, Disallowing, Resisting (+)

Illustration 20.01

The problem for this group is not on the application side of the abundance formula, it is on the *attitude* side. Coupled with all the hard work, positive thinking and good intentions, are fear, doubt, worry, lack of faith in self or in others, and/or lack of faith in a generative force. There is something that prevents this group from having absolute faith that what they desire can be theirs without some degree of striving and hard work on their part.

This notion is one of the legacies from our past, which I alluded to earlier: a legacy from misguided ancestors who were themselves struggling. What they didn't know, and so couldn't teach, is that striving sets up resistance that stops or significantly slows the energy that governs all things and leads to abundance.

Most of the people in this group have moments of faith, acceptance, and non-resistance that allow positive abundance to flow sporadically. These moments usually occur as a result of a spiritual awareness, reading a well-written motivational book, hearing a motivational message, attending a program, or going through some other profound experience that motivates them and gives them a temporary boost.

Interestingly, the term "boost" describes exactly what happens. The feeling that so many describe as a boost is in fact energy that has kicked in, according to the Law of Abundance, and has begun to flow toward positive abundance. Being on that path is always energizing and joyous. Perhaps that's why so many of the people in this group become addicted to self-help products and programs. They love that high. It is a high we are able to maintain only when we are firmly on the path to positive abundance.

Unfortunately, most of the people in this group don't have sufficient insulators in place so the highs disappear as soon as something bad happens in their life, or their attention gets riveted to one of the many troubles and woes around them and in the world at large. The negative influences bring resistance right back up and the flow of energy toward positive abundance comes to a stop. When this occurs, faith in whatever new idea or process the individual was working at is shaken, and because they don't understand why they lost momentum or know what to adjust to get back on track, people in this group often abandon the processes they have begun and move on to something new.

With each new thing that fails, as it must when resistors are keeping the individual stuck in the same place, faith in the prescribed processes, and more critically, faith in self, diminishes further. It is not uncommon for people who have failed to achieve the promised results from the programs they have invested time and money in to believe that the programs are not working because of a personal flaw, but that is rarely the case. Usually, it is simply the misapplication of the Law of Abundance.

WHAT TO ADJUST TO GET OFF THE STUCK-IN-FEAR PATH

If this describes the path you have been on, your primary goal is to make sure you have clarity and energy around what you want and enough faith/trust insulators in place to keep resistance at bay. *Refer to steps 2 – 8 from Chapter 19 (pages 231 – 235).*

STUCK IN DELUSION – THE IRRESPONSIBLE AND RECEPTIVE PATH

This is the path of total abdication of personal power to other people. We abdicate power to organizations that claim to know what is good for us better than we know. Or to "experts" who would try to convince us that their way is the only right way. Or to marketers who tell us who and what we should be so they can sell us more products and services. Or to myriad others that gain their power by stealing ours.

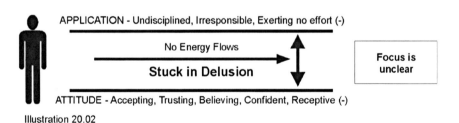

Illustration 20.02

People on this path live under the delusion that they can continue doing what they have always done and get a different result if they just pray enough, or think positively enough, or hope or wish hard enough, or follow the right crowd obediently enough.

Those who fall into this group are taking the easy, undisciplined, irresponsible path, and leaving their outcomes to some external force. They want to lose weight by taking a pill, and get fit by simply joining— but rarely attending—a gym or health club.

They want to gain financial success simply by listening to audio programs or reading a book or magazine article when they feel like it, hoping that other people's successes will rub off on them. They hope that somehow, someday, the right person will come along and tell them how to succeed without a lot of effort on their part. They are sure their prayers, dreams, and positive thinking will eventually deliver them the results they want if they just stay receptive to good things.

This group rarely takes any real responsibility for themselves or their outcomes. They regularly give their power away to other people, to programs, organizations, pills, alcohol and drugs, to the next new fad, to their concept of God, or to anything and everything that can serve as a crutch or an excuse for not taking any personal responsibility.

When those to whom they have given their power fail to deliver, as they often do, the people in this group feel even more helpless and victimized. When they are disappointed often enough, many of them shift their attitude from receptive (-) to one of frustration, anger and resistance (+), and the minute they do, they have set energy in motion toward negative abundance—*more* of what they do not want.

Those who switch to the negative abundance path from this one often become very vocal and angrily express themselves, although usually they are still not willing to take any responsibility for themselves. This manifests as loud protests of "unfair" treatment, and when irresponsible societies listen to these protestations and provide irresponsible complainers with what they bemoan not having, the whole of society takes that trip backwards towards more of what no one wants. The many social programs that give handouts without expecting any responsibility or disciplined action on the part of the recipient are examples of this backward movement.

Anthony Robbins, a well-known motivational trainer and coach, has been preaching personal power for decades. His books, *Personal Power* and *Unleash the Power Within*, are focused on the need for claiming one's own power in order to tap into and realize potential. This is a powerful and important message, yet those in this group rarely do anything with it. Why? Because it takes discipline and responsibility and they are seeking the easiest route. Plus, they are mired in fear, and don't understand what is missing or what to adjust to gain the personal power and abundance they long for. They hear about passion and may think about it, and can even witness it first-hand through high-energy people like Robbins, and some may even try to find it. But most aren't willing to do the work. They may make an attempt or two, but give up before they find their passion.

Those who walk the path of delusion don't yet realize that personal power is possible only from a place of passion, and that passion is possible only from a place of deep self-awareness and commitment to life. They don't realize that hard work and discipline, which they may be resisting or avoiding because it seems distasteful, is only difficult when *passion* is missing. They don't know that if discipline, responsibility and courageous action continue to be difficult, they are on the *wrong path*; a path that will either keep them stuck or actively add to their misery.

Where there is no passion, there is no impetus for applying one's self in a responsible, disciplined way. Where passion is absent, submitting to a life of hard work or avoiding it are the only options. While it is true that shifting from this or one of the other two erroneous paths may initially require tremendous effort, if passion is driving that effort, it still won't feel burdensome or overly difficult. Passion can see people through even extreme difficulties with amazing drive, strength, stamina, and resolve.

WHAT TO ADJUST TO GET OFF THE DELUSIONAL PATH

As with those who are on the path to negative abundance, the first thing you must do if you find yourself on this path is take responsibility for your own outcomes. Begin now to adjust where necessary to ensure that the application and the attitude sides of the abundance formula are leading you to an abundance of the things you want to have. *Refer to steps 1 – 8 from Chapter 19 (pages 231 – 235).*

RECAP OF THE 8 STEPS

1. **Take responsibility for your own outcomes.** You alone are responsible for what you think, feel, believe and do. You alone determine the quality of your life and relationships.

2. **Determine exactly what you want your life to look like.** Be sure to include personal and relationship factors (health, happiness, and general well-being), as well as financial and life-style factors.

3. **Use the checks and balances procedure** to determine how much clarity and energy your new vision has compared to the clarity and energy flowing toward your vision of the life you now have.

4. **Continue to clarify the image of your chosen life and outcomes** until they are clearer and have more energy than the circumstances and outcomes you don't want.

5. **Imagine yourself stepping into your preferred lifestyle** so that you are both surrounded by it and a part of it. Work on this step until abundance is not just a vision of your future, but an integral part of who you are, right here and right now.

6. **Trust yourself** to make good decisions and get good outcomes.

7. **Seek out others you can trust to help you achieve your goals.** Choose wisely as you grow your support network. Fill it with the people who already have what you want and learn from them.

8. **Use the techniques in Chapters 26 – 29** to release any negative energy that may be keeping you stuck or headed down the wrong path.

> *When it is dark enough,*
> *you can see the stars.*
> Ralph Waldo Emerson

CHAPTER 21

Positive Abundance, Joy and Contentment

*We choose our joys and sorrows
long before we experience them.*
Kahlil Gibran

THE NATURAL PATH TO POSITIVE ABUNDANCE

The ideal path, and the one to aspire to, is also the one everything in nature seems to be aligned with and moving toward. Evolution creates conditions that lead to greater and greater fitness. Nature is continually renewing and expanding itself. Our bodies seek health and healing.

Our inner compass is eternally trying to guide us toward happiness and well-being. Human nature is such that those who are healthy and fully functioning are most energized when they are adding to the happiness and well-being of others. All living things depend on symbiotic relationships for survival, which is nature's way of ensuring that all things work well only when working together in harmony.

Those on the path to positive abundance have learned to work with nature perfectly and nature is serving them perfectly, as it always does when allowed to.

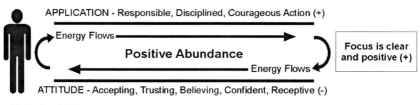

Illustration 21.01

JOY AND CONTENTMENT

If the natural flow of energy is toward positive abundance, then the natural state of life must be one of complete satisfaction, joy, and contentment. These are the feelings which our internal guidance system—that perfect compass—is constantly seeking, and trying to direct us toward.

Somewhere deep in our soul or psyche, we know that life is supposed to be joyous, not laborious. Nose-to-the-grindstone, do as told, put others first may be the messages we often get, but they feel wrong. On the other hand, the freedom to live and work in our own way, call our own shots, and have enjoy the work we do feels so deliciously right.

We resist the first set of directives and seek, or at least long for, the latter. And as we have seen, resistance is not conducive to the natural flow of energy. Where energy is not flowing, a vacuum exists, and life cannot exist in a vacuum.

When we are not experiencing joy and contentment, we can always look at our life and find one or more areas where resistance is high enough that energy is not flowing.

Where such areas exist, it is a sure bet that we are resisting life itself in some way. We withdraw out of fear, distrust, or a lack of understanding. We are not allowing ourselves to be expansive enough, passionate enough, purposeful enough, or loving enough to fully connect with the energy of life. We are allowing the resistors that have built up around certain parts of our life to diminish all of life.

When there are too many areas of resistance, energy is so diminished that people find themselves idly watching life slipping away and bemoaning what they don't have rather than savoring what they do have.

When your primary emotions are those of frustration, anxiety, and/or despair, you can be sure that you are resisting life in some way.

Use this awareness to redirect your energies and keep yourself focused on the path to positive abundance. Choose to be fully alive and joyous, not at some time in the future, but right now.

This seems backwards to those who believe that life can be full and joyous only when they have everything they desire. But before we can experience vigorous health, loving relationships, robust financial conditions, and great happiness, we must first embrace life. The position that life can be embraced only when everything is already good, slows or completely halts the very things that those clinging to this idea are holding out for.

You may be wondering how to embrace life if your life doesn't seem all that great right now. Begin by taking a Life Inventory. I recommend thinking through and then writing down your answers to the following questions. This will take some deep thought and serious self-examination, but the awareness you will come away with will serve you in very powerful ways as you adjust your energies toward a life filled with positive abundance.

INSTRUCTIONS FOR DOING YOUR LIFE INVENTORY

Use Illustration 21.01 as a guide for creating your own form or, if you prefer, you can go online and download the whole set free from the resources section at *wwwtheLawofAbundance.com*.

1. To create a form, take a blank sheet of paper, turn it sideways, and make six columns with columns 1, 3 and 5 being approximately twice as wide as columns 2, 4 and 6.

2. Head the columns "Factor," "Feelings Now," "Positive Change," "R Level," "Solution," and "Feelings Then" (see Illustration 21.01).

3. Make eight copies of this master sheet and head them "Life Inventory – Q1," "Life Inventory – Q2," and so on through "Q8." Each page will represent one of the life inventory questions.

Life Inventory - Q1
What parts of your life are currently diminishing your joy?

	Factor	Feelings Now	Positive Change	R Level	Solution	Feelings Then
1						
2						
3						
4						
5						
6						
7						
8						
9						
10						

Illustration 21.02

LIFE INVENTORY QUESTIONS

1. What parts of your life are currently diminishing your joy? (Examine every part of your life, including home, work, finances, relationships, health, fitness, beliefs, assumptions, expectations, irritants, and so forth.)

2. What parts keep you from being fully content?

3. What parts actively add to your frustrations?

4. What parts are keeping you stuck in a passionless pattern of sameness?

5. What parts are preventing you from enjoying the beauty that surrounds you?

6. What parts are keeping you from loving and being loved on a grand scale? (loving and being loved by more than just immediate family and close friends)

7. What parts are preventing you from feeling deep and sincere gratitude?

8. What parts are short-circuiting your dreams and desires?

CREATING YOUR LIFE INVENTORY

1. Beginning with question 1 and using the Q1 sheet, enter into the first column each of the factors you identify as you ponder the question. Say, for example, that when you pondered the first question ("What parts of your life are currently diminishing your joy?"), your answers were long hours commuting to a job I don't like, the job itself, growing household clutter, and no time for family, friends or self. In this case, you have identified six factors that are diminishing your joy: (1) the long commute, (2) the job you now have, (3) growing household clutter, (4) too little time with your family, (5) too little time for friends, and (6) too little time for self. All identified factors for question 1 are listed in the "Factor" column on the Q1 worksheet.

2. In the second column, record what your feelings are now in relation to each of the factors you have identified, and record them in the "Feelings Now" column. The related emotions might fall under various categories such as fear, frustration, anger, disappointment, sadness, or worry.

3. Once you have identified the emotional impact of each factor, determine what has to happen to correct the condition such that you will feel better about your results. Record this in the third column labeled "Positive Change."

Once you have identified the changes necessary, rate your resistance to doing what needs to be done (actually taking the steps to make the changes) on a scale of 0 to 5, with 0 being no resistance at all and 5 being extreme resistance. Record your rating in the "R Level" column ("R" is for resistance).

If your resistance level is high, find ways to remove the resistance when the task cannot be delegated to others. When it can be delegated, find someone else to do this task for you. Be sure to find someone who loves doing what you are resisting. If you don't have friends or family members who are happy to help, and are easily able to do so, be willing to hire someone. The money you spend to hire the work out will come back to you many times over when you are using your energies in accordance with the Law of Abundance.

Remember: when you are forcing yourself to do things to which you are resistant, you are slowing or stopping your progress toward your desired goals. But if you have put an item on your list, it must be dealt with. To ignore or avoid it is irresponsible, which also slows or stops your progress.

4. Once you come up with the best, most non-resistant way to correct the situation, record that in the "Solution" column.

5. Finally, imagine what your life would be like once the solution has been applied and the problem solved, and how you will feel when the solutions have been implemented. Note the feeling in the "Feelings Then" column again using the 0 to 5 scale (no resistant to extreme resistance).

Repeat this process for each of the eight questions. If you need more space than one "Q" sheet will accommodate, make as many copies of each as you need so you have plenty of room to record your observations.

From the identified factors in the examples I gave earlier, let's take item 3 from Q1 (growing household clutter) and walk through the rest of the Life Inventory process. Say the feelings related to household clutter are frustration and a growing sense of despair so you decide that what has to happen is for the clutter to go away. But when you rate your resistance to doing the work yourself, you find it is a 4, and maybe a 5 (which is why it hasn't been done up to now). In this case, you will need to either get creative and find a way to eliminate the clutter without doing it yourself, or you will have to find some way to make doing the work more fun and appealing.

Say you decide to try to make the chore more interesting by creating a contest for yourself in which you guess how long it will take you to completely eliminate the clutter if you work on it for one hour a week. In this self-contest, you decide you will mark the "end of clutter" day on your calendar and put yourself to the test to see how close you come to your estimate. You decide you will devote one hour per week (the whole hour at once, ten minutes a day for six days, or whatever works for you) to meeting the goal. The contest is to see how close you come, devoting one hour per week, to your estimated "end of clutter" date.

If, in imagining yourself in the described contest, your "Feelings Now" check revealed that resistance was still high, you would need to find another alternative and check the feelings around that one. For the best result, you will want to keep looking until you find an option with relatively low, and preferably no, resistance around it.

DON'T TRY TO DO IT ALL

As you look for ways to alter your current path, realize that you need not handle everything you uncover yourself. In fact, many of the things that will need attending to should not be handled by you personally. If anticipating the task sets up resistance and you can't find a way around it, doing the work yourself will only increase the resistance further.

Responsibility does *not* mean always doing the activities yourself. Sometimes it is finding a way to have someone else do the work. Your role is simply to ensure that the job is done by someone who *enjoys* it and is therefore *non-resistant* to that kind of work. When you have that person, they are highly likely to do a good job, provided you give them good instructions.

If hiring someone else seems to be the best option, but you feel resistance around hiring the job out, you may need to add "lack of trust in self" and/or "lack of trust in others" to your "Factor" column. If you are resistant to hiring out a high-resistance job, you either don't trust yourself to be able to generate the money to pay someone else, don't believe you have the ability to find the right person, or you don't trust other people enough to believe that there is someone out there that can do the job to your satisfaction.

Staying with the clutter example, you may not yet realize that allowing the clutter to remain, *and* your efforts to try to eliminate it yourself, are *both* draining away your energies and sabotaging joy and contentment. If you are resistant to the clutter *and* resistant to the task of clearing it out, you have an energy drain on both sides of the equation.

As energy continues to be depleted by the clutter, your irritation with it and your resistance to the task increases, and the ability to eliminate the clutter diminishes along with the energy. You are slowly, or perhaps quickly, spiraling toward *more* of what you do not want.

Now, imagine that you didn't have the condition that is draining your energy (in this example, the clutter). How would you feel if this condition was corrected and your environment was neat and orderly?

You are tapping into your flawlessly accurate compass when you attend to your feelings in relation to what is happening in your life. Notice how quickly your feelings shift upward toward the positive once you have let go of the things you are now resisting.

Once the feelings shift upward, notice what happens with the energy in your body and in your life. Your mind will feel more alert, your body will feel more energized, and you will be able to sustain the high energy for longer periods. You will smile a lot more because you will regularly feel joyous. You will notice the beauty in the world around you more. You will like people—all people—more because you will have given up harshly judging yourself and them. Life will take on new meaning and all that great energy will begin to manifest in wonderfully positive ways.

Once you have done your Life Inventory, answer three more questions:

1. What parts of your life bring you great joy?
2. What do you have right now that you are truly grateful for?
3. How clearly do you see and completely own your idea of positive abundance *right now?*

The first eight questions are for discovering what is preventing you from having all you want in life. Work through these and then release them.

The last three questions are for discovering what you already have. These are the ones to hold onto, focus upon and grow from.

Remember: *We manifest what we give energy to.* Be sure that what you have, are grateful for, and desire, receive more energy than what you want to eliminate and what you think you are lacking.

> *Our ultimate freedom*
> *is the right and the power*
> *to decide how anybody or anything*
> *outside ourselves will affect us.*
>
> Stephen Covey

All the genius I have lies in this;
when I have a subject in hand,
I study it profoundly.
Day and night it is before me.
My mind becomes pervaded with it.
Then the effort that I have made
is what people are pleased to call
the fruit of genius.
The fruit is the labor and thought.

Alexander Hamilton

CHAPTER 22

Genius

Genius is the power to labor better and more availably.
Deserve your genius: Exalt it.
Ralph Waldo Emerson

For years, it has been my contention that every normally functioning human being has at least one area of genius. Understanding the Law of Abundance just deepens that conviction.

Albert Einstein suggested that most people use less than 10% of their brain, and there is a great deal of evidence to suggest that is true. But even at 10%, the human brain is more powerful than the most powerful computer on earth today; a fact that I find awe-inspiring.

I have always been awed by the abilities of the human mind, and that awe increased tenfold when I put a team of programmers to work in 2000 trying to computerize a system my team and I developed for discovering the authentic nature of people. After more than two years of attempts to computerize it, various programmers informed us that the system was too complex to be fully computerized. They told us that what we were trying to get a computer to accomplish required a level of artificial intelligence that was not yet available, and may never be available as far as any of them knew.

Computers, with all their computing power, could not effectively interpret the results. Yet we are able to take a group of people and teach them how to see the relationships between the various parts, detect the patterns and interpret the results in as little as 24 hours. And once they understand how the system works and can see the patterns that emerge, their brains have the capacity to see and interpret thousands of pattern variations in nanoseconds.

They don't have to be top college professors or Mensa candidates either. They can be just ordinary people with an extraordinary passion for the work they do and the willingness to seek out and learn the most effective ways to do it. Those who excel have a genuine desire to transform people's lives, and apparently, that is all that's necessary for the typical human brain to outperform the biggest and best computers.

Genius, it appears, is really just *focused passion meeting up with a natural inclination or ability.* When natural ability is paired with a clear and passionately desired goal, an abundance of energy flows in the direction of that goal and amazing things become possible. When passion is driving actions and natural abilities are allowing them to occur with ease, there is a lot of natural motivation and no resistance to doing the work that must be done to realize the goal.

When Thomas Edison stated that genius is "ten percent inspiration and ninety percent perspiration," he was surely alluding to this totally non-resistant, passion-driven type of "perspiration." He stayed in his lab for days at a time poring over experiments, not because he had to, but because he was driven to by his own passions to perservere.

There are those, such as child prodigies, who are born with such pronounced abilities that they find their genius very early in life, but they are very rare. Most genius appears to develop around a passion we have discovered in the course of living our lives, such as was the case for Edison, Einstein and most of the other geniuses we read about.

When genius appears is not what's important. *How* it appears is what you want to be focused upon. If your particular genius has not yet emerged, you can speed the realization of it by understanding that genius appears as a result of aligning passion and natural ability, and purposefully working toward alignment.

Newton and Einstein are examples of the purposeful alignment of passion and ability. Both are considered geniuses, but both found genius as adults. Apparently, neither was remarkable as a child. In fact, it is said that Einstein didn't even talk until he was three and is reported to have been inept at some of the most basic things throughout his life.

What Newton and Einstein had in common was a great passion around understanding the physical world, combined with natural mathematical and problem-solving abilities. Their passion to know (receptiveness to discovery) and their willingness to learn (responsible, disciplined action) set into motion the Law of Abundance, and both received an abundance of knowledge of the exact kind they were seeking.

Thomas Edison did the same thing in a different arena. In his case, the passion was to understand electricity and to harness it in useful ways. He is said to have tried thousands of experiments before he found the formula that resulted in the light bulb. That is disciplined action! He eventually received patents on 1,093 different products and literally changed the history of mankind. Like Newton and Einstein, Edison found genius in the areas where he had a burning passion, but was not especially remarkable in other areas of his life.

Bill Gates had a passion for technology, and a strong desire to take what he knew about operating systems and do something really big with it. He set the Law of Abundance in motion and certainly met his goal. Not only did he manage to do something really big around operating systems, he went on to become the wealthiest self-made man on the planet at this writing. Bill Gates is a technical genius to be sure, but more than that, he is a team building and marketing genius. There are probably many people who have technical skills equal to or perhaps greater than those of Gates, but they sure don't know how to leverage those skills in quite the way he has.

Mahatma Gandhi, Mother Teresa, and Martin Luther King had a still different kind of genius. Their genius came from passion for serving humankind, protecting those who had fallen victim to corrupted power or to the harsh realities of life. Theirs was a spiritual genius.

Genius comes in all kinds of packages. Plato and Socrates were philosophical geniuses. Helen Keller, who was left deaf and blind due to an illness she suffered as a toddler, developed genius around communication in spite of her considerable limitations. Babe Ruth was an athletic genius. Mark Twain, Will Rogers, and Bob Hope were geniuses of humor. Warren Buffett is a financial genius, and Oprah Winfrey is a genius at connecting with and inspiring people.

All really great people—those who get and keep our attention—have genius in some area, and every single one of them has tapped into an ability with a passion that allowed each of them to open the flood gates of abundance.

Far too many of us leave great talents untapped for one reason or another, barely allowing even a small trickle of genius to appear, much less opening floodgates. Sometimes fear is the culprit. Sometimes we undervalue our talents because they come too easily. Sometimes we are too distracted or are scattering ourselves too thin. Sometimes circumstances temporarily prevent people from developing their talents, but there are ways around almost all circumstances if we choose to find them. Mostly, we fail to develop our genius out of lack of awareness or fear.

When fear is the factor, it is generally because we lack sufficient faith. It can be lack of faith in self, others, or the generative force, but it usually begins with and remains centered around self. That's because self-mastery is essential to healthy development. If we fail to develop ourselves adequately, it is hard to trust our own ability to succeed in ways that allow us to claim our genius.

Those who undervalue talents because they come too easily, often do so because they erroneously believe that to have value, they must work and that work has to be hard. They reason that, if it's fun, it can't be work and, if it isn't work, it doesn't count toward value. Yet it is exactly here, in natural talents, that true genius lies. And the easier the talents and abilities come, the more energy we have to expend in that pursuit.

Some people have multiple talents and think they have to choose between them. That might be true if an individual had dozens of natural talents that were unrelated, but that is almost never the case. Most people have only two or three talents, and generally, they are in some way related. When they aren't, there is almost always a way to combine them into one great pursuit.

I have a son who has natural abilities and a real genius around technology. He also has an intense interest in inventing new things. Clearly, these work together. Another son has natural art talent. He is an amazing artist, but also has an intense interest in and genius around biology. These two talents seem unrelated, but he can and does use his art talents to create scientific illustrations. He could also use his artistic talents to create documentaries around his passion for animals and nature, or produce wildlife paintings that capture the beauty of biology on canvas.

STRENGTH OF CHARACTER

When circumstances that make it difficult to tap into natural talents are the factor, strength of character becomes the defining difference. Some people manage to rise above adversity and develop their talents in spite of everything, and those who do often rise far above the crowd and become quite remarkable human beings. American author, activist and lecturer, Helen Keller, who was both deaf and blind, and French Journalist Jean-Dominique Bauby, who wrote *The Diving Bell and the Butterfly* by blinking his left eye, the only part of his body that functioned after he was paralyzed by a stroke, are examples.

Others allow their circumstances to defeat them, and when that occurs, the defeat is very bitter. for example, I know of one young man who had outstanding athletic abilities. He was an exceptional football player who could easily have made it into the world of the pros, but his family was poor and could not afford to buy the football gear he needed to play on the high school team. Further, his prideful and controlling father would not allow others to help. The boy could see no way to overcome this circumstance and began masking his frustrations with drugs. He was young and had not yet developed the strength of character he needed to rise above his circumstances.

He was able to raise money as it turns out and could have used that skill to buy the football gear he needed. Instead, he chose to use it to feed his drug habit. Eventually, he began dealing drugs and before long, the promising young athlete was nothing more than a strung out drug dealer.

Finding the best way out of difficult circumstances does not take genius. What it takes is faith in one's self. Until we have that, all the potential we have inside us remains hidden, and like an unplanted seed, it sits waiting for the conditions that will allow it to emerge.

Give your own genius the environment it needs to emerge and it *will* emerge. We all have at least one area of genius—at least one seed that, given the right conditions, will grow into an amazing and wonderful gift. You are no exception.

Within every little acorn lies the potential
for a million great forests.
Imagine what lies within the human mind!

CHAPTER 23

Values, Energy and Time

Do you love life? Then do not squander time,
for that is the stuff life is made of.
Benjamin Franklin

Clear goals are an essential part of the abundance formula and we each have to do this work for ourselves. No one else can do it for us because no one else knows our inner-most needs. Sometimes we don't consciously know either, but in the depths of our subconscious mind reside our truth, our purpose and our passion, and only we can plumb those depths.

Few people will stick with goals, no matter how profitable or high-minded they may seem, if the goals are not aligned with their passion and values. Yet, scattering energies and wasting time doing things that don't mesh with values is all too common because so many fail to plumb those depths and examine their needs and wants.

The great philosopher, Socrates, observed that, "an unexamined life is not worth living." It can certainly seem that way. An unexamined life is often be one of pain, sorrow, and a rash of seemingly endless difficulties. When we don't know who we are or what we value; when we squander a lot of time and energy on things that don't really matter and that are not leading us toward the things we desire, life becomes a daily struggle and many find themselves continually losing ground. Yet that dynamic can shift, and sometimes quite quickly, when we take the time to examine our lives and align our values with the way we are spending our energy and our time.

Even those who don't yet know where their passions lie often do know, or can easily discover, what they value. And since being aligned with our values can release energy and free up time for discovering our passion, taking the time to align with our values is very much worth the energy and time it takes.

When people lay out their values and their energy and time expenditures side by side, many are very surprised to see how much of what they are doing is not in alignment with their values. They are equally surprised at how much happier, more dedicated to goal achievement, and more effective they become once they have done the work to become aligned.

Bringing your energy and time into alignment with your values and passions is what this chapter is about. This may take some time, but doing this exercise will greatly increase your odds of discovering and developing goals that are truly meaningful and which will lead you to abundance on your own terms.

VALUES TO ENERGY AND TIME EXPENDITURE (VET SCALE)

The VET scale is like a sleek, powerful "Vette"—as in Corvette. Learn how to keep it fine-tuned and take good care of it, and it will get you anywhere you want to go in style. This exercise is designed to help you get the most from your VET—values, energy and time.

Using 100 as a measure of your total values, and 100 as your total energy and time availability, rate each factor on the scales below. The "Values" scale is the value you place on each area of your life. The "Energy & Time" scale is the average amount of energy and time you are spending on each area.

- **Career/Financial** includes anything and everything you actually do (energy/time expenditure) or desire to do (value) in pursuit of career development, meeting financial obligations, investing for your future, or amassing financial wealth.

- **Family** includes anything and everything you do (energy/time expenditure) or desire to do (value) to directly care for your family, spend time with them, and build healthy relationships. This includes spouse, children, parents, siblings, grandparents, and any other family members that are important to you.

- **Friends/Social/Leisure** includes anything and everything you do (energy/time expenditure) or desire to do (value) with friends and acquaintances, and everything you do or desire to do for fun, including activities such as travel, hobbies, movies, and reading.

- **Spiritual/Community** includes all the things you do with your energy and time, or desire to do (value) to develop or express spirituality, and to make a difference in the world, beyond family and friends.

- **Health/Fitness** includes anything and everything you do (energy/time expenditure) or desire to do (value) to stay healthy and fit physically, mentally and emotionally, including watching your diet, exercising, improving your education, improving coping skills, etc.

In this exercise, you have a total of 100 points and you must divide that total between all five categories. If you spend 50% of your energy on career/financial, for example, and 10% on family, your actual energy/time expenditure totals 60% for these two areas and you have 40% left for the other three categories. But say you would like to spend 35% on career/financial and 40% on family.

In this case, your values would have you allocating 75% of your 100% total to the two scales (35% career/financial, plus 40% family), leaving 25% to be allocated to the other three categories. Your first two scales would look like the sample in Illustration 23.01.

Notice that the energy and time (E/T) spent on the family and career/financial categories do not currently match values. Career/financial is getting 15% more time than you would prefer to give that category, and family is getting 30% less. If you shift 15% from the career/financial category to family, you still have a deficit of 15% for family, so you would still need to pull some energy and time from some of the other three categories. Or you could find ways to combine more than one value into an E/T expenditure.

Career/Financial

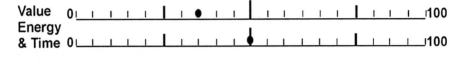

Family

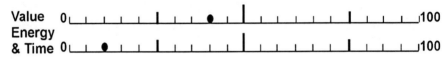

Illustration 23.01

Say you discover that you are spending 20% of your E/T watching television (the friends/social/leisure scale). In that case, finding the energy and time to devote to family might be as easy as deciding to invest only 5% of your E/T watching television. However, if you were spending only 5% of your time on leisure activities, you probably would not want to pull much, if any, E/T from that category. You would then have to find other places to get the E/T. By being creative, you could increase your E/T to values ratio so that you have what appears to be more than 100% of energy and time available, thereby getting more of everything.

For instance, you could involve your entire family in fun ways to stay fit and healthy. In this way, you are combining family, fitness, and fun. If that pursuit takes up 10% of your E/T and you are meeting three values, you have in effect tripled your E/T in relation to meeting your values needs. That's exactly what people who seem to get lots of things done are doing.

In working through the energy/time to values assessment years ago, I realized that the E/T I wanted to devote to the areas in which I placed high values exceeded my 100% allotment. I have very high family values, but also love my work, which feeds one of my Spiritual/

Community values; changing people's lives in profound and positive ways.

When I began looking for ways to combine values so I could have more and still keep my values aligned, I discovered that much of the work I was doing didn't improve people's lives in a way that was consistent with what I valued. I had spent many years designing and presenting workshops mostly because organizations saw value in them and would pay for them. These programs were more focused on helping organizations improve their bottom line results than on positively impacting the lives of the people in the organizations, though that was always the underlying intent. Also, about 60% of the E/T I was investing in my work was spent on things I really didn't enjoy. I came to realize that I was using valuable resources in the wrong way in my work, which was actually draining my energy and robbing me of the time that I wanted and needed for other things.

Besides high family, work and spiritual/community values, I place high value on staying healthy and physically fit. With all of these holding important value positions, I discovered that the E/T I needed to accomplish everything just wasn't there. I solved that dilemma by bringing my family into my business and re-focusing my work to ensure that I was truly impacting lives. By combining my work and my passion for changing people's lives with family time, I can now meet three needs simultaneously. I exercise with my husband every day so I am spending time with him as I am taking steps to keep myself (and him) fit.

By examining what I valued and how I allocated my E/T to those values, I was able to see where I was coming up short and found ways to meet multiple values simultaneously. The effect is that I now get the equivalent of 200% out of my E/T allotment, which allows me to have more of the things I value.

As values go, you really can have it all if you can find creative ways to combine them so you are managing your energy and time wisely and getting more from it. The place to begin is with an honest evaluation of how you are currently spending your energy and time in relation to your values. Once you have done that, start getting creative and see how you can fine-tune your VET to get the most from your life.

Once you discover ways to work smarter, rather than harder, you will find you get a lot more from your life and with a lot less effort and a lot more enjoyment. You may not be able get everything perfectly aligned right now, but you can begin making adjustments in that direction so your values support your goals and promote the life you long for. Use the Values Scale below (Illustration 23.02) to complete this exercise, or you can download a worksheet at *www.theLawofAbundance.com* resources section.

VALUES TO ENERGY/TIME (VET) SCALE

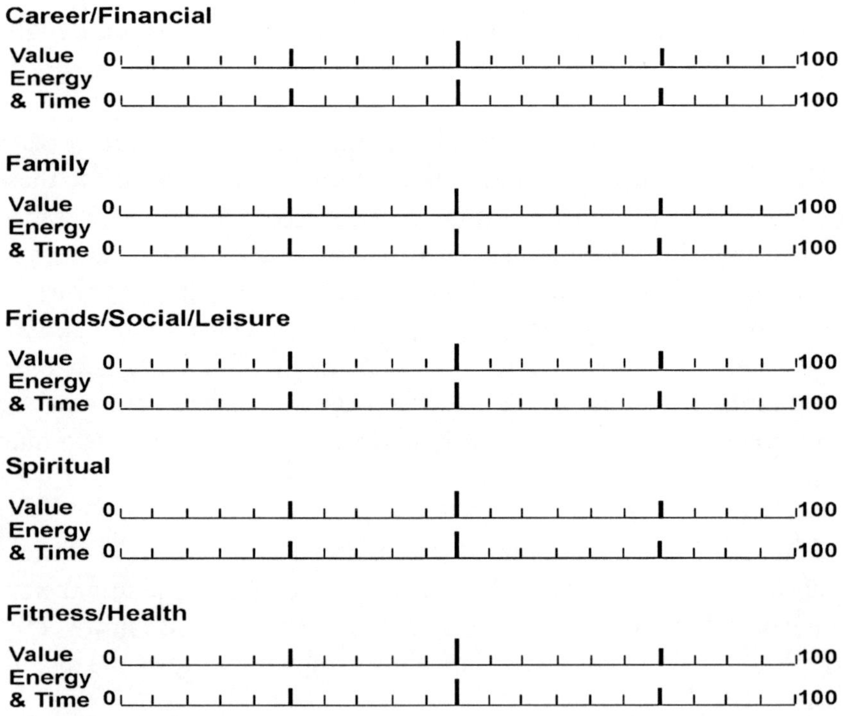

Career/Financial

Value   0 |_____| 100
Energy
& Time 0 |_____| 100

Family

Value   0 |_____| 100
Energy
& Time 0 |_____| 100

Friends/Social/Leisure

Value   0 |_____| 100
Energy
& Time 0 |_____| 100

Spiritual

Value   0 |_____| 100
Energy
& Time 0 |_____| 100

Fitness/Health

Value   0 |_____| 100
Energy
& Time 0 |_____| 100

Illustration 23.02

Now that you have an idea of what you must do to get your VET tuned up and running smoothly, it's time to discover your passion.

CHAPTER 24

Finding Your Passion

Perhaps the most important vision of all is to develop a sense of self, a sense of your own destiny, a sense of your unique mission and role in life, a sense of purpose and meaning.
Dr. Stephen R. Covey

We all came into this world with a particular set of skills, abilities, strengths, and inclinations. When we are working with these natural attributes, rather than against them, life flows beautifully. When we have also identified our true passion and begun living it, our energy levels skyrocket, and we move very rapidly toward our goals and dreams. We quickly become very effective at the things that are natural to our passion, and experience more regular successes. We are happy, content, and very satisfied with who we are and we feel in control of where our life is headed.

One of the most important quests of your life is that of discovering your true passion and finding ways to begin living in accordance with it. If you did the exercise in the last chapter, you have already taken the essential step of discovering what you must do to align your energy and time with your values. Following are some other things you can do to help you open the floodgates to your own special passion and the genius that lies within it.

FIND A WORKABLE MODEL

One of the fastest ways to develop anything is to find an effective model and use it to guide our growth. Effective modeling is not taking what others are doing and duplicating it. It is taking what we need from a working model and modifying it so that we end up with our own unique model.

Sometimes, what will prove to be our best model doesn't come from another person. It is already ours, and we just don't realize it. Many of us have at least one area of our lives that is working for us. That area can serve as a model for other areas if we take note of what we are doing right and simply recreate it.

Often the areas of great effectiveness are so easy to sustain that we don't recognize them as a model. There is a natural passion for this area and a natural drive toward it. Take gardening, for example. Many people who could easily afford a gardener, do the work themselves because they love it. Gardening is hard work, but to avid gardeners, it is not work at all. It's pure pleasure. They describe gardening as joyful— as a way to release tension, or as a creative endeavor that results in beauty and further adds to their enjoyment. They never describe all that disciplined work as drudgery.

If there is something you do just because you love doing it, imagine yourself doing that thing, and notice the degree of non-resistance in relation to it. Notice how easy it is to be responsible, disciplined, and perhaps even courageous (as in parenting and protecting your child). Notice how effortless it is to accomplish the goals you set for yourself in this area. Then take what you discover and apply it to the other important areas of your life.

FIND THE PURPOSE BEHIND THE ACTIONS

Sometimes, as we examine our life and activities, we realize that there are things we don't necessarily have passion around or enjoy doing, that nonetheless have to be done, and only we can do them. When this is the case, obviously we cannot give up doing these tasks. What we must give up, then, is the resistance to doing them. We do that by shifting our focus from the tasks to the *reasons* for doing them.

Everything we do serves a purpose or we wouldn't do it. If you can't love the task, love the purpose behind it. Love the result you get from doing the task and keep yourself focused on the purpose or the potential result. For example, no loving parent enjoys changing dirty diapers, but they do it almost always without resistance, because they are focused not on the diapers, but on the comfort and well-being of their child.

Likewise, there are unskilled laborers who don't especially enjoy the hard work they are doing, but find joy in the fact that the work provides for their needs or allows them to care for their family and secure their future. They can smile as they labor because they are not focused on the work. They are focused on what they value and on the fact that the work helps them sustain those values.

If the purpose for continuing an activity is positive, and we focus on that purpose, the energy we generate receives a boost on the active application path (+). Resistance is also lessened, which increases receptivity on the attitude path (-). The result is an upward spiral toward positive abundance. The work gets easier and we get more of what we want.

If the purpose is negative, or if we focus on the negative aspects of the task, the energy we generate is then negative (-) which acts as a resistor on the application path. It also adds greater resistance to the attitude path (+). The result is a downward spiral toward negative abundance. In this case, the work seems harder and we get more of what we do not want.

Where you cannot alter your actions so that you have passion around the task, alter your focus so that you have passion around the reason for the task.

EXPLORE ENJOYMENT

A good place to start in your search for your true passion is to make a list of the things you *really* enjoy, and/or that you are naturally good at. Here are some specific steps to discovering your passion:

1. Start by listing the things you are good at and enjoy doing. Do not include things you have been trained to do, but don't necessarily enjoy. There is a big difference between the things you know how to do, and the things which bring you joy and energize you. List only the enjoyable things.

2. Next make a separate list of the things you aren't all that good at, but which you do, or would like to do, just for fun.

3. Go through the two lists once you have generated them and asterisk the items that you believe have the potential to produce income.

4. Now compare the two lists and see if there is some commonality between them. Your great passion exists somewhere within that commonality. Pay special attention to common items on both lists that you have placed an asterisk by. These suggest a passion around which you can earn a good living.

5. Once you have the list of things you are interested in, enjoy, and at which you are naturally good, use these to create a third list of ways you might use them to make your life meaningful. Assume as you build the list that money is no object, the opinions of others would be just as favorable and you would be equally loved and respected in any of the roles you choose. Be as specific as possible. Stating that you want to make a difference in people's lives, for example, is too general. Say exactly how you envision making a difference. Use my example below as a guide to how specific you will need to be in the beginning. You can add more details as you refine and clarify your vision.

HERE IS MY STATEMENT:

For me, making a difference means setting people free to live life fully and joyously. I do that by helping them to discover what is causing them mental and emotional pain (quiet desperation), and by using specific tools and processes to eliminate the causes fast. The fast part is important for me because I want to positively impact as many lives as possible as effectively and efficiently as possible. I want the people I help to be free of the things that limit their happiness quickly so they are living the life they love as soon as possible. I want to make such a difference in the lives and outcomes of the people I work with that they are fully free and capable of affecting their own great outcomes in a very short period of time. The tools and methods I use either already exist or I create them. Everything I do and every tool I use must lead to rapid, positive change, and no tool or method can create resistance by being difficult to implement or sustain. In a capsule, the tools and methods I use must lead to healthy self-reliance and personal effectiveness rapidly and create as little resistance as possible in the people utilizing them.

Although a beginning statement like this needs more clarity, it is specific enough to provide criteria for what you will adopt or reject as you develop your mission. In my case, I didn't know up front what the tools and methods would be. I just knew they had to be fast and highly effective. If they weren't, they got tossed and I kept searching until I found or created the tools and techniques that filled the bill.

I had no idea that the tools and techniques I searched out or created aligned with the Law of Abundance when I developed or adopted them. I didn't even know the Law of Abundance existed. But as the law unfolded, I began examining my work and found that everything I do leads people toward responsible, disciplined actions that occur naturally and without resistance through setting natural energies free and directing them toward natural passions. Though I didn't know exactly how my vision would manifest in the beginning, I knew exactly what to head toward and what to avoid. That was enough to start energy flowing in the right direction and ensure that I would arrive at the exact place I intended.

MAKE IT PRESENT TENSE, POWERFUL AND YOURS

When I created my initial outline for what my life's mission must look like, I took ownership of that result then and there. Nothing else would do. Although the means for achieving the goal was not yet clear,

I could clearly see what that reality looked like and claimed it for myself and for every person whose life that goal would positively impact.

Clarity and ownership are crucial first steps, and ownership is always in the here and now. If you lack clarity and are not sure where you are headed, there will be caution and even fear in moving forward. If you can see the goal, but haven't taken ownership of it, you aren't likely to take action because you won't be convinced that the action will bear fruit that *you* can enjoy.

It would be like knowing that what you want is bushels of apples and then deciding that the only place to plant an orchard is on a farm that isn't yours and to which you believe you will not have future access. Even though your goal is to have apples and you know that, if you don't think your work would yield you that outcome, you aren't likely to put in the effort.

All achievement works just that way. As long as ownership remains out of reach or in the future, your subconscious mind will put off taking any serious actions and you will feel no urgency to begin taking the steps toward the goal no matter how clearly you can imagine the outcome. That's why positive affirmations which you haven't bought into 100% don't work. You can repeat them from now until the day you die and they will be little more than distractions. Only those you take full ownership of will move your subconscious mind, and then you, to take action.

Try writing out statements about your passions in present tense, then go back and read each one. Notice how you are feeling as you do, and note your feelings in the margins of each statement. Because they are written in present tense, your subconscious mind will respond to them emotionally as though they are already real and will report back to you the level of interest generated by the statement. If the statement agrees with what the subconscious mind knows to be a passion for you, the feedback will be positive feelings. You will feel energized, hopeful, excited and ready to get started.

If the statement does not reflect your true passions, the feelings will be less positive. You may be aware of feelings like caution, concern, doubt or resistance if the statement is pointing to a path that is wrong for you.

Using the notes you have made in the margins next to each statement, rank the statements from the most positive response to least positive. You now have some very clear indicators as to what your passions may be, and which ones hold the most power for you. Act on the most appealing ones and you are on your way to greater abundance.

ABUNDANCE IS WHATEVER BRINGS YOU JOY AND SATISFACTION

Abundance doesn't have to result in the manifestation of something physical, although you generally have some physical result from it. You can have an abundance of love for example, and while love is not physical, your body's response to it is. Research has proven conclusively that being in healthy, loving relationships boosts the immune system, reduces the likelihood of many diseases—including heart attack—and increases longevity.

You can have an abundance of fun, which is not physical either, but it certainly has physical benefits. So, as you search for effective models, look for areas of your life that are non-physical as well as physical. Don't narrow your search to just physical abundance.

Although many people equate abundance with material wealth, that isn't what abundance really is. It can certainly include a lot of money and material wealth if that is what makes you happy, but there are a lot of people in the world who don't have material wealth, yet feel that their lives are abundant. We can have an abundance of love and an abundance of freedom to spend time doing what we enjoy, but very little in the way of material wealth, and be completely happy and content. Ultimately, it is happiness, contentment, and a deep sense of satisfaction that are the true measures of abundance.

My own experience about all the blessings in my life is that the more I give away, the more that comes back. That is the way life works, and that is the way energy works.

Ken Blanchard

CHAPTER 25

Stewardship

*We did not weave the web of life; we are
merely a strand in it. Whatever we do
to the web, we do to ourselves.*
Chief Seattle

Because abundance cannot exist outside of the collective, and because only humans have the ability to purposefully direct energy, there is no question that we must accept the role of stewards of Planet Earth.

We live in a physical world where every action impacts something, or someone, in some way. Just as a pebble thrown into a pond impacts the entire pond, our actions have an impact on others, and through others, on the world as a whole. Most people don't pay much attention to the impact of negative actions unless they result in something tragic. A deranged leader slaughters millions of people, as did Hitler. A group of young men with twisted thinking fly airplanes into buildings killing thousands, as happened at the World Trade Center in New York on September 11, 2001. A mother drives her car into a lake killing her young children, as did Susan Smith in 1994. These things get our attention. But our collective actions, benign as many of them seem, are wreaking havoc on entire populations, nations, and the planet as a whole, and many are oblivious to that fact.

At the rate we are going, it may take centuries for humankind to figure out that we are responsible for more than just our own private experiences. This planet can sustain us and continue to provide abundantly only if we change our destructive behaviors and begin taking care of the world and one another. If we continue to consume and destroy faster than we create, we will surely destroy ourselves if not the planet.

"But wait!" some will protest. "Isn't this a book about a law that guarantees abundance? A dead species or a destroyed planet isn't very abundant!" True. But, as you may recall, the law is non-selective. It operates through energy, which exists in abundance and will continue to exist long after our species and Planet Earth has disappeared because energy cannot be destroyed. But the forms it takes can certainly change.

The law serves us to whatever extent we allow it to, but only to the extent we allow. We can work with the law and reap the benefits, or we can ignore it or work against it and reap the consequences. Remember, too, that abundance is not possible unless it exists collectively first. That's why people in poverty-ridden countries cannot affect their outcomes as readily as those in wealthy countries. It's also why we need to take our role as stewards very seriously. History tells us that it is possible for even a small group of people to change the world, and the Law of Abundance tells us we must try.

Stewardship begins at home, but because there are so many disempowered people in the world and so many that are irresponsible, it cannot end there. We all have our work cut out for us for awhile. Those of us who have unlimited opportunities and choices, which includes most of the people in the United States and other developed countries, have a duty to lend a hand to those with limited opportunity. And those with limited opportunity have a duty to do their best to help themselves, to whatever extent possible, as we reach out to help them.

Those who need our help are everywhere. Some are obvious; some not so obvious. A few of the obvious examples are those living in abject poverty with no means for getting out; those living in nations where governments keep them oppressed; women, children and the elderly or infirm who are abused, those who are sold into slavery and cannot escape, those with physical disabilities. Some of the not so obvious are the non-physical limitations that plague so many, such as mental and emotional disabilities. Although these are not as easy to detect, they are no less real. Obvious or not, as a worldwide community, there is very little about the human condition that we cannot positively impact if we so choose.

For every effect, there is a cause. The cause of widespread hunger and disease can almost always be traced to people, usually lots of people, who are working against the Law of Abundance. Just as there are a lot of innocent victims when the forces of nature are out of control, creating disasters such as tornadoes, floods and hurricanes, there are also a lot of innocent victims when humans (another force of nature) are out of control. They, too, create disasters through greed for power, greed for money, selfishness, the need to be right even to the point of killing those who disagree, turning a blind eye to suffering, and in myriad other ways.

Take, for example, the AIDS epidemic in Africa. There are millions of orphaned children, many of whom are themselves infected with AIDS and are dying. This condition exists not through the choices or actions of the children, but through the choices made by their parents, their government, the governments of other nations, and the choices of people like you and me.

Not only do individual actions lead to negative abundance, so too do the choices made on a broader scale by the heads of corporations and of the governments of just about every nation on earth. When governments squander billions of dollars on social programs that teach its citizens that laziness has benefits, when politically correct legal systems teach criminals that crime does pay, or when the agendas of the privileged few cause the masses to suffer, those countries and the people who populate them are squarely on the path to negative abundance. Eventually, everyone will end up with a lot of things no one really wanted. Such is the world we are collectively creating, which is currently greatly unequal, frighteningly unstable, and wholly unsustainable.

Just as individuals can look at the Law of Abundance and determine whether their actions are right, so too could corporations and governments. To make the right choices they would only need to ask the right questions, test their answers against the Law of Abundance, and insist that the answers always lead to positive abundance—active application (+) with a receptive attitude (-) directed toward clear and responsible goals.

What questions would corporations and governments need to ask? The first question would have to be "Is this a responsible action?" The only way to answer that question correctly would be to consult the Law of Abundance. For an action to be responsible, it would have to lead to responsible, disciplined actions (active application) on the part of everyone that the decision would affect—politicians, businesses, employees, and citizens alike. It would have to be a decision that was focused on clearly defined, positive outcomes that were so beneficial, and so clear and well conveyed, that the majority of people would have no resistance to the action (receptive attitude). That's a very big order to be sure, but not an impossible one.

Those with their own agendas would initially resist responsible decisions and actions that didn't fit their model, but responsibility, courageous action, and doing the right thing requires that we teach others how to be more responsible, as well as being responsible ourselves. If we collectively and consistently did that, again weighing every decision against the Law of Abundance to guide our every step, a world filled with people living abundantly would be entirely possible.

Using the Law of Abundance to inform every decision could literally change the world, because the same formula that applies at an individual level applies nationally and globally as well. Just as governments and corporations go awry when they are administered without understanding, so too do many social and charitable programs. When they simply provide handouts to the poor and underprivileged, they are failing to work within the Law of Abundance because they are requiring no responsible, disciplined action on the part of recipients. Even the giver is being irresponsible in not requiring responsible actions. The intent may be good, but the action is not rightly taken because some of the components that lead to positive abundance are missing, and the endeavor is doomed to fail eventually.

Failure is inevitable because the recipient is receiving (-), but no responsible, disciplined action is required in return. So the recipient takes the easiest route, that of returning to the giver to receive more (-). By applying the rules of the Law of Abundance, we can see that the only possible outcome here is that the conditions of the recipient stay the same or get worse. They get worse when the source of charity finally gets tired of giving without seeing any positive outcome, runs out of money, or has to reduce the amount of subsistence for some reason.

When the amount of aid the recipient has become accustomed to receiving is altered for any reason, he/she then becomes upset. Once accustomed to receiving at a particular level without giving anything in return, resistance to the unwelcome change is inevitable. The recipient is now not only stuck (-/-), he/she is moving toward negative abundance (-/+) and everyone eventually ends up getting more of what they do not want. The United States is experiencing a huge problem with welfare reform right now as a result of this formula for failure. Well-meaning charities face the same continual battles as do many well-meaning individuals.

We are the stewards of this planet and, as stewards, we must work with, not against, the Law of Abundance. What does that look like? First, we must maintain in ourselves—and require of those we would help—responsibility, discipline, and the courage to do the right thing. But the requirement, according to the Law of Abundance, cannot be a forced one because the minute we start pushing and forcing our way onto others, we have jumped off the (+/-) path to positive abundance and onto a (+/+) path to nowhere. And, if the (+/+) path causes us to begin acting irresponsibly or using energy in the wrong way, we move from the stuck path to one of negative abundance (-/+).

Teaching, therefore, must be provided in such a way as to avoid resistance on our part, minimize resistance on the part of the recipient, and ensure that all parties continue taking the right actions and doing the right things. It also requires that we allow those who choose not to act responsibly to discover that there are consequences to irresponsible, undisciplined behaviors and we must be alright with allowing them to learn from their mistakes.

It is not our duty to correct the course of those who act irresponsibly and without discipline or courage, but it is our duty not to enable their poor choices. When we stop enabling victim mentalities, those who act irresponsibly and in undisciplined ways will quickly learn that there are unwanted consequences to such actions. And since we are all motivated by the need to move away from pain and toward pleasure, such people would be motivated to learn better ways to live in the world. They would then be ready to be taught without our needing to force the issue.

There will always be people who are not willing to learn no matter how gently and caringly we provide the instruction, and it is not possible to teach those who will not learn. In that case, according to the Law of Abundance, we must accept that such individuals are not ready or willing to learn and grow. We must also respect that choice, and in staying with the Law of Abundance, leave them to their own devices to learn in ways that may be more difficult. To do otherwise would be teaching them the wrong lessons, and then we too would not be acting responsibly or courageously.

To help those who will not help themselves depletes us all, and most of us instinctively know this. Good stewardship requires that we adhere closely to the Law of Abundance and use it to inform all of our decisions and actions. That means being ever willing to help those who are willing to help themselves, but requiring that all help themselves to whatever extent is possible.

It is our duty to help those who genuinely cannot help themselves (the terminally ill, the mentally or physically handicapped, orphaned children, and the old and infirm), but these groups make up only 3% to 5% of the population. And many of these could be helped to the point of being self-sustaining with proper care.

Short-term help designed to ease the burdens of the dying, teach children and unlearned adults to be self-sufficient, assist the weak in finding their own strengths, or teach the irresponsible how to take responsibility for their own life and outcomes, is not what will deplete humanity. What depletes us now, and will continue to deplete us as long as we allow it, is turning perfectly capable people into victims. We do this by providing long-term crutches to those who are perfectly able or can be taught to walk on their own. We do it by rewarding those who regularly take advantage of others, or by taking from those who have little to fill the coffers of those who have much. Misguided actions such as these put the majority of people on the path to limitation and ensure that we continue to live lives of quiet desperation.

Those who believe that abundance means greedily amassing material wealth or gaining power over others are way off base. They may have the material things they are after, but are giving up something much more precious in the process.

A mafia boss is a good example. They often amass a lot of money and material wealth, and wield a lot of power, but they don't have personal freedom or peace of mind. Mobsters don't have bodyguards without a reason.

YOU CAN'T CHEAT THE LAW

Just as you can't secretly drive off a cliff and not get hurt, you can't secretly misapply the Law of Abundance without consequence. Your energy shifts and flows according to your own application, attitude and focus, and you can never escape that fact.

Your actions and your attitude will always be the source of energy flow in your life and your focus and intent will always impact the quality of life you experience. You can hide your thoughts, feelings, actions and intent from others, but you cannot hide them from yourself. Whatever creates resistance in you creates resistance to your energy supply and slows your progress. As long as you are working against your own ideal, there will be resistance. And where there is resistance, there will be limited abundance. That's why getting your life aligned with your values is so important.

Because we live in a physical world where the actions of others impact the whole, the actions of others are going to impact us and our actions will impact others, and it doesn't matter how innocent the one being impacted may be.

Tragedies at the hands of those gone awry will not cease unless and until we have collectively grown to the extent that we all understand and fully obey the Law of Abundance.

Yet, there is evidence that those who work within the law, even unconsciously, have a degree of protection not available to those who don't. There are people who seem to live charmed lives. Everything they touch turns to gold. Their lives are filled with fun, freedom, happiness, and love. They are healthy, fit, and full of vigor. Tragedies seem to bypass them. We wonder how on earth they do it, and they wonder how on earth the rest of us are not doing it.

Often these people try to teach us what they are doing. They instinctively know that we must take responsibility for one another and be good stewards to this planet we call home. They understand that we are indeed our brother's keeper and they work actively at modeling that truth and spreading that message.

This small, but powerfully important group of people, keeps working at making a difference in as many lives as they can, and so many of us have benefited from their efforts.

Remember, only humans have the ability to conserve energy and alter its flow in purposeful, planned ways, and having that ability indeed makes us stewards.

Sadly, we are not doing a very good job of it right now. Yet, we have the ability to direct and redirect energy in whatever way we choose. As more and more of us learn how to use the Law of Abundance to affect positive change and positively impact the lives of others, we can and will change the course of history.

CHAPTER 26

Creating the Life You Want

An aim in life is the only fortune worth finding.
Jacqueline Kennedy Onassis

Because it takes tremendous effort in the early stages of working at changing old patterns, you must be prepared to apply yourself diligently to the process of altering old ways of thinking and feeling, re-directing a negative focus, and modifying habitual attitudes, approaches, and routines. Shifting your energies from a negative or stuck path to the path of positive abundance is going to take dedicated effort initially, and if you are prepared for the initial effort, it won't surprise or derail you.

Too many people fail to fully realize how much effort it takes to change old habits, or how powerfully resistance to change can prevent them from doing things they really do want to do. The ultimate goal is to get to a place where there is no resistance at all to the things you choose to be doing. But that will not be your experience in the beginning, especially if you have not been accustomed to taking responsibility for all of your outcomes or disciplining yourself to do the right things. Remember, one factor of energy is that, once down, it seeks to stay down and, once up, it seeks to stay up. So, once you get the momentum going, keeping it going will be easy.

To prevent resistance from creating conditions that will halt energy or send it toward negative abundance, it is important that you have some workable tools available and that you stay focused on the result you are after. Avoid focusing on your resistance to the effort required during the transition period. It is not easy to change bad habits on the application or attitude sides, so expect to do some initial work no matter which side needs to be adjusted.

To quote author and corporate trainer, Brian Tracy, "Good habits are hard to develop, but easy to live with. Bad habits are easy to develop, but hard to live with. The habits you have, and the habits that have you, will determine almost everything that you achieve or fail to achieve."

Keep in mind that the feeling of hard work is temporary and can be greatly diminished by staying focused on your *reason* for making the effort. As soon as you have effectively shifted the energy to the right direction and it is flowing, the impression of effort or working hard won't exist.

Below are some essential steps for moving from where you have been to where you want to go. As you work through them, allow for the fact that these steps may take time, effort, and dedication on your part, and there may be some resistance to taking some of the steps. Do them anyway. Once you have mastered them, you will love the changes that begin to occur in your life and the ease with which your life will flow toward the things you desire.

1. **Be Persistent and Patient with Yourself.** The first thing you will need to do is develop patience. When there is a longing for something better, it's hard to be patient when it doesn't materialize right away. Sometimes our growth is so imperceptible that we have to look at our lives historically to see that we have actually made any progress at all. Know that if you patiently and steadily work in responsible, disciplined, and courageous ways toward your goals, you *must* get more of the things you desire. Remember that to keep yourself moving toward an abundance of the things you want, you will have to be persistent (disciplined application), and you will have to remain non-resistant or patient with your progress (receptive attitude).

2. **Find Your Passion.** This step powers your generator. Until you find something you can be really passionate about, you won't have enough energy and dedication to drive you through the early stages of shifting the flow of energy toward positive abundance. Change is difficult for most people, and without a powerful reason for making changes and keeping up the effort until a new habit has formed, the likelihood of abandoning the quest is very high.

If your past actions have not resulted in the life you love, don't let past actions dictate your future. If you don't already have a passion for something, it might be because you are not living true to your nature and are suppressing desires connected to your natural style, or it might be that you have too many interests and haven't prioritized them or aligned them with what is meaningful to you. If you are not already aware of your true passion, now is the time to discover it.

3. **Get Very Clear on What You Want.** This step is like your product design, and in this case, your product is your life. You are creating a specific receiver toward which your natural energies can flow. Your focus must be so keen and clear that the life you want feels more real than the life you now have. The vision you build clarity around must be a passionate intent, not just a goal.

If you don't feel a strong pull toward your goal, rethink it. It may not be the right goal for you, or some important element may be missing. Be sure each goal has a greater pull and greater energy around it than the current reality. Clarity includes a clear understanding of your authentic (as opposed to conditioned) self, as well as a clear vision of your life path and what that path is leading you toward. In other words, there needs to be great clarity around who you are and where you are headed in life.

4. **Create Clear Personal Boundaries.** This step provides your first layer of insulation so that energy is not drained away or dissipated by negative people or events. There are two parts to personal boundaries: (1) who you are and are not, and (2) what you will and will not accept from yourself and others. Create both parts by getting two large sheets of blank paper or two poster boards if you prefer.

Examples of these two sheets are available at the Law of Abundance website. You can print out the pages as worksheets or use them as guides to create poster-sized worksheets. Some people like the notebook sized sheets so they can keep them in a loose-leaf journal. Others like the poster size so they can put it on a wall where they will see it every day. Either way is fine as along as you keep the boundaries lists handy enough to refer to them regularly, and to add to as you claim or reject various things.

To make posters, draw a very large circle in the center of each poster board such that the circle takes up half of the total area.

On one poster put "I Am" inside the circle and "I Am NOT" outside of the circle. Then define and begin listing who you are (inside the circle), and who you are not (outside the circle). You are the things that create passion, joy, contentment, and other positive feelings in you. I'm not talking about instant gratification here. I'm talking about the feelings that define who you are, not what you enjoy—feelings that give you a sense of pride in yourself and lead to a deep, abiding sense of satisfaction, not just momentary appeasement.

You are all the things you have learned and which you enjoy. Remember, your compass leads you to your truth by conveying feelings to you. As you build your personal boundaries, consult your compass often. Remember to put the things that cause you to feel bad about yourself in any way outside of your "I Am" circle, in the outer regions labeled "I Am NOT." Those things do NOT belong to you and your perfectly attuned inner compass is continually trying to tell you so.

Some examples of things that do not belong to you are the negative "you" messages people have visited upon you over the years: "You can't do that," "You're too little," "You aren't smart enough," "You're lazy."

Other examples are the negative things you tell yourself and the limiting beliefs you have bought into as a result of negative messages, your own and those you received from others (which have helped to shaped yours).

Remember: if an attribute doesn't feel positive and if it isn't empowering, it isn't yours.

Inside the circle on the second poster, write "I Will Accept." Outside the circle, write "I Will NOT Accept." Then begin defining all the things you are willing to accept from yourself and others. These go inside the circle. The things you will no longer accept or never have accepted from yourself or from others go outside the circle.

This is not a one shot process. It may take you months to complete your boundaries identification. Just keep adding to the lists as things come up. Defining who you are and are not, and what you will and will not accept, will give you an amazing sense of clarity and personal power, and will eventually create conditions that keep you on track almost automatically.

When I first did this exercise, one of the things I put in the "I will NOT Accept" section was being manipulated. Once I had determined and stated that I would not accept being manipulated, I became intensely interested in learning what manipulation looked like in all its forms, and became highly aware of manipulative behaviors.

I also began studying assertiveness skills so I would be better equipped to handle aggressive and passive-aggressive people effectively. Now I am able to see and effectively respond to people who manipulate through a guise of "caring," as well as the ones that are more obvious, and I don't play that game anymore.

5. **Build Trust.** Before you can be fully abundant, you must trust that you can achieve the goals you set for yourself, and you must trust at least a few other people to help you. Although conscious awareness of the generative force isn't absolutely necessary, having it increases your ability to insulate yourself from negative influences. The reason a conscious awareness isn't necessary is because the generative force works perfectly whether you are aware of it or not.

Everyone has faith in the generative force, some consciously and some unconsciously. Conscious awareness allows you to tap into the generative force more readily and more purposefully and reap huge benefits, but conscious awareness is optional. Just as your blood circulates through your body whether or not you are aware of it, so too does the generative force perform as it does whether or not you are aware of it. You must consciously and purposefully apply your faith in yourself and others, however. If you don't, fear and doubt will creep in and you will not be able to fully achieve your goals. The ability to acknowledge and trust in a generative force expands possibilities beyond yourself and the capabilities of others, and gives you a much larger playing field. So it is wise to find ways to build trust in all three factors.

6. **Maintain a Positive, Expectant Attitude.** This step removes resistors on the positive path to abundance and acts as a conductor to boost energy along that path. It also minimizes activity on the negative path. Internationally known author and consultant Brian Tracy describes six things you can do to ensure that you have the very best attitude in his book *Million Dollar Habits* (Enterpreneur Press 2004). Here is an adaptation of his recommendations.

   A. **Focus on the future rather than the past** . Don't worry about who did what or who is to blame. Focus instead on where you want to be and what you want to do. Get a clear mental image of your ideal outcome and then take whatever action is possible right now to begin moving in that direction.

   B. **Focus on the solution rather than on the problem.** Don't waste time rehashing and reflecting on the problem. When you're faced with a difficulty, focus instead on the ideal solution. Solutions are inherently positive, whereas problems are inherently negative. You become more positive and constructive as soon as you begin thinking in terms of solutions, and you continue removing resistors from the path to abundance and boosting energy toward it.

   C. **Assume there is something good hidden within each difficulty or challenge.** Only by meeting challenges will you gain the strengths and abilities necessary to achieve big goals. In every challenge, look for a valuable lesson or the opportunity to gain a strength or skill. Assume that every set back contains a lesson that is essential for you to learn or an opportunity that you will need in the future. If you see a difficult situation as a problem, the problem side of it is what is being fed and what is growing. If you see it as an opportunity, that side is being fed and is growing.

D. **Assume that whatever situation you are facing is exactly the right situation you need to ultimately be successful.** If you are open to it, the situation will help you learn something, become better, and/or expand and grow.

E. **Direct your thoughts and choose your focus wisely.** You can entertain only one thought at a time. If you are focused on a solution, you cannot be simultaneously thinking about the difficulty or the obstacle. If you are focused on the things you are grateful for, you cannot be focused on the things you don't have. If you are focused on the goodness and beauty in people and the magnificence of the world, you cannot be focused on shortcomings.

F. **Make a solution list.** Whenever you have an unachieved goal, an unresolved difficulty, or a problem that is blocking you from getting where you want to go, make a list of every single thing that you could possibly do to correct the situation. Record every idea, no matter how ridiculous. By thinking on paper, you will activate your unconscious mind and gain control over your conscious mind so it is focused where you want it: on the solution.

7. **Think BIG.** Anyone can think small and far too many do. But small thinking is what keeps people stuck inside a self-imposed prison built of fear, which disguises itself as a comfort zone. Since you are always thinking anyway, you might as well think big. As you lay out your life plan, don't just think about what you believe is possible. Think about the things that seem almost impossible for you right now. Think about things that would require you to really stretch your boundaries and grow.

Knowing the Law of Abundance principles, you know what you need to adjust to have the things you desire. But have you considered how grand that adjustment can be? Have you expanded your ideas of abundance far enough? Give yourself permission to be outrageous, and to let your imagination soar. I'm not talking about unrealistic, pie-in-the-sky daydreaming. I'm talking about truly grand, but doable, goals that will stretch your limits, enhance your abilities, and breathe life into your most cherished dreams.

Unless you stretch your thinking beyond the thoughts and beliefs you have always held, you will find yourself in the same old place, doing the exact same things you have alway done. To experience significant growth, you must let go of limited, and limiting, thinking. Thinking big may feel uncomfortable at first, but give yourself the gift of pushing past those limitations and exploring what lies beyond. That's where the next step comes in.

8. **Let Go of Resistors.** Resistors are fear-based responses generally created as a result of worst-case scenario thinking. They prevent energy from flowing and can create energy blocks in your mind and body that, over the years, become patterns of response that are easily triggered and automatically activated. They prevent your success by keeping you stuck in old beliefs and thought patterns that are not serving you well.

To let go of resistors, you must first become aware of them and then have effective tools for managing them. Any time you become aware of a resistor, notice what you are telling yourself. What story, what-worst case scenario, what expectation of a consequence are you aware of? Sometimes it's easier to begin with how you are feeling and ask yourself, "What would I need to believe to be feeling this way?" When you have the answer, shift your focus to a better option to redirect your energy.

Every form of therapy is some means of redirecting energy, releasing blocked energy, or removing resistors. Blocks are simply a series of resistors that work in tandem with one another so as you remove one resistor, you may be positively impacting others as well.

9. **Lay Out a Plan.** This step is your blueprint. It is like a wiring schematic that directs energy along specific pathways, taking

it to where you want it to go. If you want specific results, you must have a plan to follow, and you must follow your plan. You don't want just one set-in-stone plan, though. All good plans have contingency plans that provide pre-thought-out options in case plan "A" cannot be fully implemented. A good plan also always allows room for adjustment where necessary. But it lays out and defines the interim steps according to plan "A". Only when something occurs that prevents plan "A" from moving forward are plan "B" steps substituted.

As you lay out your plan, be sure to distinguish between goals and desires. Your plan will likely contain both. Realize that for a desire to also be a goal, its accomplishment must be entirely within your control. If achieving something in your plan requires the cooperation of others, it is a desire, not a goal. It becomes a goal only when you have gotten the necessary cooperation to move forward. If you will keep these distinctions in mind as you work your plan, you will not get frustrated when a desire, which you mistook for a goal, does not materialize.

This is one of the areas where you may have some resistance and may find yourself dragging your feet. Creating a plan can seem like a daunting task, but it is definitely nowhere near as daunting as a lifetime of disappointments. You don't need to do the whole thing at once, but you do need to get started. Begin with a general plan— an outline of where you want to head, and add details regularly until the plan is specific, detailed, and exactly the way you want it.

10. **Work Your Plan.** Once you know exactly what you must do to get where you want to go, lay out goal steps to get you there. Work backwards: yearly first, then monthly, weekly and daily. Use a daily planner to lay out the daily steps you will need to take to reach your goals. And take steps every single day. This process will definitely require discipline, but remember: to have an abundance of what you want you must purposefully boost energy along the positive application path, and self-discipline is the way to do it. Once you have learned to take the daily steps without resistance, abundance is yours.

Since the path to positive abundance cannot flow freely until you have removed resistors, the next few chapters are devoted to things you can do to affect that outcome

If, in working through the steps in this chapter, you find you are unable to move through them effectively on your own or to sustain momentum, one of the greatest gifts you can give yourself is a great coach or mentor to get you past the initial resistance and help you develop essential skills. You can find links to good coaches in the resource section of *www.theLawofAbundance.com.*

Human nature has been sold short.
We all have a higher nature which includes
the need for meaningful work, for responsibility,
for creativity, for being just and fair, and for
doing what is worthwhile, and preferring to do it well.
Abraham Maslow

CHAPTER 27

Releasing Energy

Energy and Persistence alter all things.
Benjamin Franklin

Energy meridians in the human body have a long history. The Chinese were mapping them as early as the Shang Dynasty (1766 – 1123 BCE) and the Zhou Dynasty (1122 – 249 BCE)[20]. For thousands of years, traditional Chinese medicine has treated the human body as an integral system of interrelated energy networks, each having different physiological functions.

The Western World is now beginning to take Chinese medicine more seriously because methods such as acupuncture have at times proven more effective than Western medicines and have no adverse side effects. Over the years, a number of other effective techniques have sprung up around the release of energy blocks as well.

Unless you plan to become an acupuncturist or reflexologist, knowing the exact energy meridians or paths in the body is not necessary. What is necessary is to be able to identify an energy block when it occurs in your own body and have the resources to release it.

Energy blocks in the body appear to be related to the subconscious mind's need to create patterns or habits that enable us to function effectively without conscious thought. When we hold a thought or belief long enough, the subconscious mind assumes that it must have value, and like repeated actions, stores it away as an unconscious habit to be repeated automatically whenever the right stimuli are in place.

Energy blocks are resistors that occur in response to negatively charged thoughts or stressful events. Most people don't deal with negative emotions very effectively. That's because, as children, we are taught to avoid or resist them so we better conform to social expectations.

Because modern societies are so outer focused, many people aren't aware enough of their feelings to monitor them, and those who are aware often don't know what to do with the feelings that come up. Rather than recognize them as a signal to make an alteration, they tend to see them as unacceptable and suppress them.

Beginning around age three, most children are taught that they should not cry or openly express anger or other negative emotions, so by the time we reach adulthood, most of us are quite adept at suppressing our emotions, which we do until they get so uncomfortable that they just erupt from us.

When we repeatedly suppress negative emotions, they grow stronger. Just as adding more weight to barbells builds muscles, so too does adding more resistance to an already resistant feeling build its capacity to block the flow of energy.

Feelings of resistance come up as feedback from that infallible compass we all have. They come up not so we will resist, suppress, or inappropriately express them, but so we will know that we are off track and can correct our course.

If we see negative feelings and the resulting resistance as guideposts to be attended to rather than as something to avoid, and if we attend to them rather than suppress them, they will not build up and come out in negative ways or become energy blocks. Since most of us do not attend to our emotions effectively, energy blocks are a problem for most people, and usually they have been building since childhood.

Each time we suppress a feeling, resistance increases. In response, we resist harder and the blocked feeling resists right back, gaining even more strength. Eventually, in an attempt to get our attention, the negative feeling, and the resistance we have built up around it, turn into aggression or depression, or manifest as physical symptoms that aren't so easy to ignore.

Medical science suggests that as much as 90% of all illnesses are psychosomatic or psychologically based—all in our head. The reality is they are not all in our head, they are in our blocked energy system. They occur when suppression of the body's natural energy flow creates patterns that run in continuous loops. Once loops form, they habituate, and because they are running automatically, we aren't even aware that they are there.

We are usually aware of the effect, but not of the energy blocks that cause the effect. And, because we are focused on the effect and trying to alter our outcomes from there, we remain stuck, running the same old behavioral loops over and over again and nothing we do seems to help. That's because we are working on the wrong thing.

We can't alter the cause of a problem by trying to eliminate the effect, and if we aren't aware that there is some underlying cause, we never address it and it never changes.

We can't do anything about things we can't see, which is why the physical body eventually enters into the picture. Illness demands our attention and we have to attend to it. The problem is, most people continue to attend to the effect, in this case the symptoms, rather than the cause, so blocks seldom get removed and the illness remains or returns.

The goal of our inner compass on every level, from the initial hint of anxiety or resistance to the full blown disease, is to get our attention so we can correct our course. Once you understand this and learn to pay attention, you then have the opportunity to deal with stessors directly and effectively by altering your course and getting back to the place where your compass is reporting that all is well. This is typically felt as a sense of inner peace or balance, happiness, more energy and more robust physical health, and feelings of well-being.

You will feel better mentally and emotionally, almost immediately.

Physical responses can also occur immediately, but they can also take time. Just as it takes longer for suppression of feelings to affect the physical body, it can also take longer for it to respond to freed energy.

Be patient. Patience keeps the receptive energy flowing, which allows the releasing and balancing process to continue. Specific methods for releasing blocks are covered in chapters 28-30.

The words of the tongue should have three gatekeepers:
1~Is it true?
2~ Is it kind?
3~ Is it necessary?

Arab Proverb

CHAPTER 28

Realigning Your Energies

Go confidently in the direction of your dreams.
Live the life you have imagined.
Henry David Thoreau

In the early stages of becoming aware of your inner compass you may not be aware of the actions, attitudes, or self-talk that generate particular responses, but you can and should be aware of the response itself. You become aware by monitoring your emotions. It is emotions—how you feel in relation to events, people, thoughts, beliefs and actions—that your internal compass uses to give you feedback and let you know when you are on track and when you are off. The primary, and perhaps only, purpose of emotions is feedback and guidance.

The goal in realigning your energies is not to be top-of-the-world 100% of the time. Life happens and we respond. And, since life is not perfect, there will be times when we are less than joyous. It is counter-productive to strive for constant joy or to allow its absence to cause stress. Stress slows or stops the very energy we need to get back to joy.

Being off track isn't always a reflection of our personal actions or decisions. We can be doing everything right personally, and have every factor in place for traveling our own unique path, and still get thrown off by an unexpected loss or tragedy.

We are feeling beings who are impacted by the world we live in and the actions of others. Sometimes those actions hurt or are not to our liking. Sometimes life's events have such great and long lasting impact that it takes us awhile to recover emotionally. The loss of a loved one is an example.

While it's true that how we handle tragedy and loss is largely a matter of our approach to it, all but the most hardened react to tragedy and loss with pain and sadness. And during such times life is not exactly the way we want it. We are emotionally derailed, not because of something we have personally done, but because we are human.

Yet those who have a strong, healthy inner core are able to bounce back from tragedy and loss quicker than those who do not. Nonetheless, we all get derailed occasionally, and to expect that life will be perfect is to set ourselves up for times of resistance, which will slow our energy and our progress. People who think life should be perfect all the time are the ones who find themselves devastated when things happen that they could not see coming and would not have chosen.

The reality is that we are just one part of the great symphony of life. We play one instrument—ours—and that's all we have control of. If we play our own instrument beautifully, and choose the orchestra we play in carefully, the odds are good that we will experience beautiful music most of the time. But if other people in the orchestra play discordant notes, we will be impacted by them unless we are both deaf and blind.

The goal should not be to track perfectly all the time no matter what. It should be to stay on track most of the time, and to be aware of what pulls us off course so we can make the necessary adjustments to get back on as quickly and effortlessly as possible. To do that, we must first be fully aware of what it feels like to be on the right track, or off, in the first place. And to get there, we must be aware of our feelings, what those feelings are pointing us toward (their meaning), and what actions, attitudes, beliefs or self-talk generated the feelings.

As you might imagine, that is much easier said than done. Many people have suppressed and ignored their feelings for so long that attending to them is difficult and can feel downright scary. Many are unable to hear the self-talk that feeds emotions, and many more cannot determine what beliefs or attitudes led to the self-talk even if they can hear it.

The good news is that you don't need to start at the source, and you don't need to force a thing. The best way to get there is to begin with the response itself and work backwards from there. In time, attending to your feelings and determining their source becomes almost as easy as breathing.

When you notice a negative feeling, for example, rather than trying to dismiss it, allow yourself to explore it. Approach it as an adventurer looking for clues to a treasure might. Did the feeling occur in response to something you thought, something someone said, a tone of voice, or an expression? Perhaps it was an expectation of how things ought to be. Pose questions to your subconscious mind and just allow the answer to arrive. You will be surprised at how accommodating your subconscious mind can be when you are not trying to force something out of it, and at how stubborn it can be when you are.

Once you begin noticing what triggers negative responses, you will find that the triggers occur in predictable patterns. And once you can see the patterns, you can find strategies to circumvent them. If, for example, you find that a trigger occurs as a result of something you consistently tell yourself, you can decide on a more effective message to counter-balance the negative response. Then, whenever you become aware of the triggered feeling, you will know that the old message is running and you can purposefully introduce the new one. If you do this enough times, the old trigger will lose its energy and disappear.

If you find that a trigger occurs in response to a tone of voice, a particular look from someone, or some other external stimuli, look deeper because emotional triggers always have an internal source. The external stimuli triggered the response, but it is not the source of the response. As you notice your response to the external trigger, ask yourself, "What would I have to believe for this tone of voice (look, etc.) to trigger this response in me?" Once you are aware of the belief that triggered the response, ask "What message would I have to be giving myself to maintain this belief?" Once you find the message that maintains the belief, change the message. It's your life, and as an adult, you get to write the chapters that will become your biography. Not just future chapters, but all of them if you so choose.

The subconscious mind "thinks" in stories, complete with images, sounds, feelings, tastes and smells. Every significant event that has ever occurred in your life has its own story, or is a part of a bigger story. Energy is generated around these stories and it is the energy, either positive or negative, "good" or "bad", that we become aware of and that drives us forward or holds us back.

We have a large library of stories, from the ones we bought into as children, to the ones we are buying into today. And they don't have to be logical or make any sense. In fact, quite often they aren't at all logical and they don't make a lick of sense. It is the illogical nature of the stories that drive the behaviors which we see as problematical, but which we keep repeating anyway.

All addictions fall into this category as do all destructive behaviors. And as long as we believe we are powerless to change them, we are. Think about the term "powerless." Remember that a negative or resistant attitude carries an active (+) charge. When we are trying to rid ourselves of destructive behaviors through active or resistant means, we are just adding resistant (+) energy to energy which is already resistant (+), and as you know, two like energies do not flow. The result is a buildup of resistance which becomes an energy block that is going nowhere and we are truly *powerless*.

TECHNIQUES TO REALIGN ENERGIES

There are a number of techniques you can use to realign your energies and remove blocks. I have personally experienced or witnessed the results possible with the ones I am recommending in this chapter. All have potential. All are worth checking into.

Every person is different, and what works beautifully for one person may not be effective for another. Some people are completely open to getting quick, easy results, while others are convinced that it can't be that simple and need more complex procedures. Some people are fine with making shifts mentally and/or emotionally, while others need to do something physical. Still others need to combine the two into a ritual. You may need to experiment with one or two techniques before you find the one that works consistently for you, so I have provided the names of several that are good, but different in their approach.

The method presented in the next chapter, which I call the *Energy Release Technique* (ERT), is a quick self-administered method that works very well for many people. Another technique that I have had great success with personally and with others is that of rewriting life stories. This method works because, while your subconscious mind acts in response to the stories it maintains, it absolutely does not care whether they are based on external events that actually occurred, or on a story you created. As long as the story aligns with the subconscious mind's awareness of potential, which is vast, the stories are all the same to it. If you don't like the messages you uncover as you begin monitoring your emotions, change them to something more positive and beneficial to you. If you are paying attention, that perfect inner compass of yours will tell you whether your subconscious mind bought the new story or not.

Let me give you a personal example. My image of my parents years ago was that they were both dysfunctional. In my external experience, they were, and as long as I held that image internally, my internal "parents" (protectors) who cared for the internal children (thoughts and feelings) were also dysfunctional. I didn't like the results I was getting from two dysfunctional inner-parents so I rewrote the story.

I transformed my father from a struggling entrepreneur, who was rarely happy and who never managed to create the life he wanted, into a highly successful businessman who was confident, content and highly satisfied with his life. I transformed him into a great businessman and a kind, loving, gentle, and wise father. I transformed my mother from a loving and charismatic, but insecure person, into a highly confident woman with a strong, healthy sense of self. She kept her loving, charismatic attributes and still thoroughly enjoyed her children and her friends, but her new self also enjoyed and had great confidence in her personal abilities, and her life in general.

Clearly, I still have memories of the unevolved parents, but they are just memories now. There is no emotional attachment to them and they are not the ones minding the "children." My emotional attachment is now to the transformed parents. My new image of them led to my creating a new life story and caused profound shifts in my feelings, and, therefore, my results, around a great many things. Even some I had not expected.

I discovered that the subconscious mind will only accept a story with some validity to it when I did this exercise for myself, and have consistently seen the same response when working with hundreds of other people. In my own case, I initially thought that two parents who were successful in business and worked together in a family business would give me two good role models for building a successful family business. So I tried to create a mother who was a successful business woman in addition to her other attributes when recreating my childhood story. My subconscious mind completely rejected that idea, apparently because my mother never worked outside the home in the way I imagined, and never gave any indication that she wanted to. She occasionally worked in family owned restaurants with very casual environments, but I wanted the image to be one of a high powered businesswoman. That image didn't fit her reality, so my subconscious mind rejected it. The attributes I was able to give my parents in the rewrite were those that reflected their true potential, which my subconscious mind was already able to see, but which my old stories had kept me blind to.

Examine the stories you hold to be true. If you don't like them, present a new story to your subconscious mind. One to your liking and your benefit. If you make the story detailed enough to build an emotional charge around it, your subconscious mind will work with the created story as easily as with the real one.

Find your potential and that of your family members and give yourself the gift of an ideal past. You will love how it impacts you now and in the future. As a plaque I once saw in a friend's office proclaimed "It's never too late to have a happy childhood." How true.

CHAPTER 29

The Energy Release Technique

The energy of the mind is the essence of life.
Aristotle

The Energy Release Technique (ERT) works by giving you a means to stop resisting the negative emotions that are blocking your energy. It allows you to move to a place of allowance or acceptance and introduces receptive energy (-) into an area where overly active energy or resistance (+) has created a block. Introducing the receptive energy encourages balance and provides the plus/minus (+/-) combination necessary for energy to flow in the right direction.

Just as physical health is dependent on balance, so too is emotional and mental health. As you introduce the receptive energies through ERT, you are balancing your body, mind, and emotions and aligning them so that you get positive results on every level.

Blocks show up, not surprisingly, as negative or resistant feelings. Many of these can be released rather quickly, often with just one try. But making a permanent shift may take more than one attempt where a lot of resistance has built up.

If you introduce enough receptive energy (-) to balance the active energy block (+), the block will completely disappear. If the receptive energy introduced is not sufficient to balance the block, it will be reduced, but won't completely disappear. In that case, you will need to repeat the process until the block has been completely neutralized and disappears. Once blocks are released, they become useful energy and you will feel the effect as an increase of energy in your physical body, an increase of mental energy in the form of clearer, sharper thinking, and a lighter, happier emotional state. Be patient with yourself and with the process. Remember, when you lose patience, you are adding resistance which is counter-productive.

Blocks that are resistant to releasing usually just need more receptive energy to balance them out. In some cases, blocks that seem to return after you think you have released them are not the same blocks. In other cases the release was not complete. In still other cases new resistors have developed in the same region as a result of similar beliefs, assumptions and self-talk. Know that negative feelings are always feedback that shows up for one reason: to alert you to the fact that you are off your path. Find the cause of the returning feeling and remove it, and the blocks will not keep building up. With a little practice, you can prevent resistant thoughts and feelings from building into energy blocks.

STEPS FOR THE ENERGY RELEASE TECHNIQUE (ERT)

1. Think of a situation where you feel stuck, limited or are getting negative results.

2. Notice the dominant feeling that comes up in relation to the thought or image, such as fear, worry, anxiety, regret, embarrassment, or shame.

3. Locate that feeling in your body. Where is it? In your stomach? Your neck? Your back? How is that part of your body responding to it? If it is in your stomach, for instance, is your stomach responding by knotting up or perhaps with frequent indigestion?

4. Once you have identified and located the feeling, allow it to express fully, rather than resisting it. Completely and totally accept it. You may notice increased resistance as you attempt this, especially if the feeling is fear, grief, shame, or some other feeling you worry about releasing. To cease resisting it and just accept it may feel scary. Try it anyway. Remember, all you are doing is introducing receptive energy (-) to balance out the overly active, resistant energy (+). You are not destroying anything, you are simply balancing and releasing the energy to do what it is there to do. And, according to the Law of Abundance, it is always there to do something positive.

5. Create an image of what complete and total acceptance might look like and surround the negative feeling with that image. Wrap it in the acceptance as you might wrap an infant in a warm, cozy blanket, or surround the feeling in a beautiful bubble and fill the air inside the bubble with love and acceptance.

6. As you enfold the negative feeling, mentally state to the feeling that you fully and completely accept and appreciate it, and are open to hearing its story. Allow the feeling to respond to your offering in any way it chooses. If you try to direct how the feeling is to respond, you are not being totally accepting of it. Allow the feeling to choose its own response and, whatever it is, fully and completely accept the response and extend gratitude for it. Often, all that is necessary to release the block is the acceptance. Sometimes however, the response is to inform you of the purpose for the block and give you the opportunity to change a detrimental circumstance. Listen. What you learn can be immensely useful in moving you toward an abundant life.

7. Once you are aware that the feeling has responded and released, recall the situation where you felt stuck, limited or have been getting negative results and again check your response to it. If there is no negative or resistant emotional response—none at all— then the block is gone and will not return. Be sure it is gone, though, not just reduced. If it is just reduced, you will want to repeat the exercise remaining completely accepting of whatever is there until you are absolutely certain any negative response is gone. You will be certain when you are not able to call up the negative feeling anymore. You will remember it as a thought, but you will not feel it as an emotion.

Once you can no longer call up a negative feeling in relation to the memory, that particular block is gone for good, and your thinking and behaviors will automatically shift in the direction you prefer. You will be amazed at how completely effortless the change in your behaviors will be. It occurs so naturally and effortlessly that many people are not aware of the shift until they notice, often with surprise, that they are no longer responding or behaving in the same old ways.

FOR PAIN RELIEF

ERT often works to relieve headaches, back pain, tense or painful muscles, and other aches and pains because most of these are also a result of blocked energies. Blocked energy covers a very wide range of illnesses and diseases so this technique can improve many conditions. Always use alternative methods, including this one, as an adjunct to traditional treatments, however. *Do not use this or any other technique as a substitute for medical treatment.*

A good approach to pain relief is to mentally enter into the pain as a curious explorer. Resistance is the typical response to pain, but your goal is to release it and to do that, you need to balance out the already overly resistant energy. So don't resist it. Allow the pain to express fully so you can explore it. As you mentally move through the pain, exploring it, curiously examining it, fully allowing it, it will often greatly diminish or disappear altogether.

As with negative feelings, address the pain with acceptance, appreciation and gratitude. I generally approach pain as I might a beloved infant that is fretful or hurting; soothing, comforting, caring deeply about its pain. This almost always works to completely relieve the pain. Even painful, tensed up muscles tend to relax and release both pain and stiffness when resistance is removed.

IF AN ENERGY BLOCK DOESN'T GO AWAY COMPLETELY OR SEEMS TO RETURN

If ERT isn't completely releasing negative energies and removing resistors, there are a couple of reasons why:

1. **You are not introducing enough receptive energy.** Some negative feelings are really hard to be receptive to, such as anger, righteous indignation, grief, regret, or fear. But to introduce enough receptive energy to balance out the active energy and release these emotions, you must fully accept them.

You cannot fool yourself into believing you accept what you are feeling if you don't. If release was not complete on the first try or if the feeling seemed to release, but then returned, don't be discouraged, simply repeat the process.

2. **You are on the wrong path.** The primary reason that resistors recur is because you are continuing to do things that are keeping you on the wrong path. The purpose of your inner compass is to keep you on your true path and it is not going to stand by silently and allow you to head off in the wrong direction. So, if you keep trying to release a feeling and it keeps coming back, examine your life in relation to the feeling. What are you doing, thinking, or believing when the feeling appears?

Know that whatever you are doing that brings up the emotion is wrong for you and is throwing you off your path. You will either have to change course or learn to live with the discomfort and the realization that you will never know abundance fully as long as you continue to follow that same path.

Choose to make the proper adjustments and the feeling will shift to something positive, or disappear. It may take some time and you may go through a process of trial and error to get there, but if you keep adjusting you will eventually succeed. Most things release almost instantly, however, and the rewards are immediate and lasting.

*The best preparation
for a better life next year is
a full, complete, harmonious,
joyous life this year.*

Thomas Dreier

CHAPTER 30

More Techniques for Removing Blocks

Courage is the mastery of fear,
not the absence of fear.
Mark Twain

REMOVING FEAR OF FAILURE

Many people allow fear of failure to prevent them from moving forward. But there are really only three ways to fail, and continuing to try and falling short is not one of them. The three ways to fail are:

1. **Continuing on a path you know is wrong for you** because you committed to it once upon a time. Strangely, there are people who will subject themselves to a lifetime of misery because they think that to abandon a bad choice which they made when they had less knowledge or awareness would mean that they failed. Ceasing to drive down a road that will lead you over a cliff is not failure. It's success. It is taking knowledge that you didn't have before you saw the cliff's edge and acting on it wisely. Staying in a bad job or career, or in a bad marriage that has little hope of getting better, are common examples of this way to fail.

2. **Giving up before you reach a goal you really want to reach.** In this instance, an individual makes several attempts, and because they didn't get the result they wanted after several tries, gives up and settles for less. Imagine what would have happened if you had taken this approach as a baby just learning to walk. How many times do you suppose you fell down before you succeeded? Not achieving the intended goal on the first, second, third, or even thirtieth try does not suggest failure. It suggests that there is still more to learn to achieve success.

3. **Settling for less.** This way of failing occurs when people fail to alter their course after they realize they are capable of achieving more. Choosing the lesser path just because it is predictable and not all that bad, even though you know it is not the most beneficial or desirable path, is a choice for failure and regret. In this case, the comfort zone is a prison, not a safe haven.

THE NO-FAIL FORMULA

Here is a formula you can apply to everything you do that absolutely guarantees that you will not fail, provided you follow it consistently. This is called the "No-Fail" or Triple A formula. Triple A (or AAA) provides a helpful way to recall the steps. I don't know who originated this formula, but I am indebted to whoever it was. It looks like this:

- Attempt
- Assess
- Alter

To use it, decide what you want to accomplish and set out to make it happen—make an *Attempt*, then *Assess* your results. And if they are not exactly what you wanted, decide what might have gone wrong and make an *Alteration*. Once you have altered your course, go back and make another attempt. Assess the new results, and if you still didn't get the desired results, make another alteration. Continue to do these three things until you get the results you want, and you absolutely cannot fail. You may run out of life before you manage to achieve a really grand goal, but you won't have failed, you will just have run out of time. You never fail as long as you keep assessing the reason you got the last result, making adjustments and trying again.

Everything you have ever mastered was mastered exactly this way. All of science works on this principle too. Scientists learn early on that they must assess the reason an experiment failed and adjust their approach in order to succeed. And, like Thomas Edison with his ten thousand tries at creating a light bulb, they continue adjusting and retrying until they learn what they need to learn to get a good result.

Great scientists have also learned to keep the concept of failure focused on the experiment, not on themselves. They say an experiment failed and try a new formula. They do not say "I am a failure" and give up in defeat.

In that none of us have explicit instructions for living our lives, life is pretty much a series of experiments. Those who approach it that way realize that every failed attempt puts them that much closer to success if they are paying attention and working the formula. Which, by the way, plants them firmly on the path of responsible, disciplined, courageous actions.

The resistance created by contradictory thoughts, self-talk, and mental images must be removed before energy can flow freely and your desired results can manifest. Guilt or remorse over past mistakes are resistors that are defeating in more ways than one. The better you are at letting go of past mistakes, the faster you will be able to remove resistors, maintain a receptive mindset, and keep energy flowing toward an abundance of all the things you desire.

OTHER METHODS FOR REMOVING BLOCKS AND ELIMINATING OLD PATTERNS

There is a field of mind/body medicine that has emerged in the past few decades called energy psychology that focuses on the subtle energies of the mind and body to affect cures. Many of the techniques are thousands of years old and a few are newly developed. All have the effect of releasing blocked energy. Unblocking energy is such an important step in accelerating progress that I am providing several of those methods for you to try.

Like the Energy Release Technique, the top two on the list can easily be self-administered. Both require more training than ERT to prepare you to self-administer them, but they are not difficult to learn. Some people get a better result when a trained practitioner takes them through these processes initially, but that is not necessary. The others on the list, while effective for many, generally do require the help of a trained practitioner or the assistance of another person. Information is readily available on each technique, both on the internet and in public libraries.

Here's the list:
- The Sedona Method
- Emotional Freedom Technique (EFT)
- Accelerated Mind Patterning (AMP)
- Neuro-linguistic Programming (NLP)
- Behavioral Kinesiology (BK)
- Hypnotherapy
- Acupuncture
- Acupressure
- Reflexology

RECAP – THE STEPS TO POSITIVE ABUNDANCE

1. **Take full responsibility for yourself, your life, and your outcomes.** Only through right action can your dreams and desires (kinetic energy) act on potential energy to unleash it so that the things you dream of having can manifest in the physical world.

2. **Find your passion and claim your power.** Without passion for what you are doing and a feeling of personal power in pursuing it, there will be resistance which will prevent energy from flowing freely. To find your passion, it is essential that you know who you came into the world to be rather than who you have been conditioned to be. Your passion lies at the core of your true nature. To find your passion, you must first know your truth.

3. **Realize that only ONE path leads to positive abundance,** and when you take responsibility for your outcomes and allow the energy you send out to flow freely back to you, you will receive abundance far in excess of what you need. Allow yourself to

have and enjoy anything and everything you desire, because you deserve it, but share your excess wealth so that abundance continues to flow to and through you and the whole world will be more abundant.

4. **Remember: the ONE correct path** is *active* (+) application (responsible, disciplined action and the courage to do the right thing), coupled with a *receptive* (-) attitude (accepting, believing, trusting, allowing, confidence, non-resistance) directed toward a well designed receiver. Keep adjusting application and attitude to keep yourself on that path.

5. **Realize that fear or anxiety around a desired outcome hinders or stops the flow of energy** toward that outcome, as do negative thoughts and feelings. Refocus your thinking toward faith in your ability to achieve the desired outcome.

6. **Be certain that what you want is crystal clear** and that there is more energy around what you want than around what you don't want. Run the checks and balances process frequently to ensure that there is greater clarity and energy around the things you want. Clarity and definiteness of purpose are essential to getting what you want.

7. **Check your areas of focus and the strength of the energy** surrounding *each area* of your life, not just overall. If you have a clearer picture of limitation than of abundance in any area, work on clarifying your picture of abundance. What *specifically* does abundance look like for you in that area?

    Make the picture very, very clear—far clearer than the picture of lack or limitation. This may take time and require some effort in some areas, but it is essential that you have energy flowing toward what you want if you want to experience abundance in that area. And it is clarity that creates the conduit along which energy flows.

    Keep checking the strength of your image of desired things in relation to the image of what you don't want, and keep working

on the positive end of the spectrum until you feel the energy
flowing consistently in the direction of your desire.

8. **Develop a life plan with the precision of a blueprint** so energy
    has clear channels along which to flow and is not being dissipated
    along undefined channels.

9. **Develop the three areas of faith: self, others, and a generative
    force.** The path you have chosen will then be well insulated, and
    negative factors won't easily pull you off course.

10. **Regularly move to a place of gratitude** for what you have now,
    and of certainty about your ownership of everything you desire.
    Gratitude keeps your thoughts and feelings positive and boosts
    energy along the positive abundance path. Taking ownership
    right now makes abundance a current reality rather than
    something to be gained in the future, which never arrives.

11. **Know that if you adhere to the Law of Abundance, you will
    experience an abundance of the things you desire.**See that
    which you desire as a bank account which is already yours.
    Your only task it to decide how large the account is, then find
    a way to get to it and claim it.

12. **Learn from the masters.** We all have available to us a vast store
    of knowledge and wisdom. Make it a point to tap into it as often
    as you can. By studying all kinds of subjects (philosophy, the
    sciences, all forms of religion, the arts, etc), you can develop a
    depth of knowledge and understanding that will lead you to your
    own wisdom.

    Wisdom is a priceless gift which you give to yourself. Once it is
    yours, no one can ever take it from you, but you can share it freely
    and it increases in the sharing.

PART 4

Epilogue and Appendixes

We come to beginnings only at the end.
Genuine beginnings begin within us,
even when they are brought to our
attention by external opportunities.

William Throsby Bridges

*Divine discontent is the means by which
the Law of Abundance activates energy
and provides the impetus for action.
Action turns energy into substance.
If you are not yet fully satisfied, be glad!
You are still in the mainstream of life.*

Epilogue

A Chronology of Events:
How I Arrived at the Law of Abundance

Setting the Law of Abundance into motion through passion and having a clear vision of the desired outcome can have amazing and often unexpected results. Seemingly unrelated events become stepping-stones that lead to your heart's desire. In my case, they led me to the law itself.

Like millions of other people, I spent many years chasing every rainbow and trying every new method that came along hoping it would lead to success. But, it was not until the Law of Abundance became clear to me, that I fully understood why I had not achieved the results I sought.

Just as the folks who are trying so hard to teach us how to be successful have each stumbled upon the formula that set the Law of Abundance in motion for them, I unknowingly did the same thing. It happened when I read and had such an impassioned response to the Thoreau quote, "*The mass of men lead lives of quiet desperation.*"

But, unlike some who report success in a year or two, my journey didn't unfold quite that way. For me, the journey from Thoreau to the Law of Abundance was a long, circuitous route because, like most people, I didn't yet have the whole picture and hadn't just lucked into the formula in its entirety. In fact, nearly thirty years passed from the day I read that quote to the day I discovered the Law of Abundance.

I experienced many successes along the way, but at nowhere near the level or speed at which I had imagined it. Since discovering the Law of Abundance, things have begun to unfold much more rapidly and predictably. Now, when I am not getting the results I desire, I can look at the principles that unfailingly drive the Law of Abundance and know exactly what I am doing wrong. I can then make purposeful corrections to get the results I am after.

Have I suddenly become a billionaire with mansions, big yachts and fancy cars? No. That isn't me. That is someone else's dream. My dream is to be an instrument for positive change in the world and I am blessed to be able to do that every single day of my life. I have a wonderfully loving and supportive family and friends whose lives I am privileged to share and positively impact, and who certainly return the favor. And I have an entire network of people who regularly use the systems, books and programs I have created, so I am able to reach far beyond what I could ever personally do, and can even affect positive change while I sleep. I live comfortably and all my personal wants and needs are met.

My ultimate desire is the same today as it was in 1976 when Thoreau's quote woke me from the trance I was in. The difference is that with the knowledge I have gained through the Law of Abundance, what has been a long, slow process is now accelerating rapidly and, when I am not moving in the exact direction I choose, I know exactly why and can make purposeful adjustments that ensure I keep moving in the right direction.

The Thoreau moment was the catalyst that set me on my life path, but it was through a series of serendipitous events that I would eventually arrive here. Yet, as I look back, I realize that all the elements for bringing me to the exact spot in which I now find myself; here writing this book, were set into motion in that one moment.

In that moment was born the passionate response that led to the vision of a world filled with happy, satisfied people rather than desperate ones. This provided the focused passion, a clear vision and, although I was not conscious of it at the time, a specific goal. My deep determination to find an answer set in motion the active application part of the abundance formula. The belief that an answer existed created a receptive attitude.

Unbeknownst to me, every element needed to set the Law of Abundance into motion was in place and each worked perfectly, as the law must, to bring me to the exact destination I was seeking; a formula with the power to abolish human desperation.

The passion I felt for changing the condition of humanity provided the impetus for me to begin reading everything I could get my hands on concerning success, satisfaction, personal growth, healthy relationships, mental and emotional health, growing businesses, or any other area where I could see that a lack of that particular thing might result in desperation.

I began interviewing people who were successful and those who were not to see if I could glean any clues. I wanted, *needed* to understand the root cause of mass desperation and the reason why so few people were truly joyous. I was relentless in my search.

By 1984, searching and researching was not enough and I began building a business for the specific purpose of helping people move toward joy, satisfaction and their own brand of success. I enlisted the help of my daughter Gina, and together we developed and delivered workshops. Our initial focus was on improving business functions (sales, customer relations, team building, employee effectiveness, etc.) because I could see so much desperation in so many workplaces.

After many years of interviewing people, doing research and delivering workshops in business settings, I realized that the primary problem was not the external actions that so many people focus on and try to fix, but the internal programs, personal perceptions and beliefs that drove the actions.

Most people, I discovered, failed to get their desired results not because they weren't trying or didn't care, but because they didn't know exactly what their employer wanted or needed from them and often didn't even know what they wanted personally. Few had a clear sense of where they were headed or needed to be headed, and most lacked clear goals.

Lacking goals was such a common occurrence that I began exploring that phenomenon specifically and was amazed at how prevalent this was. Most people could not tell me what gave their life meaning or what they were passionate about, though almost everyone reported a strong desire to have meaning and passion in their life.

Delving deeper, it soon became apparent that the reason most people didn't have goals, meaning or a clear purpose in life was because they lacked a deep, authentic sense of self. It stands to reason that without self-awareness it is not possible to know what will fulfill us. Self-awareness at a deep, core level is essential for managing life as well as managing self. Without these elements life becomes chaotic or feels pointless.

Much of psychological research suggests that everything we experience in life is filtered through our own vision of ourselves. Our self-perception determines our confidence level; how we approach situations; how we relate to other people; how we feel from moment to moment; and what we will or will not allow into our lives, including success and joy, or misery and despair.

With an understanding of how essential awareness of self and others is to all success, Gina and I began using off-the-shelf personality assessments in our workshops and, while they helped people better understand their behaviors and the behaviors of others, they failed to go deeply enough to explain ineffective behaviors or suggest more beneficial ones. Worse, there was no way to determine whether the results were accurate to the individual's truth. This was distressing because we had discovered that people frequently reported traits on assessments that were incongruent with what they were reporting non-verbally.

At the time, I was studying psychology and was a serious student of both personality and non-verbal communications. I had become very good at reading people and knew I could trust non-verbal reporting far more than I could trust the assessment results. In my studies I had learned that nearly 93% of our communications are non-verbal and that, although people can lie to themselves mentally and to others verbally, few people lie non-verbally. The truth is always there if you know what to look for.

This knowledge induced me to start questioning those whose non-verbal communication was different than what they reported on the assessments and, in every instance, the individual would report lack of true self-awareness. Many instinctively knew that the self they claimed was not the self they longed to be, but didn't know how to get to that ideal self or even exactly what it looked like. They only knew there was something missing; something they wanted desperately to find.

Some reported they were still trying to discover what they were supposed to be when they grew up. And this sentiment came from people in their thirties, forties, fifties, and older, more often than from those in their teens and twenties. Usually teenagers and people in their twenties are still too outer directed and have not yet begun the inner search for self. They don't really know who they are any better than the more mature folks, but they aren't as aware of that fact yet.

The reason so many of the people in the "lost-but-searching" group had no long-term goals or plans for the future is because they didn't know what the future should or could look like. They just lived from day to day hoping they would someday find their purpose, but had no idea where to even begin looking.

On the other hand, those whose non-verbal communications were congruent with what they were reporting usually told a very different story. Many in this group were already successful in life and those that were not yet there, at least had a clear and comfortable sense of self. They knew where they were headed and were confident in their ability to eventually reach their goals. This group was very much in the minority though and the drive to know why induced me to keep searching.

I explored numerous other assessments trying to find something that would get past the facade the majority of people had built around themselves and identified with, but to no avail. In an attempt to get more accurate results, I began combining assessments that measured different aspects. Perhaps by looking from multiple angles, I reasoned, we could get past the false mask and discover an individual's truth.

Over several years of testing and questioning, very distinct patterns began to emerge in relation to those who reported that they had a clear sense of self and were confident of the direction they were taking in their lives. These were truly authentic, fully functioning, well-directed people, and whenever we had the opportunity to interview the family, friends, and/or co-workers of this highly effective group, they always confirmed the level of effectiveness the individual expressed.

I assembled a team and we began doing research around these emerging patterns. We added a new dimension that no other assessment had ever included, which allowed us to see the traits the individual claimed to have, how effectively those traits were developed, and how much stress existed around the use of those traits. We could also see whether the claimed traits were being expressed in positive or negative ways, or somewhere in between.

The system that eventually evolved proved to be highly predictive of self-awareness, sense of direction, satisfaction, contentment, personal effectiveness and overall success in life. We found that where these factors existed in large measure, there also existed a sense of purpose, passion, and meaning. The people in this group had the personal resources, always internally and usually externally, to handle any challenge or crisis that might arise so they approached life's events with courage and confidence. This group was definitely not living lives of desperation.

Another interesting factor that emerged around other patterns was that the successes people reported were directly related to the areas that our system presented as effectively developed. For example, if there was healthy development around the traits that relate to people and relationships, but not around the traits that relate to accomplishment, the individual tended to have great relationships, but not a lot of money or career enjoyment.

If they had developed the area that relates to achievement drive, but not empathy or other people-related traits, they were often doing well in their careers, but not in their relationships. If both areas were well developed, they had both. Those who reported healthy levels of development across the board tended to be effective and content in every area of their lives to the degree that development had occurred.

With this knowledge, Gina and I began working one-on-one with those who did not fit healthy patterns; those who were unclear as to who they were or where they fit into the scheme of things; those who were living lives of quiet desperation. We spent endless hours helping people discover the conditioning that had pulled them off course (usually as children) and helping them find their own authentic path.

The results were astounding! People began telling us how profoundly we had changed their lives. Many of them begged us to take the system we had developed into high schools, colleges, prisons, large corporations, the military and other arenas where they could see that people were still lost and searching.

It didn't take long to realize that we had something really powerful and unique; something the world, not just a few thousand workshop participants, ought to have access to. However, it also became apparent that we could not do this on our own.

In 1996, two decades after that Thoreau moment and a great deal of research later, the CORE *Multidimensional Awareness Profile* (CORE MAP) was born. It took a lot of help from a dedicated team of people, including Gina, my son Ron, Gina's husband, also named Ron, a team of programmers and researchers, and the patience and support of my husband, George, but at last, here was a tool that could truly get to the *core* of things.

We applied for, and in December of 1999 received, a patent on the CORE system and, using it, we have been privileged to witness profound transformations in thousands of lives. CORE MAP is a system that requires a trained analyst to decipher the results so we developed a training model and in 2001 began teaching and certifying others to use this phenomenal tool. They too began changing lives.

Today we have a growing network of trained analysts nationwide and many thousands of testimonials from people whose lives have been positively and profoundly altered. With this dedicated team we are now collectively eliminating lives of quiet (and sometimes not so quiet) desperation in greater and greater numbers. Our goal is to take the CORE system to the whole world.

We have found that, for many, being able to see their true nature and the conditioning that has prevented them from living fully is all it takes for them to make that quantum leap forward and claim their authentic, joyous self. But sometimes, early conditioning was so severe that the old patterns just won't budge without effective intervention.

To address that problem, I began studying processes designed to produce rapid change such as hypnotherapy, Neuro-linguistic Programming (NLP), the Silva Mind Method, Kinesiology, etc. Each process I examined had benefits and drawbacks and I wanted to eliminate the drawbacks if possible.

It had taken me more than twelve years to go from lost to found in my own life and to get rid of the patterns that were derailing me and that was way too long in my opinion. My long, arduous journey has made me an advocate of brief therapy and the briefer, the better. If something can be accomplished in a few hours, why spend years at it? My goal was to find something that was very fast and very effective in eliminating old patterns and I wanted it to work 100% of the time. Although I was aware that I might have to settle for less, I knew I wouldn't be satisfied with less.

My life has been full of serendipitous events and it was just such an event that led me to the discovery of what I was looking for. During training for certification in hypnotherapy, I was the chosen subject for a demonstration of post-hypnotic suggestion. The trainer hypnotized me and suggested that I would not remember my last name when he brought me out of trance. He suggested that I choose a number as a substitute and use the number when he asked me to report my last name. As he made that suggestion, there immediately came an image of the other students laughing at my loss of memory and of my mother pointing her finger at me and saying very emphatically,

"Don't you embarrass me." My mother was always very concerned about presenting the right image and my subconscious mind decided that not embarrassing my mother was more important than pleasing the trainer and I over-rode his suggestion.

The trainer was astounded that I was able to do that and I was enlightened as to why many of the modalities I had studied didn't always work. In that moment I understood that we all have our own answers and our own solutions and realized that the powerful subconscious mind will not allow "solutions" that don't fit with its agenda. With that awareness, I set out to develop a process that would help people find and implement their own solutions quickly and easily.

Over the next five years, I developed, tested, and retested a process I call *Accelerated Mind Patterning* (AMP). I was thrilled to see even my early "guinea pigs" getting outstanding results. And, as I refined the process, I was privileged to witness some seemingly miraculous changes occur in people's lives; changes that occurred instantaneously and better still, were almost always permanent. And the effectiveness has been very close to 100%.

While the results were phenomenal, the AMP process had a drawback too. I found it could not be self-administered because the conscious mind always tries to run interference. The process had to be facilitated and, unlike CORE MAP, I wasn't sure how to teach others to facilitate it. I came to realize that, although the AMP process is extremely effective, it is not a practical way to change lives *en masse* without effective training programs and large groups of people trained to administer it. Since I was after mass transformation, I continued my search.

In early 2006, a friend and business associate introduced me to a method that appeared to produce rapid change and which could be self-administered called the *Emotional Freedom Technique* (EFT). Almost simultaneously, another friend mentioned *The Sedona Method*, which appeared to produce essentially the same results as the EFT method. As I studied them I could see that, while they used very different methods, both had something in common with one another, with hypnotherapy, Neuro-linguistic Programming (NLP) and with the Accelerated Mind Patterning (AMP) method I had created. I didn't know what yet, but the notion that there was a commonality, and that there was something very important about that commonality, played in my mind for weeks.

Then at 3:15 a.m. one morning I awakened from sleep with a start, and with a keen awareness that I needed to understand energy and how electricity worked. I was not too inclined at that hour to get up and do any research, but there was such an urgency to begin right then that I could not go back to sleep. So, dutifully, I got up and went to the computer to look up the principles of energy and electricity (or energy flow).

As I sat there in the wee hours of the morning, wondering what on earth I was doing there, what electricity and the principles of energy had to do with anything, and reading what I would have typically found to be very dry, boring technical information, the answer to everything I had sought to understand for thirty years suddenly became crystal clear.

Staring at electrical schematics, I finally understood why "the mass of men lead lives of quiet desperation." I knew why the methods for change I had been pondering for the past few weeks work the way they do. I could see why all human initiatives either work or fail to work. And at last, I understood how we could all completely eliminate desperation from our lives if we chose to. Right there in those schematics was the answer I had been searching for and I knew that I had been handed the greatest gift of my life.

As the whole complex system unfolded, it became clear that this was truly the master law under which we all operate; the key to the abundant universe. Here was the master formula; complex, yet eloquently simple; mysterious, yet completely self-evident; hidden and yet it had been right there in front of us all the time.

The wise have been pointing us to this one truth in one way or another for millennia and humanity has used its rules for thousands of years to get every amazing result we have ever gotten. Yet somehow, we had all missed the fact that the same formula that works to guide and direct energy in homes and cars and all the conveniences to which we have become so accustomed; the same law that keeps the universe functioning so perfectly, also guides and directs the energies and outcomes of humanity.

Sitting there studying the laws that govern energy, I realized that programs like AMP, EFT, NLP, the Sedona Method and others work because they all help to remove resistance and realign the energies of the mind and body. They work instantly because energy aligns or realigns instantly. Acupuncture and acupressure work for the same reason. Hypnosis works because it helps to change old, negative, stories into new, more positive ones that allow the subconscious mind to let go of resistors so that energy flows more freely.

I understood that since everything is energy, everything is subject to the principles that govern energy, and to the law that ensures that each principle is absolutely consistent and totally predictable. I realized that people were as much a part of the energy equation, and therefore of the laws governing energy, as anything else in the universe and I could see how we fit perfectly into that law.

There in the wee hours of the morning, I suddenly realized that here at last was that unfailing formula I had been searching for; the one that literally had the power to set us all free; to end desperation for anyone and everyone who chose to use it. At last, the answer which that quote from Thoreau had set me in search of was mine. And now it is yours as well.

Live abundantly!

Share your favorite teachers, thoughts, quotes, stories and resources at www.theLawofAbundance.com

Appendix 1

Additional Resources
LEARNING FROM THE MASTERS

Throughout history, we have had master teachers and visionaries providing us with advice and modeling successful patterns for us to follow. Tapping into their wisdom and depth of knowledge can greatly speed your progress as you create the life you want.

SOME MASTER TEACHERS AND VISIONARIES FROM AGES PAST (IN ALPHABETICAL ORDER BY FIRST NAME)

Abraham Maslow
Albert Einstein
Alfred Adler
Aristotle
Benjamin Franklin
Bertrand Russell
Carl Jung
Carl Rogers
Charles Darwin
Confucius
Copernicus
David Hume
Descartes
Emily Dickenson
Erwin Schrödinger
Galileo Galilei
Gautama the Buddha
George Berkeley
Helen Keller
Henry David Thoreau
Immanuel Kant
Isaac Newton
Jesus of Nazareth

Lao-tzu
Leo Tolstoy
Leonardo da Vinci
Mahatma Gandhi
Margaret Mead
Martin Luther King
Maxwell Maltz
Mother Theresa
Nichola Tesla
Nicolaus Copernicus
Niels Bohr
Neitzsche
Paul of Tarsus
Plato
Pythagoras
Ralph Waldo Emerson
Socrates
Solomon
Spinoza
Thomas Edison
Thomas Jefferson
Voltaire
William James

FOR A LIST OF CURRENT TEACHERS AND VISIONARIES, AND OTHER HELPFUL RESOURCES

Go to www.TheLawofAbundance.com. There you will find:

- Internet links for finding tools and exercises you can use to improve outcomes personally and in relationships. and lists of philosophers, psychologists, spiritual leaders and scientists, and their works.

- Recommended books , audio programs and workshops to assist you on your journey to the life you desire and deserve.

APPENDIX 2

Test your Knowledge of the Law of Abundance

EXERCISE 1

Use the scenarios below to determine the energy path for both application and attitude. Use (+) to indicate a positive or active path and (-) to indicate a negative or receptive path. Then indicate whether that combination will result in an energy flow toward positive abundance (+ Flow), negative abundance (- Flow) or in being stuck (No Flow).

1. You are being bullied. You 'turn the other cheek' and remain passive. You do not defend yourself or resist the aggression in any way. The bully knocks you to the ground and walks off. You maintain an attitude of humility and try to understand the bully's behavior.

Application __ Attitude __ = __ + Flow __ - Flow __ No Flow

2. You are being bullied and you meet aggression with aggression. You get angry and get into a fight with the aggressor. You both end up bruised and bloodied.

Application __ Attitude __ = __ + Flow __ - Flow __ No Flow

3. You are being bullied and you firmly resist the action. You let the bully know his behaviors are not acceptable to you, while remaining calm, collected and purposeful in the way you respond.

Application __ Attitude __ = __ + Flow __ - Flow __ No Flow

4. You are being bullied. You 'turn the other cheek" and remain passive, but inside you are seething. You would love to take this guy down, but you fear that, if you do anything, he might just get meaner.

Application __ Attitude __ = __ + Flow __ - Flow __ No Flow

EXERCISE 2

An Erroneous Approach to the Law of Attraction

You decide what you want, ask God or the Universe or the Generative Force for it and wait patiently for your dreams to come true. What part of the Abundance formula is missing here?

_____ The Positive Application Line

_____ The Receptive Attitude Line

See next page for answers

EXERCISE 1

Scenario 1:
Application Receptive (-); Attitude Receptive (-) = No Flow

Scenario 2:
Application Active (+); Attitude Active/Resistant (+) = No Flow

Scenario 3:
Application Active/Responsible (+); Attitude Receptive (-) = Flow toward positive abundance (+ Flow)

Scenario 4:
Application Receptive/Lacking Courage (-); Attitude Active/Resistant (+) = Flow toward negative abundance (- Flow)

EXERCISE 2

What's missing?

The Positive Application Line (responsible, disciplined action, the courage to consistently do the right thing). Without the positive application line, we cannot impact potential energy in the physical world. Although we may experience a shift in attitude that can eventually compel us to act, nothing will occur externally until we (or someone else) take action. And even in the rare instances when our attitude compels another to take action on our behalf, we still have to take some action to claim and sustain anything in the material world.

APPENDIX 3

About The Author

Sherry is an internationally known consultant, presenter, trainer, and author, and a leader in the field of human potential. She is president and CEO of NaviCore International, Inc. a research, development and consulting firm focused on the creation of world class products for accelerating human growth and development, increasing motivation, and maximizing performance and personal effectiveness. Sherry has been immersed in learning the dynamics of successful living and the many aspects of human nature since 1976 through both formal and independent study of the world's great sciences, philosophies, psychologies and religions. She holds a Ph.D. in psychology.

She is the originator and co-developer of the highly acclaimed CORE *Multidimensional Awareness Profile* (CORE MAP), a system for deep, meaningful analysis and an exceptional developmental tool used by coaches, therapists and trainers worldwide. She developed the Energy Release Technique (ERT) and Accelerated Mind Patterning (AMP), both tools that rapidly transform lives, even where years of traditional therapy has failed.

The many transformations she has witnessed have convinced her that all people have an abundance of everything they need to be completely successful and wholly joyous in life. She asserts that those who have not realized their great potential have failed to do so only because portions of their potential is buried under a lifetime of non-beneficial conditioning. Sherry's work continues to demonstrate that, once the old conditioning is released, what always emerges is exactly what the individual wants and needs to be happy and content. From a place of authenticity, acceptance develops, responsibility increases, dreams and goals become clearer and, in keeping with the Law of Abundance, positive abundance increases.

Sherry resides in Dallas, Texas with her husband, George.

Bibliography

1 pbs.org/wnet/hawking/html/home.html

2 Stapp, H.P. (1993). A quantum theory of the mind-brain interface. *In Mind, Matter, and QuantumMechanics,* Springer, Berlin, pp. 145-172.

3 Elizabeth A. Thomson (2005). E=mc2 Passes Tough MIT test. eb.mit.edu/newsoffice/2005/emc2.html

4 Conservation of Energy. en.wikipedia.org/wiki/Conservation_of_energy

5 F. Heylighen, C. Joslyn and V. Turchin (editors): *Principia Cybernetica Web* (Principia Cybernetica, Brussels) URL: http://cleamc11.vub.ac.be/Entropy

6 How Things Work. rabi.phys.virginia.edu/105/2002/ps9s.html. See also, Thermodynamics of chemical equilibrium. www.chem1.com/acad/webtext/thermeq

7 Botany online: Physical Chemistry – Thermodynamics. www.biologie.uni-hamburg.de/bonline/e18/18a.htm

8 Electric Current. hyperphysics.phy-astr.gsu.edu/hbase/electric/elecur.html

9 History of Radio. history.acusd.edu/gen/recording/radio.html

10 University of Chicago, chronicle.uchicago.edu/050414/cacioppo.shtml

11 Cynthia, Wall. *The Courage to Trust,* New Harbinger Publications, 2004

12 Pascal's Wager. Stanford Encyclopedia of Philosophy, plato. stanford.edu/entries/pascal-wager

13 Electromagnetism Practical Physics. www.practicalphysics.org/go/Topic_7.html?topic_id=7

14 Electric Circuits, 2000, 2002. School of Computing and Software Engineering, Southern Polytechnic State University – www.spsu.edu/cs/faculty/bbrown/web_lectures/circuits

15 What is Electricity? www.eia.doe.gov/kids/energyfacts/sources/electricity.html

16 Altering the flow of electricity. www.chester.ac.uk/~mwillard/teacher_education/electric.htm

17 National Measurement Institute. www.measurement.gov.au/index.cfm?event=object. showContent&objectID=91201B56-BCD6-81AC-1A5C90DA48F6D939

18 Psychological Comparisons Between Women with Rheumatoid Arthritis and Their Nonarthritic Sisters, RH Moos, GF Solomon - Psychosomatic Medicine, 1965% - Am Psychosomatic Soc

19 The Biology of Belief: Unleashing the Power of Consciousness, Matter and Miracles by Bruce H. Lipton Publisher: Mountain of Love (2005) ISBN 0975991477

20 Energy Meridians. www.tuberose.com/meridians.html

Printed in the United States
204283BV00002B/1-84/P